A PROPER PERSON TO BE DETAINED

Also by Catherine Czerkawska

Non-fiction

The Way It Was

For Jean:
Poems, Songs and Letters by Robert Burns
for his wife, Jean Armour

Precious Vintage

Fiction

The Posy Ring

The Curiosity Cabinet

The Jewel

The Physic Garden

Bird of Passage

The Amber Heart

Ice Dancing

A Quiet Afternoon in the Museum of Torture

Plays

Wormwood

The Price of a Fish Supper

Quartz

Burns on the Solway

The Secret Commonwealth

Catherine Czerkawska

A PROPER PERSON TO BE DETAINED

THE STORY OF A MURDER AND ITS AFTERMATH

CONTRABAND

Published by Contraband,
an imprint of Saraband,
Digital World Centre,
1 Lowry Plaza,
The Quays, Salford, M50 3UB
and
Suite 202, 98 Woodlands Rd,
Glasgow, G3 6HB

www.saraband.net

ISBN: 9781912235537
eISBN: 9781912235544

1 3 5 7 9 8 6 4 2

Designed and typeset by EM&EN
Printed and bound in Great Britain by Clays Ltd, Elcograf S.p.A.

FSC www.fsc.org MIX Paper from responsible sources FSC® C018072

The publisher acknowledges support from the National Lottery through Creative Scotland towards the publication of this title.

Supported by The National Lottery® through Creative Scotland

For Elizabeth and John Manley,

who were cheated of life,

and for my friend Sooh Sweeney,

without whose generous help and expertise in genealogy all this would have been much more difficult.

I am come of the seed of the people, the people
  that sorrow,
That have no treasure but hope,
No riches laid up but a memory
Of an ancient glory.
My mother bore me in bondage, in bondage
  my mother was born,
I am of the blood of serfs;
The children with whom I have played, the men
  and women with whom I have eaten,
Have had masters over them, have been under
  the lash of masters,
And, though gentle, have served churls;
The hands that have touched mine, the dear hands
  whose touch is familiar to me,
Have worn shameful manacles, have been bitten
  at the wrist by manacles,
Have grown hard with the manacles and the
  task-work of strangers,
I am flesh of the flesh of these lowly, I am bone
  of their bone.

'The Rebel', Padraic Pearse, 1915

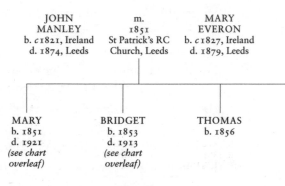

JOHN
MANLEY
b. *c*1821, Ireland
d. 1874, Leeds

m.
1851
St Patrick's RC
Church, Leeds

MARY
EVERON
b. *c*1827, Ireland
d. 1879, Leeds

MARY
b. 1851
d. 1921
(see chart overleaf)

BRIDGET
b. 1853
d. 1913
(see chart overleaf)

THOMAS
b. 1856

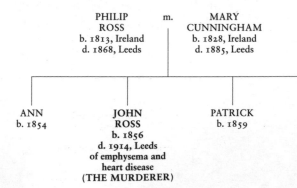

PHILIP
ROSS
b. 1813, Ireland
d. 1868, Leeds

m.

MARY
CUNNINGHAM
b. 1828, Ireland
d. 1885, Leeds

ANN
b. 1854

JOHN
ROSS
b. 1856
d. 1914, Leeds
of emphysema and
heart disease
(THE MURDERER)

PATRICK
b. 1859

Family Trees

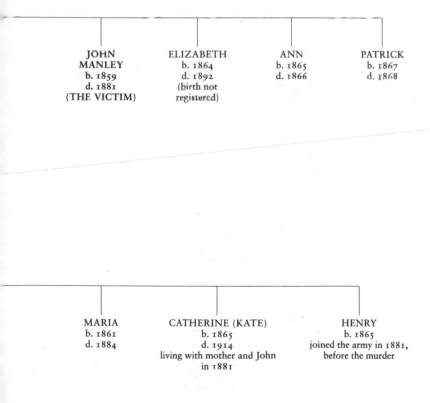

JOHN MANLEY
b. 1859
d. 1881
(THE VICTIM)

ELIZABETH
b. 1864
d. 1892
(birth not registered)

ANN
b. 1865
d. 1866

PATRICK
b. 1867
d. 1868

MARIA
b. 1861
d. 1884

CATHERINE (KATE)
b. 1865
d. 1914
living with mother and John in 1881

HENRY
b. 1865
joined the army in 1881, before the murder

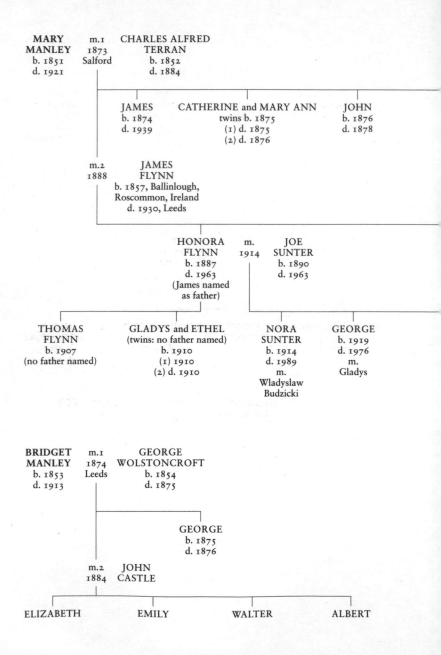

MARY MANLEY
b. 1851
d. 1921

m.1 1873 Salford

CHARLES ALFRED TERRAN
b. 1852
d. 1884

JAMES
b. 1874
d. 1939

CATHERINE and MARY ANN
twins b. 1875
(1) d. 1875
(2) d. 1876

JOHN
b. 1876
d. 1878

m.2 1888

JAMES FLYNN
b. 1857, Ballinlough, Roscommon, Ireland
d. 1930, Leeds

HONORA FLYNN
b. 1887
d. 1963
(James named as father)

m. 1914

JOE SUNTER
b. 1890
d. 1963

THOMAS FLYNN
b. 1907
(no father named)

GLADYS and ETHEL
(twins: no father named)
b. 1910
(1) 1910
(2) d. 1910

NORA SUNTER
b. 1914
d. 1989
m.
Wladyslaw Budzicki

GEORGE
b. 1919
d. 1976
m.
Gladys

BRIDGET MANLEY
b. 1853
d. 1913

m.1 1874 Leeds

GEORGE WOLSTONCROFT
b. 1854
d. 1875

GEORGE
b. 1875
d. 1876

m.2 1884

JOHN CASTLE

ELIZABETH

EMILY

WALTER

ALBERT

JANE FRANCES
b. 1878
d. 1879

ELIZABETH
b. 1880

JOHN THOMAS
b. 1882

MARY
TERRAN
b. 1885
(no father named)

TIMOTHY
b. 1889
d. 1925

THOMAS
b. 1891
d. 1894

MICHAEL
b. 1893
d. 1958

VERONICA (VERA) m. ERNEST WATSON
b. 1924
d. 2005

KATHLEEN IRENE m. JULIAN CZERKAWSKI
b. 1926 / b. 1926
d. 1998 / d. 1995

CAROL
b. 1963

JANE CATHERINE and DAVID
twins b. 1964

CATHERINE LUCY
b. 1950

Preface

On Christmas Night in 1881, my great-great-uncle, John Manley, whose parents had migrated from Ireland some 30 years earlier, was stabbed in a Leeds street, after a foolish quarrel. The single wound was fatal and he died within minutes. He was just twenty-two years old, and the murderer was only three years older. The two men had known each other for years and may even have been friends. This book began as an attempt to tease out the truth of that tragedy, to understand what happened and why, to establish whether the stories passed down through my family were accurate, or half-truths, shaped into a tale for family consumption. This is a true story about a crime, or as nearly true as I can make it. But it turned out to be about so much more than that. This is a story, especially, about the women in the family who were affected by a crime that seemed to trigger even more tragedy in lives that were already being lived on the very edge of an abyss of poverty and despair. It is a tale that is at once deeper, darker and even more tragic than I could ever have imagined.

1. *Family Photographs*

On Christmas Night in 1881, twenty-two-year-old John Manley was drinking in what is described as a 'beerhouse' called the Railway Hotel, on York Street in smoky Leeds. There were plenty of other railway hotels, inns and taverns in Leeds, including one called the Old Railway Inn on Marsh Lane, very close to York Street, but this was an area where there were numerous public houses and beerhouses, and names were often replicated, or nearly so. The landlord, as we know from the subsequent trial of the man accused of the murder, was John Hardaker, and in that year, he was running the Railway Hotel at 58 York Street, very close to Brussels Street where John Manley was living with his sisters Bridget and Elizabeth. Their Irish-born parents were both dead. Their elder sister Mary lived just around the corner in Little Off Street, with her husband Charles Terran, a son, James, and a baby daughter, also named Elizabeth, after her young aunt.

John Hardaker was thirty-five years old and on the night of the census in 1881, his household consisted of his wife, Annie, a ten-year-old daughter, Alice, described as a scholar, a young domestic servant called Hannah Cooper and, intriguingly, his or his wife's nine-year-old nephew, also a scholar: Reginald J Beacham from New Orleans. It's hard to resist pursuing Reginald's story: how had his parents come to be in New Orleans? Were they part of that earlier wave of migrants who had finally made it to the promised land of America? You find yourself wondering how the child came to be living above a beerhouse, in a seedy part of Leeds, with his uncle and aunt. Next door at 56 York Street sits a 'public house' called the Red House Inn, so the two pubs were side by side. There is a picture of this building, taken in 1901, twenty years after the murder, an impressive and handsome Georgian town house, running to three storeys, with a balustraded roof, ornamental urns on pedestals, and a gas lamp outside. This looks like a hotel with some letting bedrooms, but on the night of the springtime census in 1881, there are no guests, only the publican and his family.

In the photograph, there are what look like crumbling brick buildings on either side of the Red House Inn, either of which could be an ale house. It may be that the Railway Hotel had closed by 1901, although the Red House Inn was still in existence. Even in 1881, however, the distinction between beerhouses like the Railway Hotel and public houses such as the Red House Inn had become one of status rather than reality. Beerhouses were meant to sell only beer, but in truth the rules were complicated and poorly enforced, and it became all too clear during the subsequent trial that the Railway Hotel was selling spirits as well as ale. Nevertheless, landlord John Hardaker was running a fairly tight ship. Ten years later, he is living elsewhere in Leeds. He and his wife are lodgers in somebody else's house and he is described as a 'traveller', which covers a multitude of occupations from travelling hawker, the lowest of the low, to commercial travellers selling goods for a particular company. Perhaps the murder and subsequent publicity had adversely affected his business.

The enthusiastic industrialisation of Leeds, throughout the nineteenth century and earlier, coupled with the need for workers and the associated requirement to provide somewhere for those workers to stay, had resulted in a domestic landscape in which heavy industry sat cheek by jowl with countless streets of tiny back-to-back houses. Even in 1908, by which time some slum clearances had taken place, a glance at the Ordnance Survey map for this area reveals a criss-cross of houses in narrow streets, with their associated patchwork of yards, courts, squares and 'folds' that would once have been farmyards. There are mills of all kinds: wool, flax and grain. There are iron works, gas works and foundries. There are buildings associated with textiles, chemicals, leather and pottery as well as all of the heavy machinery essential to the new industries, the construction and servicing of locomotives and the transport of coal from nearby pits to the city. Tall chimneys abound and change the shape of the skyline. The pubs and inns have multiplied, too, in response to the need for some means of escape for those working and living nearby. Beerhouses had originally been one of various worthy ways in which the Victorian authorities tried to control the tendency of working men and women to drown their multitude of sorrows with strong alcohol. In an effort to discourage the disastrous prevalence of cheap gin, the government had removed the tax on beer earlier in the century and issued licences to growing numbers of beerhouses so that they could sell ale alone, often made on the premises. Long before 1881, however, many of these had either closed or become conventional public houses. Perhaps the name 'beerhouse' stuck in this case because the Railway Hotel is repeatedly called that in the newspaper reports, with their various and occasionally conflicting tales of the murder.

When I was young, pubs were mysterious, forbidden places. Doors would swing open and there would be a gush of cigarette smoke and beer fumes, sometimes accompanied by sounds of hilarity and raised male voices. Until I was seven, we lived next door to the Goodman's Arms on Whitehall Road, on the south side of the river Aire, but I was never allowed inside. My grandad Joe, never a big drinker, would go in there for an evening pint sometimes, with his angling friends, but I wasn't aware that anyone else in the family accompanied him. Alcohol wasn't forbidden. My nana, Honora, had the occasional glass of Sanatogen Tonic Wine, and there was always a bottle of 'black beer' in the house for medicinal purposes. This was a sweet, malty concoction, dating back in one incarnation or another to the sixteenth century. Captain Cook is said to have favoured it for its health-giving properties, although its commercial production came much later. It was made close to home, in Wortley, Leeds, by an old company called Mather's, and mostly drunk in very small quantities, in warm milk or cold lemonade. This meant that although the actual alcohol content was 8.5 per cent, it was always used as a cordial. Its syrupy sweetness made it virtually undrinkable on its own, and its iron and vitamin C content were high, too. It had survived well into the twenty-first century as an historic beverage, and ceased production only a few years ago, thanks to the Chancellor getting rid of various anomalous tax exemptions. With the 'simplified' price doubling overnight, black beer become economically unviable and production ceased.

Even pubs like the respectable Goodman's Arms were to be avoided as far as my nana was concerned. I don't remember her ever venturing inside. If I summon it, though, I can still smell the interior through the open door, as people came and went, can still catch a glimpse of it, the lights, the coal fire, warm and inviting on a winter's night. The Railway Hotel, where Irish men and women were drinking on that long-ago Christmas Night, must have smelled the same, of beer and tobacco smoke, with the addition of warm and infrequently washed clothes and bodies.

I began with pictures, the desire to populate my mind's eye with images of the time, the place and the people. In all of the pictures from the streets where John Manley and his sisters once lived, York Street, Brussels Street, Off Street, you can see that the stones and bricks would have been covered with a thick coating of soot. When I was a child, I thought all buildings were black. Many years later, I realised that the natural colour of millstone grit, a coarse-grained sandstone found throughout Leeds from the Town Hall to the railway bridges, is honey brown. But even in 1881 the stones would already have been blackened by years of industrial pollution. It would have been a very short walk from Brussels Street, where John lived, to the Railway Hotel, outside which he would die, bleeding out within minutes from a stab wound under his left ear, drowning in his own blood.

*

I was born in Leeds and spent the 1950s there, before we moved to Scotland in the 1960s. For most of my early childhood, we lived in a part of the city that was just as industrialised and just as polluted as the district where the Manley family lived. We were a working-class family, but although money was always in short supply, we would not have judged ourselves poor. The house was warm and clean. There were no infestations, except once, when my grandfather, who dealt in fishing tackle and sold maggots for bait, neglected to put a big container of them in the fridge where he kept them dormant, and – nature having taken its course – filled the house with bluebottles. My grandmother was not pleased.

There was an old-fashioned range for baking and heating. There were always books in the house, and a big wireless with knobs to twiddle and exotic names like Luxembourg and Hilversum on the dial. We had one outside toilet between a family of six – my grandparents, my aunt, my parents and myself – but it was ours, it was fresh and it smelled only of bleach. There was always enough food on the table. My grandmother baked several times a week and taught me how to do it, too. Nobody went hungry. Even if many of our clothes were, like all our food, home-made, they were good clothes. My aunts and my grandfather worked in tailoring. They despised poor-quality cloth made from recycled wool and would not entertain it at any price. One of my earliest memories is of seeing my aunt and my mother handling off-the-peg clothes in some city centre store, and using a single, disparaging word – 'shoddy' – before moving on. They would buy good worsted remnants and sew things for themselves instead.

There was plenty of love in that tall, narrow house. I was never aware of anything else. I was the first child of my generation in a warm, kindly, quarrelsome and demonstrative family. They spoiled me because I was seriously asthmatic and couldn't breathe properly. Illness seemed a normal condition to me. When my temperature soared and I saw visions of horsemen galloping over the foot of the bed, when all the fairy tales and folk tales and extracts from the classics in my old Wonder Books came back to haunt my fevered mind, my mother would put cool cloths on my head and sing to me for hours. I knew all about Robert Louis Stevenson's Land of Counterpane, although I would never have called it a counterpane. It was a bedspread and that was that.

My parents and I lived next door to my grandparents, in a flat above the two small shops owned by my family: one a sweetshop and one from which my grandfather sold fishing tackle. In the warm, dim bedroom we three shared, my mother's eyelids were drooping with weariness but she would not desert me. The drugs made my arms and legs jerk, jittery as a puppet. Often it felt as though my limbs were growing large, ballooning out, or that the walls of the room had receded into some unimaginable distance. In the bedroom was a big mirror, fixed to the dressing table. When the light from under the door shone on it, it glowed with a livid grey aura. I thought that it had turned into a giant mouse, and screamed.

Sometimes, when I was very small, my nana, Honora, would take me into her big bed in the afternoons for a nap. There would be the strange clandestine feeling of bed in the daytime, with the traffic noise outside and the vague light filtering in and the smell of feathers from the eider-down. There were birds outside, singing their dusty city song, sparrows with soot in their throats. Then the heavier thump and trundle of traffic in Whitehall Road. I was never very good at napping in the afternoon. I always fidgeted and she would push me out.

'Go on down then, if you're not going to sleep.'

The narrow house, the adjacent shops, the two-roomed flat above, with a stone-flagged yard and wash-house outside the back door, these were my world and it seemed big enough for me. The main road at the front door was judged too dangerous for play. Sometimes, in the evening, I would venture down the single steep flight of stairs from the flat, through the fishing tackle shop, with sawdust on the floor, through the sweetshop to my grandparents' part of the house. The lamplight from outside – gas lights in my very early years – shone in on the big scales and jars full of pear drops, acid drops and cough candy. There were bars of Fry's Five Boys chocolate too and I was sometimes allowed to take one. The shop smelled of mints and tobacco. If I was on my own, I would run through, afraid of what might come after me.

One foggy night when I was wheezing as usual and tucked up with plenty of pillows and blankets on the settee (like 'counterpane', the word 'sofa' was unknown too), my father was late coming home from the night school he went to after work. My mother, cooking cauliflower cheese, grew irritated with worry. The supper dried up and filled the room with the smell of burnt vegetables. Tongues of dirty yellow fog crept under the door and curled around the light. When my father came in, he had a big wad of bandage and plaster over one eyebrow. His face looked green under it. A car had hit his bicycle in the fog and he had been tossed over the bonnet. He had had to have stitches in the cut on his forehead, had been lucky it wasn't worse, the doctor said. My mother's anger dissolved into retrospective panic. I was shocked. Anything could happen. All of your worst fears might be realised. People were fragile then, all blood and bruises. It could happen over and over again and probably would.

I loved my family unconditionally. Nobody was ever cross with me or, if they were, I don't recall it. I remember falling asleep on my nana's soft lap or sitting in my little chair, watching my grandad work in his fishing tackle shop and pestering him with questions. I remember Saturdays spent in the countryside with my father, or playing with my Aunty Vera on the rag rug in the living kitchen, or helping my mother make fancy paperchains in the weeks before Christmas. We would sit together in the dim light of our room upstairs, with the gas fire making its soft popping sound and *Journey into Space* (the title always intoned in a sepulchral and menacing voice) on the wireless. I remember struggling to breathe and my grandad, Joe, distraught, saying he wished he could 'give it to the milkman's horse'. Milkmen still had horses in those days.

And yet, when I think back to that time, to my nana and my mother, Kathleen, and my aunts Vera and Nora, I'm aware of a thread of something wild and strange running through all of them, these women with their mixed Irish and Yorkshire Dales heritage. To describe it as steel would be a cliché and besides, it would be inaccurate. This was different: at once more fine, more flexible, almost invisible, unless you glimpsed it in certain lights or inadvertently came up against it: spider silk, a female thread, one of the strongest and toughest natural fibres in existence. They say that a Boeing 747 could be stopped in flight by a single pencil-width strand of spider silk. True or not, there have been times when I was uneasily aware of this female strength, this not entirely comfortable resilience, to which I have fallen heir, like it or not: a determination not to be messed with, never to give in or give up. An angry determination not to suffer fools at all, never mind gladly. That was what ran through the women in our family and, as far as I know, it still does.

Among our small collection of family photographs, there's a post-war 1940s picture of my mother, Kathleen, and her sister, Vera, with two friends whose names I don't know: four young women marching confidently down the street, arm in arm, smiling at the cameraman. I love this picture and find myself returning to it again and again, as some kind of antidote to the many nineteenth- and early twentieth-century pictures from working-class Yorkshire I've gazed at over the past few years. These other, grimmer pictures are often posed, static images of groups of working people, women and children in mills or other factories, bearded men in industrial settings, individuals or groups posed outside crumbling brick walls. Time has lent a kind of artistic gloss, a weird beauty, to these images.

One of these staged pictures actually hangs on my wall. It must have been taken in the very early 1900s, or the late 1890s. It shows a group of road menders, some standing, some seated on stools with a background of greenery, trees in leaf. These labourers are in grubby working clothes, a uniform of sorts: baggy, muddy, corduroy trousers, flannel shirts – almost all of them are wearing waistcoats and boots but there is a great variety of hats. Most have beards or moustaches, and one or two of them are smoking their pipes or chewing on them, the way pipe smokers often do. They are quite obviously a team. They stare defiantly at the photographer, some with their arms folded. Seated in the front row is a big man with a full white beard, a battered hat and what looks like a leather waistcoat. He is clutching a large black tar barrel on his knee. I know the names of two of these men and, although the man with the beard and the barrel is one of them, I know only his nickname. He's Tarry Arse the Fiddler. The man sitting next to him is my great-grandfather, James Flynn, sometimes known as Michael, from Ballinlough in County Roscommon, Ireland. He was a paviour, who laid paving stones, a skilled occupation that, for its time, paid well enough. In 1891, ten years after the murder, he's living in Hound Street, in the Quarry Hill area of the city, with his new wife, Mary, and her family from her previous marriage. Some of the houses here had been built in the late 1700s, but by the mid- to late 1800s, massively overcrowded, without proper sanitation and with frequent outbreaks of disease from wells polluted by sewage, this was not a healthy area. James had aspirations, though, and learned how to read and write at a time when many could not. There he is in the picture: small and self-possessed, compact and strong, with a round, knobbly 'billycock' hat like a kind of industrial bowler and a neat moustache, a waistcoat, too, neatly fastened. He looks as though he's impatient with the process of photography, anxious to be up and doing. There are always jobs to be done.

Mostly, though, these nineteenth- and early twentieth-century images of working-class people in Leeds and its surrounding towns are oddly impersonal and often downright exploitative, so that when you look more closely, you notice the skeletal thinness of the young women and children, the raggedness of their clothes, the way in which some of them are haggard with illness or injury or with extremes of poverty. It's as though the photographer was more interested in their working environment than he ever was in them. There is a whole swathe of pictures of squalid housing, streets and yards of back-to-back terraced houses, where the people seem to be incidental, there only to show the scale of their environment. Back-to-backs were exactly that: rows of houses built back to back and at this time generally of substandard construction. The very poorest were flea- and cockroach-infested, bug-ridden. Bed bugs would throng the ceilings with their curious coriander scent. The people trapped in these photographs, as though by chance, gaze at the camera without interest, faintly hostile if anything, certainly suspicious. They must have been told to stay still – these are very old images – and so they do, mostly unsmiling, leaning on walls or doors, giving an impression of nothing so much as overwhelming fatigue.

Another image, this time from the excellent Leodis website, caught my eye before I knew that there was any family connection with the place: Off Yard near Off Street, looking towards Brick Street. To the left are bricked-in railway arches, to the right yet another row of back-to-backs with a window in the foreground, wooden shutters folded back against the wall. The windows in these houses are unexpectedly large and multi-paned, given that the rooms were so small. They must have been designed to let in such light as was available, bearing in mind that the alleyways were narrow, and industrial buildings blotted out the sun. The ground-floor rooms often seem to have had these external wooden shutters, for security or warmth or perhaps both.

There are two particularly disturbing things about this picture. One is the dirty brick wall, some five or six feet high, that seems to have been built only to divide one section of the street from another, but look more closely and you can see that the wall flanks a narrow passage with cracked paving – we'd have called it a snicket, when I was a girl – that leads off to the left, past what may be an outside privy. All of these houses in the notorious Bank area of Leeds had been built to take advantage of every spare foot of space, so access to houses was often by means only of these narrow passageways. In the foreground, in it but not quite of it, virtually propped against the shutter, or at least steadying herself against it with her elbow, stands a diminutive young woman. She looks as though she would like to slide right out of the picture but has been told to stand still. Like the Red House Inn, this image too dates from 1901 and the photographer seems to be more interested in the configuration of the street than in the girl. She is incidental, like all of her kind. It must be winter, because she's bundled up in dark clothes, a full, shabby skirt with flannel petticoats beneath and one of her black boots showing, a short fitted jacket and, over it all, a knitted shawl, covering her head and shoulders, the light stripe across her shoulders and a coat of whitewash on the wall behind her the only bright elements in the picture. Her little hands are tucked up beneath the shawl, against the cold; you can see something of her hair, and a thin, dirty, unhappy face. But she's doing as she's told, standing still. An even closer examination of the figure reveals that she is, in all probability, stooping forward a little, the way you do when your back aches incessantly. There is about her an impression of despair so intense that you can practically feel it seeping out of the picture, more than a hundred years later. There are plenty more like this. At first, you, the viewer, approach them with curiosity, only to find yourself experiencing some painful combination of sympathy and outrage. The very worst, the most upsetting, are those highly posed pictures of inmates of workhouses or asylums in their uniforms with attenuated and horribly vulnerable or simply vacant faces, the faces of people who have abandoned all hope, because there is none.

Perhaps this is why I find myself so drawn to that later photograph of my mother Kathleen, her sister Vera and their friends. It's a good picture, professional rather than a snapshot. It was taken in Douglas, Isle of Man and they must have gone there on holiday together. The picture must have been taken post-war, in the mid- to late 1940s. Kathleen would be about twenty and Vera twenty-two, roughly the same age as their great-uncle John Manley when he died. Both are unmarried. They are in the centre of the shot and all four of them are striding out, the two on the left with left foot first, the two on the right with right foot first. Perhaps the photographer, enchanted by such lovely, vivid young women, choreographed the image like this.

All of them have fashionably long, wavy or curly hair, victory rolls, pin-curl waves. All are smart. Vera is wearing a pretty print summer dress, probably one she made herself, and Kathleen has on a closely fitting striped top and cardigan and a pleated skirt. She's carrying a camera over her shoulder. They are wearing flat, comfortable sandals for walking and they look supremely happy and self-assured. Looking at it now, I realise how rare it is to see that confident expression on old pictures of ordinary working women, although that's what they were. They would certainly have been labelled working class, and Leeds Irish working class at that. It is ahead of its time, that image, and it's their joyfulness that both inspires and breaks your heart, coupled with their determined self-confidence. They know how good they look and they are enjoying themselves. They have all the poise of their youth. The war is over. They are, in this moment, absolutely happy and sure of themselves.

2. *Nothing Short of Deliberate Murder*

The events of that Christmas Day in 1881 are described in graphic detail in various recorded and some published accounts. There is an inquest, a magisterial enquiry and, of course, a trial. There are long reports in several Leeds newspapers. This was a time when the press covered such cases in extensive, but reasonably accurate, detail with very little recourse to sensationalism. This was so much the case that some time later, Sir William Vernon Harcourt, Secretary of State at the 'Home Department', or as we would call it the Home Office, when considering the sentence, would ask for a copy of a full newspaper report of the murder, as well as the judge's report on the trial. It was clear that he also wanted to assess the political temperature in the city, and perhaps the popular opinion of the verdict. On that occasion, the *Leeds Mercury* was supplied, but most accounts of the trial, although varying in detail here and there, and throwing up a few anomalies, tell a consistent, albeit complicated, story.

On 25 December 1881, a group of young Irish people had been spending the holiday in company. For people in their situation that meant getting out of the cramped, cold, bug-ridden and ill-lit rooms in which they lived a life of sorts in the notorious 'Bank' area of Leeds: Marsh Lane, Brick Street, Off Yard, Mill Street. There was a whole series of courts and yards running parallel to the railway viaduct carrying the NER Leeds to York line. Proposals to construct this line had first been mooted in 1863 and now the railway viaduct, sixteen feet high and with a span of some thirty feet, had been built through the larger yards and, incidentally, through the churchyard of St Peter's Church, with small regard for those buried there or their surviving relatives.

By 1881, Bank and its surrounding area was a warren of alleys and dead ends, dominated by the railway. In September 1865, when John Manley was a little boy, T. Clifford Allbutt, physician to the House of Recovery (the place of last resort for poor people with infectious diseases), wrote to the *Leeds Mercury* expressing his concerns regarding the epidemic of typhoid fever in Leeds and in particular of the 'squalor, the deadliness and the decay of a mass of huts which lies in the town of Leeds, between York Street on the one side and Marsh Lane on the other; a place of dark and cruel habitations, which is within a stone's throw of our parish church and where the fever is bred'. He went on to say, 'if the railway should clear all these yards away, we at the House of Recovery should have little to do', going on to assert that 'fever, like mushrooms, best flourishes on dunghills in a low, dark nook'.

Should their dwellings have been cleared away, the people inhabiting them would have had nowhere else to go. When, in the future, slum clearances were instigated, the same problem arose. Overcrowding and poor maintenance began all over again. The evolution in manufacturing, the overwhelming mechanisation, had happened without any significant planning for the housing, let alone the welfare, of those workers who had become nothing more nor less than factory fodder: too often seen as a necessary evil. Caring factory owners and managers, such as the philanthropist Titus Salt, were rare. He had built Saltaire in 1851, near Shipley, also in West Yorkshire, and this village with its good housing and various benefits for workers and their families, including educational and recreational initiatives, was seen as a model of good practice. Unfortunately, few others followed his example.

Skilled Yorkshire hand weavers, only a few years earlier, had worked independently from home or from small weaving sheds, selling their wares to the city cloth merchants, who had been their customers rather than their masters. As in Scotland, they may not have been wealthy, but they were self-regulated, and they had self-respect. The radically changed relationship must have been bitter indeed. It wasn't the advent of new machinery that they hated, so much as what it stood for in all its unregulated race for profits: the steady degradation of their trade and with it, since it was cheaper to employ women and children in the new manufactories, the degradation of family life. People had always worked hard and there had always been lean times of the year, but they had, at least, been able to work together. Children had been expected to work for their keep, but in the new factories they were involved in hard physical labour for long hours, often at the imminent risk of life and limb, and were frequently beaten to make them go faster. It's no coincidence that in rural areas, before the Industrial Revolution, although pregnancy outside marriage was believed to be inadvisable and immoral, it was not the disaster it would later become. There would be one more mouth to feed for sure, but when people worked from home, on a small tenant farm, or in a cottage industry such as weaving, a child might be accommodated and quickly absorbed. The additional expense would soon be obviated by the extra pair of hands the child would provide, threading needles, winding bobbins or scaring birds. These were not normally jobs that would be done twelve or thirteen hours a day, summer and winter alike, as they were in the new manufactories.

It's no use pretending that rural and village life had been some kind of golden age. Miserable poverty, destitution and disease had always existed. The lead miners of North Yorkshire, the slate miners of Wales, the coal miners and the tin miners were used to privation and cruel treatment. But textiles had at least afforded a measure of independence to those for whom it was their livelihood. No longer. It was in these circumstances that the masters who were making considerable sums of money from the new technologies welcomed the incoming Irish migrants as another source of even cheaper labour.

These Irish, escaping the Great Hunger in their own villages, had already been shamefully betrayed. This was no famine in the accepted sense, brought on by drought or flood. Successive failures of the potato harvest meant hunger for a large percentage of the population. Grain may have been grown in Ireland but it wasn't used to feed the native Irish. It was shipped to Britain. Meanwhile, in the countries to which so many Irish people, especially the young, fled, the ground was laid for a shift in perceptions of the poor. Small workhouses had once been places of last resort, a refuge for the old and the infirm. The ascent of industrialisation had given rise to a middle class of people who thought well of themselves, and judged those who seemed unwilling or unable to help themselves as indigent. There had always been some notion of the deserving and the undeserving poor, but now it formed the basis of a set of policies that informed the whole system, a notion that has never quite left us. My Irish forebears, living on the northern bank of the River Aire, were certainly judged to be the undeserving poor.

Bank and its adjacent districts were hotbeds of fever and had been for many years, but it wasn't until the turn of the century, in the early 1900s, that the areas housing so many people were properly designated as unhealthy and scheduled for demolition. The truth was that they had never been little havens for the working classes, as I have seen them wishfully described. They had always been built with more thought for potential income than the comfort of the inhabitants and, with little to no regulation, the bare minimum to support life was provided. Throughout the previous hundred years, levels of industrial pollution had increased exponentially. The River Aire and its associated becks or streams were filthy; recipients of every variety of refuse, human and industrial. The air was full of sulphurous smoke and the middle classes who reaped the rewards of increasing prosperity were moving ever further out of town, in an effort to find more congenial surroundings. As it was sometimes termed, they were living 'above the smoke'. For the first seven years of my life, I lived below the smoke. It took my parents a while to find a way out, but they did. No similar means of escape was open to the nineteenth-century poor.

In this context, then, pubs and beerhouses must have been welcome refuges, the only real outlet available to these people, especially in winter, with light and the heat of a good fire, the comfort of such alcohol as they could afford, and almost certainly music as well: penny whistles, perhaps a fiddler, some kind of percussion: spoons or bones or maybe a bodhrán. Voices most of all. I don't know whether any of the Manleys sang, but my great-grandfather James Flynn certainly did. This was a time when comic songs and rebellious songs but perhaps most of all sad songs of emigration and regret were sung, not just in pubs, but in music halls as well, although even such inexpensive entertainments might be beyond the means of these people for much of the time. Pubs and beerhouses might have an upstairs room in which there would be singing and dancing. Middle-class observers at the time write of prostitutes and factory girls dancing together (they seem to make very little distinction between the two and their disapproval of both shines through) with their bare arms and tawdry jewellery. They did not approve of what they saw and termed it depravity.

Not only was it Christmas Day when the altercation took place, but that year it fell on a Sunday. I don't know if this meant that the following day would be a holiday, since the expectation of a holiday on 26 December is a fairly recent innovation in the working year and factory owners were reluctant to slow or stop the machinery. At any rate, Christmas Day itself was certainly a day of holiday and celebration. John Manley and his friend James Rooks, who lived at Mason's Buildings, in the adjacent Quarry Hill area, had been spending the day together. James worked as a cloth dresser, cutting the surface of the cloth after it had been in the fulling mill, a skilled occupation for a young man. John Manley was working as a dyer's labourer. He would be employed to move dyestuffs, mix dye baths under the instructions of the dyer, and haul the dyed textiles onto draining slabs: a heavy, dirty and largely unskilled job. Other reports tell of him having 'no regular avocation'. This probably means that he had no fixed situation, but undertook heavy, casual work in the dyehouses of the flax mills where his sisters also worked. Picture John: slight and wiry and cheerful, dressed in his Sunday best, with his red hair and his perpetually stained hands from the dye. We know so little about him. Did he have aspirations? What were his hopes and dreams? Did he have his eye on a pretty girl? All we know is that he had had a good day, and that he was about to become notorious, not because of anything he had done, but because of his status as victim. Picture the pair of them, John and his friend James, a bit unsteady on their feet, but pleased with themselves.

This was the second of two sessions in the Railway Hotel, the first in the middle of the day, from 12.30 till closing time at 2.30pm. They had then spent the afternoon drinking together, and had decided to return for opening time at 6pm. So James could say, with absolute truth, that they had been in only one pub that day. He doesn't specify what they had been drinking in the afternoon, nor where, but it may have been whisky.

'Manley was not sober,' he admits. 'But then none of us were. I knew what I was doing.'

Drink had certainly been taken, but they weren't obviously drunk. If they had been, the landlord, John

Hardaker, would not have served them. He seems to have run a decent pub and, as soon became apparent, he was not afraid to turn people out if they showed any signs of drunkenness or aggression. Rooks reported that the pair of them had been together from nine in the morning, which suggests they may even have been at mass in St Patrick's, doing their duty before the pleasure of a holiday. Or would they? In these communities, those born in Ireland attended mass as a matter of course. Of those born in Britain, children, women and old men attended mass more often than young men, but Christmas Day may have been an exception and Irish families traditionally go to church on that day. Midnight mass, late on Christmas Eve, may have been a possibility. At some point during that day, they must have eaten, whether in Brussels Street with Elizabeth and Bridget, or at James Rooks's house, or elsewhere, we don't know, nor do we know what kind of Christmas dinner they may have had.

Roast beef was a Christmas favourite in northern England, but not for the poor. Potatoes would certainly have featured, possibly cabbage cooked with a little bacon, maybe even a rabbit stew if they were lucky and had been able to afford the meat. Bread was a staple and eaten in large quantities. Beef bones or spare ribs would be made into a stew, padded out with potatoes and onions. Salt herrings would be cheap and plentiful and would go well with potatoes. Meat and potato pie would be a double way of eking out a small quantity of meat with vegetables and pastry, if they had access to an oven. Yorkshire pudding too is a good filler but needs a hot oven. The Manley family at that time were very unlikely to have had the kind of range my grandmother had, years later, in her house in Lower Wortley, south of the River Aire, and may have used a communal bakehouse if one were available. Think of the young Cratchits in *A Christmas Carol*, who 'came tearing in, screaming that outside the baker's they had smelt the goose and known it for their own'. The Cratchit potatoes were cooked on the stove, the pudding – 'a small pudding for a large family' – in the copper where the washing was done. The Irish incomers were very fond of tea, a liking that persists to this day in my family, but tea was more expensive than coffee and it's surprising how often the poor, even children, subsisted on a diet of coffee and bread. Even Henry Mayhew, writing about the London Irish forty years earlier, describes how often they drank coffee. Presumably the caffeine helped to keep them going. Although alcohol was freely available to those who could afford it, and was cheaper and more readily available than meat, money was always in short supply, so it's probably true that the two young men were by no means drunk, just not very sober.

Other friends had gathered in the cheerful warmth of the pub. There was John's younger sister, Elizabeth, with her friend Mary Ann Burke, and a few other young men. Bridget was not present and was probably at home in Brussels Street nearby. Mary Ann was a single woman who lived in Phillips Yard, again not very far away. She was nineteen years old, worked as a flax spinner and lived with her parents, both of them born in Ireland, and several siblings. Although she seems to have been Elizabeth's friend, her eyes were on John Manley. Unlike any of the other witnesses, she described his clothes in some detail. He was wearing a light coat, light trousers and waistcoat and a 'billycock' – bowler-type – hat. He was, in short, all cleaned up and dressed for the holiday, fancying himself as a young man about town.

John and James were sitting at the right-hand side of the pub in what they called the 'dram shop', which could be accessed only through the tap-room, where the beer was served. Dram shops had once dealt in small tots or 'drams' of gin, but by this time, other spirits would have been available – more evidence that the Railway Hotel was somewhat more than a beerhouse. The young women witnessed what went on. John and James were bickering about fighting. 'Fratching' is the word sometimes used for this and implies a low-key quarrel, a squabble, rather than anything more serious. They were doing what all young men who are 'not sober' do and taunting each other, good-humouredly. There had been a fight, earlier that day, in a different pub, not one frequented by the pair. Word had got out and the two young men had heard about it. The fight had, as Rooks said, 'come off that day' and they were bickering about it.

At half past nine, not long before closing time, John Ross came in with two friends. These two men seem to have been much the worse for liquor and when they immediately began to make a nuisance of themselves, John Hardaker stopped them in the passage, refused to supply them with drink and turned them out. Ross, conciliatory and by no means as drunk as his friends, said he was looking for somebody, and asked to be allowed to 'just glance into the tap-room'. The landlord agreed to this, although he still refused to serve him with drink, to 'fill for him', as the expression went. However, perhaps because Manley and Rooks knew him, Hardaker didn't turn him out immediately. Ross wandered into the room where Manley and Rooks were sitting and said he would smoke a pipe before leaving. The pipe itself would have been a cheap clay version. Some of these were plain, some had harps or faces on them. Some traditional pipes were carved from bog oak, but, bearing in mind that these were poor people, a clay pipe would have been much the most likely. Pipes with Irish motifs were not always made in Ireland. At least one pipe maker in Leeds manufactured his pipes with the word Dublin stamped on them, because he knew that Irish smokers, men and women, preferred to use Irish pipes. Ross sat down and smoked his pipe and listened in on the conversation for a while. This was not unusual. Manley in particular knew Ross well, as did Elizabeth, and there had never been any quarrel between them. In fact, Elizabeth pointed out later that they had been friends for years. At this time and after a troubled youth, Ross was living with his mother and some of his siblings in Somerset Street, not far away from Brussels Street, in a similar warren of slum housing.

Manley and Rooks carried on discussing the earlier fight, one they had only heard about but had not witnessed, since it had taken place in or outside a different pub. There had been a scuffle, and a man named Anthony McDonald had struck another person, a friend of theirs named Rory Brannagan.

'If I'd been there,' bragged John Manley, 'I wouldn't have let it happen. I'd have hit McDonald myself first.'

It's worth noting that a large family called McDonald were living in close proximity to the Manleys, at number 6 Brussels Street, in rooms once occupied by the Manleys when their parents were alive. There's no Anthony, although it's possible that he came from the same family. It's possible, too, especially in view of later developments, that there was some animus between the two families, although not, as far as we can tell, between Ross and Manley in particular.

Rooks and other observers admitted in court that he and Manley were still 'fratching' about the fight, although it was good-humoured enough at this point. Fighting was at least as commonplace then as it is late at night in certain British towns and cities nowadays and, then as now, drink was usually a factor in the aggression. Young millworkers from Irish migrant families were notoriously quick-tempered, readily resorting to fisticuffs – that much about the stereotype was true – but serious injuries were rare, and most of the encounters were street scraps, soon begun, quickly over. Besides, the English lads were just as likely to fight as well. Religious tensions were not unduly high in Leeds at this time, although they existed, but there was no serious sectarian element to these fights. Irish migrants congregated in certain areas, but this was as much for economic reasons as anything else. They couldn't afford to live in better housing and they were more likely to fight among themselves than with outsiders. Stories of gang fights between young millworkers from different localities, male and female, abound in northern towns and cities at this time, and very young gang members did carry knives. However, I was surprised by how seldom fights resulted in death, even in cities like Manchester, where gangs of teenage 'scuttlers' horrified the largely powerless authorities by staging pitched territorial battles with belts used as weapons, and knives employed too, on a regular basis. There were deaths from time to time, but injuries, from minor to serious, were far more common.

The young men drinking in the Railway Hotel were a bit too old for these pursuits and, besides, they knew each other well. Descriptions of Ross's dress, however, suggest that he might have fancied himself as some kind of gangster: he was portrayed in the *Police Gazette* for 30 December 1881 as being five foot five or six inches tall, with dark brown hair, dark eyes, a fresh complexion, prominent forehead, dark eyebrows, sunken eyes, slight moustache and a squint. He was dressed in dark cord trousers with bell bottoms, a slightly frayed and shabby black coat and vest, a Turkey red plaid scarf, dirty shirt, old shoes and a rough bully cap with a knob on the top. The scarf and bell bottoms were sometimes the mark of gang membership. But they could just as easily have been the mark of his holiday best.

I find something heart-rending about these descriptions of their clothing: Manley in his light coat, trousers and waistcoat; Ross trying to live up to the demands of the day, but quite without the resources to do so. The description seems to paints a picture of a young man – he was still young – at once vulnerable and braggardly. He cuts quite a figure. His clothes are dirty, and in the middle of a chilly Leeds winter, his coat is shabby and his trousers are frayed, but he's defiantly wearing his Turkey red plaid scarf in honour of the season. The Irish were well known for a love of bright colours, when they could get them.

Ross, who seems to have been approaching that stage of drunkenness where young men spoil for a fight ('trailing the tail of his coat', my grandmother would have called it), interrupted the conversation between Manley and Rooks to say that Manley would *not*, in his opinion, have been able to hit McDonald.

'Yes I could,' said Manley.

'No you could not,' said Ross.

Ross then compounded the argument by proclaiming, 'I could slug the pair of you,' but Manley said he didn't want to fight. 'I'm not a fighting man,' he said.

Ross thereupon produced sixpence (although how he had any money left at all after a day's drinking is a wonder) and said he would fight Manley for it, since it was all he had.

Manley laughingly refused, declaring, according to Mary Ann Burke who was nearby, that he would 'rather fight for fun than for sixpence'. Ross challenged Rooks instead. James Rooks may have considered himself more of a fighting man, but at any rate, Manley produced his own sixpence and the lads agreed that Rooks and Ross would have a 'bit of a fight' the following morning, by which time tempers would have safely abated, and in any case, hangovers would probably have precluded fighting. I think we can assume that all parties were thought to be too drunk at this stage to do more than issue threats. Sadly, this was not quite the case and Manley seems not to have had the faintest notion of his danger.

Ross began to lose his temper and swore that he would pay the pair of them. Manley sensibly pocketed his sixpence again, but by this time Hardaker had caught sight of the sixpences and, afraid that they meant fisticuffs, which such bets all too often did, switched off one of the lights, announced closing time and turned the three men out into the street, along with the other Christmas revellers. All of the witnesses swore that there had been no physical fighting at all inside the pub. The group consisted of the three main participants, as well as Mary Ann Burke and Elizabeth Manley, Edward Kilvington and a few others who are not named. More people were loitering outside. Perhaps word of the quarrel had spread. Elizabeth set off down the street, planning to go home. Mary Ann lingered beside John Manley. Ross, wary of taking on two men at once, was still issuing threats that if he had anyone on his side to help him, he would fight the pair of them, Rooks and Manley both. The conversation about fighting continued for a few minutes, becoming more heated, at least on Ross's part, all the time. However, it was clear that no blows had yet been struck and Manley had not threatened anyone. In fact, he was standing 'in anything but a fighting position' as witnesses reported. He had one hand in his coat pocket, and the other down by his side. The only light on the scene was the big gas lamp over the pub door, but that would have been reasonably bright so the witnesses would have seen what happened next clearly enough.

Ross, still spoiling for a fight, said that he could beat them both and the 'fratching' continued. There are several versions of Ross's words, given by various witnesses. He said he would 'pay' the pair of them. Edward Kilvington, a moulder, was also in the pub. He lived at 9 Lumb Street, another unhealthy area with little or no sanitation, some few hundred yards away. He knew both men, saw the quarrel and testified that he heard Ross say that if he had had a knife he would have 'put it through Manley's heart'. Rooks, on the other hand, heard him say, 'If I had a knife,

I could rip the pair of you.' Perhaps he issued all of these threats, although the last seems the most credible.

Edward Kilvington, who had been the first to leave the pub, noticed that Manley was standing behind Rooks and that he was talking to a young fellow behind him, perhaps with his head turned. Unfortunately, at that moment, Ross put his hand in his pocket, discovered that he did indeed have a knife, a pocket knife such as men used for cutting tobacco. He had smoked his pipe a little while earlier. This may not even have been the kind of folding knife we envisage today when we think about a pocket knife. A tobacco knife was a rudimentary wooden-handled knife with a very sharp fixed blade that could be used for chopping pipe tobacco into shreds from a roll or twist.

On impulse, Ross drew the weapon and struck a sudden and violent blow at Manley. The weapon was driven deep into the other man's neck, felling him instantly. Mary Ann Burke saw the knife sticking out of his neck, but it dropped to the ground. Ross turned around and ran away, dropping his cap in the process. Kilvington picked it up but Ross didn't stop for it. A man named Patrick O'Doherty, a cloth dresser who lived on York Street, seized Ross by the collar of his coat and shouted at him, 'What did you do that for?' but a panic-stricken Ross pulled out of his arms. O'Doherty took a swing at him but didn't know whether he had hit him or not. Ross rushed away along the street with O'Doherty after him. He chased him for some thirty yards, but eventually gave up and came back to see what had happened to John Manley.

Elizabeth was already some paces away, 'at the bottom of the street about nine or ten yards from the hotel,' she said in court, when she heard a scream and a woman, probably Mary Ann, raise a cry of 'Murder!' She turned back, just in time to see Ross running past her, and her brother lying on the ground, bleeding, although she saw no knife.

'You've killed my brother!' she cried as Ross passed her.

He was not seen again for several weeks.

Seventeen-year-old Elizabeth gave evidence at the trial that Ross and Manley 'had been good friends, as far as I know', an assertion that was repeated by other witnesses.

'They had known each other for years,' they said.

*

There are no photographs of John, or even of Elizabeth, not even a surviving official photograph of her, although it might have been expected and I searched for one. I'm left with words. We know from later descriptions of Elizabeth that she was five foot three inches tall, weighing just under eight and a half stone, but at the age of seventeen she may have been even more slight and slender than she was a few years later. Elizabeth's teeth were described as irregular but this in itself would not have been unusual. She had brown hair, grey eyes and a pale complexion, as did my own mother. The Irish genes in my family are very strong. I look like my mother and my cousins. I find myself imagining that Elizabeth may have looked a little like all of us, but there are no pictures. It's striking how often that 'pale complexion' crops up in official records. These were people who lived and worked in gloom and, even when outdoors, seldom breathed fresh air.

Nobody in our family ever mentioned Elizabeth, although they spoke briefly about the murder. It wasn't until

I began to look at official records that I discovered anything about her. She had been excised from family history, as surely as though she had never existed. My grandmother, Honora, generally known as Nora, was born to John and Elizabeth's elder sister, Mary, in 1887, six years after he was murdered and while Elizabeth was still alive, although I'm certain that Honora never met her. Nobody of that generation met Elizabeth. It's doubtful whether my nana knew anything at all about this missing aunt, although she used to describe Elizabeth's brother, her late, unknown uncle, as having 'a lovely head of curly red hair'. We can assume this is true, because Mary would certainly have spoken about her much-loved brother. Honora in turn told the story to her own children, and they, my mother, Kathleen, my aunts, Nora and Vera, and my uncle George, spoke about it to me and my cousins. Like many such family stories, it had been passed down shorn of most of its detail, until it had become a tradition, a myth of sorts.

'There was a murder in the family. John was killed in the street at Christmas. He was very young. His murderer got away with it, because he was protected by his friends.'

I'm struck by how some of this is true but some isn't. Or rather, by how many of my assumptions about the events of that night and the dreadful repercussions, proved to be imprecise. Only vaguely true. And much more complicated than I might have supposed. There were times when this process seemed to involve a constant revision of conjectures in the light of further research. It's natural to draw conclusions from limited evidence, but all too often, they're wrong.

Nobody ever mentioned Elizabeth at all.

3. *But Little Above the Savage*

In Leeds, the addresses of the main players in this tragedy, traced through census entries and other official and unofficial reports, centre around Brussells or Brussels Street (spelled with a double 'll' in many but not all documents), Off Street, York Street, Marsh Lane and Brick Street. They were part of the area called Bank or The Bank, on the north bank of the River Aire, and also those districts round about, including Quarry Hill and Richmond Hill, beyond and between the railway line and the river. It has been described as a rough area where the police walked in threes, although the Catholic priest could go about the streets in absolute safety. People looked out for each other if they could, but then it was certain that nobody else would.

It was at that time a labyrinth of streets and yards, with as many back-to-back houses as landowners and developers could possibly squeeze in, so as to maximise their rentals. The alleys and tunnels that we called snickets or ginnels gave access to the back part of each terrace. Roads were narrow, too, and pavements were narrow or non-existent. Developers were determined to utilise every available space and these streets and yards were often in close proximity to railway bridges or looming mills, with cracked paving or dirt lanes rather than roads. Some of the houses were very old indeed, timber-framed houses that had once been good town houses, long before the railway line sliced through everything in its path, leaving the remaining dwellings cheek by jowl with looming viaducts.

Goits were man-made water channels that had originally been constructed to divert river water so that it could be used to power industrial engines, and then, like a traditional mill lade, rejoin the river. Many of these had now, with the expanding population and rampant overcrowding, become little more than broad open drains. They might run between the houses down towards the river, with rickety wooden bridges here and there allowing residents to cross. They might become clogged up with refuse and sewage and would have stunk, especially in summer. They were a powerful source of infection. A handful of existing photographs date from the years of the 'sanitary inspections' at the turn of the century, 1899 or thereabouts. Residents must have been sent into the street while such inspections were carried out, and the sheer numbers of people, especially children, gives some idea of the overcrowding experienced on a daily basis.

Writing for a government report in 1845, James Smith says:

> By far the most unhealthy localities of Leeds are close squares of houses, or yards as they are called, which have been erected for the accommodation of working people. Some of these . . . are airless from the enclosed structure and being wholly unprovided with any form of under-drainage or convenience, or arrangements for cleansing, are one mass of damp and filth. . . . The ashes, garbage and filth of all kinds are thrown from

> the doors and windows of the houses upon the surface of the streets and courts. The privies are few in proportion to the inhabitants. They are open to view both in front and rear, are invariably in a filthy condition and often remain without removal of the filth for six months.

Even in the 1870s, the sanitary arrangements had hardly improved, and privies were still few in proportion to the numbers of inhabitants. In general, there was little in the way of street lighting, with the occasional gas lamp illuminating a yard or street corner. Smog was commonplace, air and water pollution widespread and intense. Winter nights were very cold and very dark indeed. Freezing yellow fog drifted into these low-lying buildings as it did throughout my own childhood, making the occupants cough and wheeze. If they blew their noses, supposing they were lucky enough to have handkerchiefs, the linen or cotton would be blackened. The houses were small and cramped, nothing like the later, more sturdily built back-to-backs, some of which could be warm and comfortable. Instead, each 'house' would consist of one small room (maybe fourteen foot square) upstairs, and one room down, with shutters at the windows, and with a cellar below, sometimes with the very top of a window at street level to let in a little light but more often with a grate at pavement level. The cellar, being utterly inhospitable, and even more bug-ridden than the rest of the house, would be rented out more cheaply than the other rooms. A casual glance at the 1881 census reveals a widow named Mary Flynn, aged 60, a 'sewing hand' or 'seamstress', living in a cellar in Balls Yard with her twenty-two-year-old lodger, a flax spinner named Bridget McNulty – two women, young and old, struggling to survive like troglodytes, below ground. Bridget would have escaped to the mill each day, but Mary probably worked from home.

Whole families, as well as lodgers, might live in one or two rooms at the most, perhaps in one cramped and damp cellar, without piped water or any sewerage system. The best they could hope for was some kind of outside privy, serving many people. This could be as basic as a hole in the ground with a wooden screen offering a modicum of privacy. Often there were no facilities at all, and human waste would be collected in a bucket and emptied onto or – if you were lucky – into a communal midden, with a metal hatch that could be locked and unlocked by those many residents who had to share it. There would be a fireplace in each room, but fuel was scarce. Many people could hardly afford furniture. There might be a corner cupboard with some crockery, a few holy pictures adorning the walls, the Blessed Virgin Mary, the Sacred Heart and the saints, with halos around their heads. Rosary beads would be treasured, but beds might be a luxury and were always shared. For some poor souls, a heap of straw and rags might be the only bedding. As the nineteenth century progressed, the overcrowding and filth became ever more shocking. There were outbreaks of cholera and typhus. Individuals in authority issued critical reports and recommendations but little would change until the end of the century. They, after all, did not have to live in these surroundings.

Many of those writing about the poverty of Britain's industrial cities would reserve their particular opprobrium for the Irish. In 1832, James Philips Kay, a Manchester physician, offers a description that seems to be more judgmental of the victims than of those who ignored or profited by the conditions in which these often unwilling and homesick migrants found themselves, a condition from which it was virtually impossible to escape.

> A whole Irish family is often accommodated on a single bed, and sometimes a heap of filthy straw and a covering of old sacking hide them in one undistinguished heap, debased alike by penury, want of economy and dissolute habits. Frequently the inspectors found two families crowded into one small house, containing only two apartments, one in which they slept, and another in which they ate; and often more than one family lived in a damp cellar, containing only one room, in whose pestilential atmosphere from twelve to sixteen persons were crowded.

A little later in the century, Friedrich Engels displayed much righteous sympathy for the English working man, but that compassion clearly didn't extend to Irish immigrants, who were beyond the pale of his expectations. This was in spite of the fact that he seems to have lived very happily for some years with an Irish factory worker called Mary Burns and, after her early death, with her sister Lizzie, all of which makes his vitriol even more extraordinary.

> These Irishmen who migrate for fourpence to England, on the deck of a steamship on which they are often packed like cattle, insinuate themselves everywhere. [The vermin reference is unmistakable.] The worst dwellings are good enough for them; their clothing

> causes them little trouble, so long as it holds together by a single thread; shoes they know not; their food consists of potatoes and potatoes only; whatever they earn beyond these needs they spend upon drink. What does such a race want with high wages? The worst quarters of all the large towns are inhabited by Irishmen. Whenever a district is distinguished for especial filth and especial ruinousness, the explorer may safely count upon meeting chiefly those Celtic faces which one recognises at the first glance as different from the Saxon physiognomy of the native, and the singing, aspirate brogue which the true Irishman never loses. I have occasionally heard the Irish-Celtic language spoken in the most thickly populated parts of Manchester. The majority of the families who live in cellars are almost everywhere of Irish origin. In short, the Irish have, as Dr Kay says, discovered the minimum of the necessities of life, and are now making the English workers acquainted with it.

Physiognomy – a belief that you could judge the character from the face – was fashionable at that time, and Engels didn't much like 'Celtic faces'. The Irish are a good-looking race, but Engels didn't seem to think so, nor did he appreciate what he called the 'Irish-Celtic' or Gaelic language he had heard spoken in Manchester. The suppression of Irish and Scots Gaelic over several hundred years is still one of the most shocking features of the relationship between Ireland and Britain. Throughout the seventeenth, eighteenth and nineteenth centuries, when Ireland was caught between dispossession and plantation, the Irish language, and those who spoke it, had no official status. The result of this was that by 1800, nobody with any political, social or economic ambitions would have chosen to use the Irish tongue, especially in the public sphere. When a language is spurned by the upper echelons of a society, the cultural memory contained within that language is weakened too, in what is one more form of colonisation.

In the early years of the nineteenth century, before John Manley's parents came to Leeds, there were still some four million Irish speakers living on the island of Ireland. But they were the poor, just as those who spoke Gaelic in Scotland were poor. During the nineteenth century, much as happened in Scotland too, English became the main language of the island of Ireland, with Irish-speaking areas increasingly isolated and marooned. When famine and economic privation, clearances and evictions affected the poorest areas, people thought they should speak only English, to prepare their young people for the exile that they knew must come. Like Scots and Scots Gaelic, the Irish language was associated with poverty, ignorance and backwardness. Engels seems to have shared this belief.

Quite apart from his prejudice against the appearance and language of these 'Celts' as opposed to 'Saxons', it never seems to have occurred to him to wonder why these migrants might be so poverty-stricken, to ask himself if there was a reason why they were relegated to the worst possible dwellings, to wonder who might have built those houses and might be profiting from them. And yet Engels seems perfectly capable of sympathy for the English working man. He rambles on in this vein for some considerable time.

> Filth and drunkenness, too, they have brought with them. The lack of cleanliness . . . which is the Irishman's second nature, becomes terrifying and gravely dangerous through its concentration here in the great cities. The Milesian [*i.e. Irish person*] deposits all garbage and filth before his house door here, as he was accustomed to do at home, and so accumulates the pools and dirt-heaps which disfigure the working-people's quarters and poison the air.

Most of these houses had no running water and little to no sanitation. He's aware of it, because he gives full vent to his feelings about it in his other writings, but when it comes to the Irish, it's no excuse. As Engels sees it, it's all because of immigration.

> The filth and comfortlessness that prevail in the houses themselves it is impossible to describe. The Irishman is unaccustomed to the presence of furniture; a heap of straw, a few rags, utterly beyond use as clothing, suffice for his nightly couch. A piece of wood, a broken chair, an old chest for a table, more he needs not; a tea-kettle, a few pots and dishes, equip his kitchen, which is also his sleeping and living room. When he is in want of fuel, everything combustible within his reach, chairs, door-posts, mouldings, flooring, finds its way up the chimney.

These people couldn't afford fuel and, in the middle of winter, might have frozen or run the risk of starving to death.

> Moreover, why should he need much room? At home in his mud-cabin there was only one room for all domestic

> purposes. . . . So the custom of crowding many persons into a single room, now so universal, has been chiefly implanted by the Irish immigration. And since the poor devil must have one enjoyment . . . he betakes himself to the drinking of spirits. Drink is the only thing which makes the Irishman's life worth having . . . so he revels in drink to the point of the most bestial drunkenness. The southern, facile character of the Irishman, his crudity, which places him but little above the savage, his contempt for all humane enjoyments, in which his very crudeness makes him incapable of sharing, his filth and poverty, all favour drunkenness.

This is the heart of the matter for the writer. These immigrants are 'not English', damned for being fit only for the lowest possible work, damned for not aspiring to greater things, but also damned for depressing wages among the more civilised natives who would otherwise be content with these unskilled occupations.

> With such a competitor the English working-man has to struggle. . . . Nothing else is therefore possible than that . . . the wages of the English working man should be forced down further and further in every branch in which the Irish compete with him. . . . For work which requires long training or regular, pertinacious application, the dissolute, unsteady, drunken Irishman is on too low a plane. To become a mechanic, a mill-hand, he would have to adopt the English civilisation, the English customs, become, in the main, an Englishman. But for all simple, less exact work, wherever it is a question more of strength than skill, the Irishman is as

> good as the Englishman. Such occupations are therefore especially overcrowded with Irishmen: hand-weavers, bricklayers, porters, jobbers, and such workers, count hordes of Irishmen among their number, and the pressure of this race has done much to depress wages and lower the working-class.

If this sounds oddly familiar, it's because this belief has never really gone away. It's curious that he judges hand-weaving and bricklaying to be unskilled but he knew nothing about the practicalities of such occupations. Even if the Irish do aspire to a better way of life, it will certainly be impossible for them to achieve anything worthwhile, because as he sees it, it is just not in their nature.

> And even if the Irish . . . should become more civilised, enough of the old habits would cling to them to have a strong, degrading influence upon their English companions in toil. . . . For when, in almost every great city, a fifth or a quarter of the workers are Irish, or children of Irish parents, who have grown up among Irish filth, no one can wonder if the life, habits, intelligence, moral status – in short, the whole character of the working-class assimilates a great part of the Irish characteristics. On the contrary, it is easy to understand how the degrading position of the English workers, engendered by our modern history, and its immediate consequences, has been still more degraded by the presence of Irish competition.

Engels did in fact visit Ireland, touring the country with his Irish common-law wife in 1856. 'The land is an utter desert which nobody wants,' he wrote, although presumably some people still wanted it. He might have been expected to have some sympathy for the indigenous population, having seen what they were reduced to, but he seems able to make a fine distinction between his idea of 'the people', about whom he can make sweeping pronouncements, and real people, with their inconvenient needs, their inconvenient behaviour.

> By consistent oppression they have been artificially converted into an utterly impoverished nation and now, as everyone knows, fulfil the function of supplying England, America, Australia, etc., with prostitutes, casual labourers, pimps, pickpockets, swindlers, beggars and other rabble.

Also, he might have added, factory hands of all kinds, especially those who will do the jobs that nobody else wants to do. He seems to have modified his views somewhat over the years, but couldn't really lose his prejudice. Outrageously, he even attempted to write a history of Ireland, but, after describing the Irish language, which he had attempted to learn, as 'philological nonsense' (that is, not Germanic and therefore tricky for him), he gave up.

There are a few more sympathetic observations from this time. One such came from journalist Henry Mayhew, who influenced Dickens and Thackeray. 'The reason there appears to be a greater proportion of the Irish among the thieves and vagrants of our own country, admits a very ready explanation; the Irish constitute the poorest of our people,' he wrote in the mid-1800s, and at least he saw fit to speak to the people he intended to write about.

Only a few years after Engels was describing the bad habits of my forebears, the 'Irish filth' in the persons of my great-great-grandparents, John Manley senior and Mary Everon, were crossing from Dublin to Liverpool, paying fourpence to be packed 'like cattle' on the deck of a steamship. Although emigration had been fairly steady until that time, the 1840s and 50s saw an exponential increase. People were panic-stricken and desperate to escape hunger, disease, privation and death. By late 1847, roughly the time at which John and Mary must have risked the crossing to Liverpool, the political climate even in Ireland had changed and migration had essentially become forced exile. The British government, with characteristic indifference, had more or less washed their hands of this troublesome sister island, deciding that they bore no responsibility for it whatsoever.

The streets my forebears came to were very far from being paved with gold. Even in my early childhood in Lower Wortley, the area called Bank had a terrible residual reputation for poverty and a lack of sanitation. Camp Field in Holbeck, had a similar reputation and people would do their best to get away, especially if they had children, but it wasn't always or even often possible. Stories were told of ceilings and walls 'running wick' with cockroaches, or covered in bugs so numerous a pin could not be put between them. Demolition and wholesale burning was the only way to destroy them. Most of these houses had been demolished by the mid-twentieth century, in determined waves of slum clearances, but it was never far from the memories of older family members, always spoken of as somewhere shameful from which they had escaped. The terrors of the poor law too were never quite forgotten. Even in old age, my English grandfather, Joe Sunter, who had been threatened with the workhouse as a young boy, flatly refused to go into St James's hospital, which he always associated with its previous function, and consequently went blind from a diabetes that would, by then, have been treatable.

Hunger, eviction, disease and the inevitability of an early death in their native Ireland had driven John Manley senior and Mary Everon to seek a better life in Leeds. They would have made the passage, arduous at that time, each of them with a few friends or family members. We know from Mayhew's writing that those who came earlier and managed to make a little money would sometimes pay for the passage of those who had stayed at home. We know that John senior at least had brothers and sisters living in Leeds. Who can say that John and Mary hadn't already met on the ferry, or even formed an acquaintance of sorts in Ireland. They would have walked across country, sailed from Dublin to Liverpool and then travelled to Leeds on foot, a journey of some seventy-four miles, along turnpike roads across the Pennines. Only those with some funds, perhaps those who had managed to sell off a parcel of land, however small, could afford to take a passage to America, although for some of these migrants it may still have been a dream, an aspiration, one they passed on to their children. The poor had no means of transport other than their own two feet, so it's to be hoped they came to England in spring or summer. On the whole, and if it were possible, they would have wanted to move on from Liverpool, a city that was already massively overcrowded and disease-ridden.

Leeds seems always to have been their ultimate destination. John senior's occupation was given as farm labourer when his first daughter was born, my great-grandmother Mary, after his marriage in 1851. But then so many of these young men thought of themselves as farm labourers because that had been their occupation at home in rural Ireland. It was all John had known, although industrial Leeds was a far cry from whatever he had left behind. Mayhew notes with his usual perspicacity that when asked if they would like to 'go back to their own country', most people he interviews say, 'what would be the use?' There's a fatalism about them. 'If I was sick, I don't know what I'd do, but I would send for the praste, and he would counsil me,' (sic) he writes of one young Irishwoman, living in utter poverty, in London. She had come to the city to join her brother who had sent for her, but being unable to find him, she has simply had to fend for herself. Her parents in Ireland are dead. She eats sporadically and sometimes barters apples for herring. 'I could read a little once, but I can't now,' she tells him. Even Mayhew, with so much good will, doesn't seem able to make the connection between the long-term effects of famine and acute fatigue. 'All these people seemed to be so utterly devoid of energy, and the men moved about so lazily that I couldn't help asking some of them if they had tried to obtain work,' he writes.

For John senior and Mary, and those like them, the contrast between their lives and heritage in rural Ireland, however beset by extremes of poverty and hunger, and their new lives in industrial Leeds, must have been absolute and shocking. Many of these people would have spent months, if not years, suffering from culture shock, accompanied by stress and depression, homesickness for the place they had lost, mourning for family and friends they would never see again – and still they soldiered on. No wonder so many of their songs were sad. No wonder even their children and grandchildren still thought of Ireland as 'home'. When I was attending Holy Family Primary School in Armley, we used to sing 'Hail glorious Saint Patrick, dear saint of our isle', a hymn written around 1853 by a nun called Sister Agnes from County Cork. We sang it without a second thought and implored Patrick to look down on 'Erin's green valleys' with only a vague notion of where those green valleys might be. At that time, my father, who still missed his native, rural Poland, would take me on a threepenny bus ride into the countryside outside the city at Old Farnley most Saturdays in spring and summer. There were green valleys in plenty, woods and fields and becks, and those are what I had in mind whenever we sang about Erin.

Records seem to be silent about John and Mary's exact place of birth, which is given only as Ireland. The tradition in our family was that our Irish forebears came from a small town called Ballyhaunis in County Mayo, although my great-grandfather, James Flynn, who plays only a minor, albeit faintly heroic, part in this story, hailed from just over the border in Ballinlough, Roscommon. The two small towns are a few miles apart so perhaps there was a family connection. The surname Everon – Mary senior's name – crops up in a multitude of variations, including Heron, Hefferan, Heavren and Hearne, and seems to originate in County Offaly, and to be derived from the name meaning 'descendant of *Uidhrin*', which is in turn a diminutive of a name meaning 'pale grey', like Elizabeth Manley's eyes. Like my mother's eyes, too.

4. *Disease of the Heart*

John Manley senior was born in Ireland in 1820 or 1821. I have been unable to find a record of his birth. Driven by hunger and all of its accompanying horrors, he migrated to England, where he married Mary Everon, on 19 March 1851, in the impressively large St Patrick's Church, built in Burmantofts twenty years earlier to serve the needs of the growing Catholic population of that part of Leeds. Several new churches dedicated to the patron saint of Ireland were built in Yorkshire at about this time, as a response to the overwhelming influx of Irish migrants; where churches were established, some form of Catholic education, religious education in particular, would certainly follow, although it would be a long time before literacy was widespread, before people began to sign documents in their own hand, instead of making their 'mark' on marriage, birth or death certificates.

At the time of their marriage, John had been living in Crispin Street while Mary was already living a short distance away in Brussels Street. For a while, the newly-weds lodged in Crispin Street with other members of the Manley family. Not surprisingly, as soon as a room became available, the young couple moved from what would have been very cramped quarters back to Brussels Street, and it was here that they set up house together and spent all their married life, albeit not always in the same part of the street.

John and Mary Manley soon added to the growing population. Their eldest daughter, my great-grandmother, was born on 6 November 1851, a scant eight months after the wedding. This was not uncommon, in spite of the stern moral precepts of the Victorian age and the Catholic Church alike. A second daughter, Bridget, came along in 1853. A son named Thomas, after John's father, was born in 1856, while a second son, John, was born in 1859. Elizabeth Manley, of whose short life I know so much – but not nearly enough – was said by her elder sister Mary to have been born on 15 August 1864, but another sister, Ann, is registered as having been born on 9 April 1865 at 10 Brussels Street, which suggests that Ann must have been very premature.

Or perhaps there was some other explanation.

Elizabeth was not registered at all, or at least not under the name by which we know her, which leaves us with something of a mystery as to the circumstances of her birth. There are several possible explanations for this lack of registration, the simplest being that Mary Manley senior just didn't get around to doing it. She may have been unwell after the birth, and she and her husband may have postponed it indefinitely. It wasn't unknown. Another more intriguing possibility, especially in the light of what followed, may have been that Elizabeth was somebody else's child. When an older child of the family gave birth to a child outside wedlock, the new baby might simply be treated as the parents' own, and brought up as a member of that family. Mary Manley junior is the only sister old enough to have been Elizabeth's mother, and even she would have been very young, perhaps fourteen years old. But it's possible, it was not unknown, and may help to explain why, in later years, Mary Manley junior shaved some six years off her age on official documents. Informal adoptions were also fairly commonplace and Elizabeth may have been the child of another family member or even a lodger, but this seems less likely. Official records are silent, and so is the family. A further son, Patrick, was born to John and Mary in 1867. Neither Ann nor Patrick lived very long, each dying in infancy in the year following their respective births. Their mother Mary Manley senior registered all of these other births except Elizabeth's, but couldn't read or write, making her mark on the entry instead of her signature.

During this time, poor John Manley senior's occupations followed a downward trajectory, from farm labourer on his arrival to hopeful blacksmith's labourer, to hawker a few years before his death. Engels would surely have approved of this confirmation of his theories. Hawking involved buying small quantities of items as cheaply as possible and selling them on the streets. Hawkers might go from door to door, but more frequently they would look for a pitch in a busy part of the city where, given the large numbers of mill hands and other factory workers employed, the footfall would be high, even though wealth was in short supply. Nevertheless, it was a thankless task in which the hawker, male or female, ran the risk of being accused by the heavy-handed police of anything from vagrancy to theft.

If found guilty, vagrants, rogues and vagabonds might be fined or imprisoned. Items sold or 'hawked' might be matches or brushes, pots and pans or even apples. Oranges were a favourite in London, although people there had access to a fruit market, which might not have been so easy for the Leeds Irish. The main requirement was for something that could be bought in small quantities, carried by hand and sold on. Drapery and broadside ballads, of which more later, were sold in this way, too. Hawkers made very little income and during the long, cold and heavily polluted winters it must have been a hellish occupation for small reward. Hans Christian Andersen's 'Little Match Girl' (first published in 1845), who 'did not dare to go home, for she had sold no matches . . . and her father would surely beat her', was no figment of the storyteller's imagination.

The Manley family lived at various numbers in Brussels Street at different times, so in 1851 they were living at number 5, while by 1861, with a bigger family, they were at number 10. Many of these numbers within Brussels Street may refer to rooms, rather than individual houses, and the family would have shifted about the street as needed, or according to the vagaries of family finances. In 1871, a few years before the elder John Manley's death, the family were living at 6 Brussels Street, the space later occupied by the big McDonald family, which suggests that for a time they may have had the luxury of a whole house to themselves, consisting of a single downstairs room for cooking and eating, an upstairs room for sleeping, and a cellar.

The 1871 census gives us a little more information about the family. John's wife, Mary senior, was working as a mill hand, as was his eldest daughter, Mary junior, then aged nineteen. There was a woollen mill called Bank Top Mill, not too far away from Brussels Street, close to John senior's previous lodgings, and it may have been here that the women of the household and young Thomas found work, but Irishwomen tended to work in flax rather than in woollen mills. By this date, almost all of the flax-spinning jobs in Leeds – dirty, unpleasant and poorly paid – were undertaken by young Irish women. Commentators complained that the Irish were undercutting native labour, but the truth was that this was labour few English people wanted to do, as long as alternatives were available. And alternatives were certainly available. English girls were moving on to better-paid woollen and worsted mill work, although it should be stressed that none of this work was anything but difficult, exhausting and sometimes dangerous. Conditions improved as the century progressed and as politicians found their consciences, but were still far from ideal.

Bridget was a scholar, although she was seventeen years old, mature for that description. Thomas was both a scholar and a cloth dresser, so he was working at least some of the time and may have attended one of the mill schools that had been set up by then. Permission for part-time attendance at these schools was often used as an incentive, a reward for good behaviour, to encourage workers to toe the line. Like his sister Bridget, Thomas was of an age where he might normally have been in full-time work, so his scholarship was probably minimal. John was eleven, and also described as a scholar, as was Elizabeth, although once again there is some discrepancy about her age, which is here given as nine, although in later years, her elder sister, Mary, is very definite in her assertion that Elizabeth was born in August 1864, which would make her seven years old at the time of this census. The family had also taken in lodgers: Rose Tookel (probably O'Toole), a twenty-seven-year-old mill hand, born in Ireland, and her two children, aged two and four months, all three of whom may well have lived in the cellar, since the rest of the house would have been crammed with people. No Mr Tookel is mentioned.

There was some discrepancy about the description 'scholar' on these census returns and the actual fact of attending school. Roman Catholic priests were, on the whole, enthusiastic about the education of their flock, as long as it was a 'good Catholic' education, and many of them were keen to combat the perception that the Irish incomers were unintelligent as well as feckless. Religious education would certainly have been mandatory and may have taken place on Sundays when families, but especially women and children, would be expected to attend mass. Bridget, in spite of being called a scholar, may have been at home most of the day, undertaking the difficult and time-consuming household tasks, the washing, the cleaning and cooking, all of which would have been a challenge in these surroundings. She may also have been looking after her younger siblings, John and Elizabeth, who would not have been attending school with any regularity, and Rose's very young children as well. This would allow John and Mary Manley senior, as well as their eldest daughter Mary and lodger Rose, to work long hours at whatever brought in enough money to keep body and soul together. Elizabeth would be next in line to undertake this task while Bridget went out to work. It was the only way in which they could accommodate a family and survive.

In 1873, Mary Manley junior, John and Mary's firstborn, married Charles Terran, in Salford, present-day Greater Manchester, although the rest of the family were still living and working in Leeds. Charles himself, twenty-one years old at the time of the marriage, the same age as his wife, had been born in Duke Street, Leeds, another child of the Bank area. His mother was Phoebe Nicholson, and she too had been born in Leeds, circa 1825. Irish workers had often come to England, Scotland and Wales as seasonal agricultural labourers, but even during the first quarter of the nineteenth century, with Ireland's population increasing rapidly, many of them had stayed on permanently, so perhaps Phoebe's parents had been among these earlier migrants. Phoebe had worked as a cap maker. She might have made cloth caps for men, or night caps, dress or widows' caps for women. Henry Mayhew found female cap makers to be poorly paid and exploited by shopkeepers. They worked long hours in terrible conditions for a few pence each week, often on spec.

'My readers will no doubt have noticed announcements in shop-windows of "Widows' cap hands wanted" or "Cap front hands wanted" or some similar intimation,' writes Mayhew, in the *Morning Chronicle*, in 1850. He continues:

> To the uninitiated, the modest looking placard seems to make public the fact that there is employment for a certain number of work-women, and of course at a regular wage, as their services are in demand. Such, however, is not the case. These 'wanteds' are to intimate that the purveyors of caps may carry in their wares, and the placarder may, of course, buy or refuse to buy at his option. 'Only do that, sir,' said a competitive tradesman

to me, 'and you'll have a hundred of them in an hour, with all sorts of caps. Where they come from to my place I don't know, haven't a notion . . . they're nothing to me. They come with their goods in boxes, and of course I make the best bargain I can with them.'

Phoebe's husband, James Terran, was a tailor, so perhaps they worked together. James's own father, however, had been a cattle dealer, which may help to explain his arrival in England. When Phoebe married James in St Ann's Church, she couldn't write, but her tailor husband signed his own name. It would probably be incumbent upon a tailor to have some knowledge of reading and writing, and James did. Phoebe and James were living in Harewood Court, near Kirkgate Market in the commercial heart of Leeds, but they too moved around, to Union Street and then south to Duke Street, where their son Charles was born in 1852. He was baptised in Mount St Mary's Church and when he grew up, he had a number of occupations, including general labourer and 'puddler', which meant that for a time at least, he was working with molten iron, in a furnace. This was an occupation that proved fatal to many. The strenuous work, coupled with the heat, and above all the poisonous fumes, meant that most of the men working in the industry at that time had a short life expectancy. They died in their thirties.

It's probable that after Charles and Mary had become engaged, Charles had been offered work in Salford and that Mary had moved to be with him. Salford, where they were married, was as industrial as Leeds, so the change wasn't much for the better. Moreover, with children coming along, there was no family support, and they didn't stay away for long. Their children were all born in Leeds; the first, James, named after his paternal grandfather, arrived in April 1874. Mary's father, poor John Manley senior, died of chronic bronchitis in that same year, at the age of fifty-three, worn out by the endless, thankless struggle to make any kind of living as a hawker. Bronchitis is not normally a summer disease, but in an environment as polluted as this one, the seasons would have made very little difference. The following year, Mary gave birth to twins, Catherine and Mary Ann, but they didn't survive for very long. When baby Catherine died, aged five weeks, of 'debility from birth', the doctor who signed the death certificate was a young man named Charles Henry Harral, a physician and surgeon. Giving birth to twins was a precarious undertaking at this time, and it's possible that the girls, Catherine and Mary Ann, had been premature. Harral was also the son of a tailor and clothes dealer who, like James and Phoebe Terran, traded from premises in Kirkgate in the centre of Leeds, although apparently with more success. The simple profession 'draper' is written on Charles's birth certificate. We can assume that, if not wealthy, they were certainly comfortably off, the kind of shopkeepers who might buy the caps that Phoebe made. Charles Harral was to play a significant part in the life of the Manley family only a few years later.

*

In 1874, meanwhile, we see the beginnings of another story that promised much, but turned to tragedy for the family. Only a couple of months after her father died, twenty-year-old Bridget Manley married George Wolstoncroft and moved with him to his house in Bachelor Street, nearby. People seemed to circulate within a very small area. George was an engine tenter, a skilled occupation, a young man with prospects. In June of the following year, Bridget gave birth to a son who was named George after his father, but only two months later, on 17 August, little George's father died of pulmonary tuberculosis. Half a year later, the eight-month-old baby also died of convulsions. This commonly recorded cause of infant death was often the outcome of some other fatal disease. The convulsions were the result of fevers and various infections, all too often caused by living in insanitary surroundings. This is also borne out by the fact that so many of these deaths seemed to occur in summer rather than, as might be expected, in winter. But hot weather would only exacerbate the possibility of infection. Such water supplies as there were might be contaminated by sewage.

This was a truly dreadful decade for the Manley family.

In 1876, Mary Terran gave birth to a baby boy named John, named after his grandfather and his uncle. But a year later, the little boy died of 'rachitis', the name for rickets, another wretched disease of privation, at 74 York Street. His father, Charles, puts his mark on the certificate, and attested that he was present at the death.

John Manley senior was followed five years later by his wife Mary, aged fifty-two, who died in February 1879 at 5 Brussels Street. These ages were considered reasonably good at this time and in this place. Expectations did not extend beyond this and were often considerably lower. She died of 'disease of the heart' and, this time, her nineteen-year-old son John was said to be 'present at her death', although he too, in spite of his supposed 'scholarship', was unable to sign his own name, and instead made his mark for the registrar. In view of what was to become of John Manley junior, and his sister Elizabeth, the fact that their parents were not alive to experience these tragedies may have been something of a blessing.

It was in this same year, 1879, that Mary Manley lost the fourth of five children she had borne since her marriage. Her firstborn, James, survived, but she had lost, in quick succession, twin girls, Mary Ann and Catherine, John Terran, who had died at only one year old, and then a little girl called Jane Frances, who was born in 1878 and died in 1879. Another girl, named Elizabeth after her aunt, was born in 1880. So Mary and Charles Terran, with their two surviving children, James and Elizabeth, were living not far away from Mary's younger siblings, John and Elizabeth Manley. By the end of 1881, with Christmas coming, Mary was pregnant again. The child would be born the following July and named John Thomas, after Mary's two brothers.

On Christmas Day that same year, Elizabeth Manley went with her brother John and a group of friends to the Railway Hotel in nearby York Street. Before the night was over, her brother would be knifed by one of his friends and would die in the street, before her eyes.

5. Very Much Obstructed

In the minutes immediately following the attack, a doctor was sent for. In the middle of all the panic, somebody ran to fetch help, while Manley's friends carried him home to Brussels Street. Charles Henry Harral testified that he examined John Manley at 10.25 on Christmas Night, very soon after the stabbing, but there's no indication of whether he saw him at home in Brussels Street, or on the pavement outside the public house. Charles was the doctor who had signed the death certificate for one of Mary Terran's twins. The speed with which the doctor arrived is rather surprising, but he must have been somewhere close at hand. The pub wasn't very far from the house in Brussels Street, so he could have arrived promptly at either place. He was still a young professional man, thirty-two years old: an apothecary or doctor surgeon. The two professions had once been differentiated, with the barber surgeon being something of a human butcher, a 'sawbones', and the apothecary concentrating on medicines, usually of his own making, but now doctors were beginning to practise both forms of medicine and to register as competent in both aspects of the profession. He may have been on a retainer from the police or the poor law authorities and he appears to have been shocked by what he saw. He immediately confirmed that John Manley was dead, and that he had died of a deep stab wound behind his left ear.

I think those young people standing outside the pub would already have realised this for themselves. Most if not all of them would have witnessed deaths in the family, or among colleagues, although seldom such a violent and tragic death as this one. Glancing through various death certificates, I was struck by how many of those registering a particular death, whether of a parent or child, and making their 'mark' since they could not write, were noted as being 'present at the death'. This is an experience, especially at home, that is by no means as commonplace nowadays as it was for our forebears. Familiar it may have been, but it was no less painful for all that. People died young by our standards. Even into the twentieth century, illnesses such as diphtheria, enteritis and the ever-present threat of tuberculosis were claiming the lives of children. However, violent deaths like John Manley's were a rare occurrence. The volume of blood alone would have been enough to convince bystanders that there was no hope. Elizabeth was clearly in shock.

Messages were immediately sent to Superintendent Ball at the police station on Millgarth Street, less than half a mile away. I can imagine the panic-stricken relatives sending for a doctor before thinking of anything else, but Hardaker, the publican from the Railway Hotel, with young children in the house, probably sent a message to the police station. Ball detailed several police officers to arrest Ross but, not surprisingly, he had disappeared, and they were unsuccessful. He had not been so foolish as to go home to his mother's house in Somerset Street either, but seems to have taken refuge elsewhere. Somebody must have been sheltering him, however briefly. It's difficult to imagine him, by this stage, as being anything other than sober and terrified of the consequences of what he had done, cowering in some cellar in that warren of back-to-back houses, and wondering where on earth he could go next. Recognising that the bird had flown, Ball asked Chief Inspector James Nortcliffe, an experienced officer, to take over the case, and he immediately extended the manhunt and circulated descriptions of Ross to various neighbouring towns. There were no photographs, of course, but they mentioned his height, his dark hair and squint, his shabby coat, his clogs and red plaid scarf, although if he were wise, he might have dispensed with this last and somewhat recognisable article of clothing as soon as possible. By the time all of this was being reported in the *Yorkshire Post* on Boxing Day, there was still no sign of him.

Charles Henry Harral, the surgeon who had been called to Brussels Street and had certified that Manley was dead, undertook to do the post mortem in or next door to the Manley house, on the following day, Monday, 26 December. Harral was a newlywed, with a young wife who hailed from London, but he wasn't destined to have a peaceful family Christmas. The examination was conducted at 4 Brussels Street, probably in a ground-floor room to take advantage of the light. Besides, moving the body would have been inadvisable. And then there would have been the wake to think about, if wake there might have been in a case like this. The post mortem must have been a harrowing event for those family members who were present, but they were few, and perhaps the poor didn't merit the dignity of better surroundings. The presence of Harral is interesting. This was long before the days of any National Health Service and I'm curious about this young doctor who was a member of the Royal College of Surgeons, who worked among the poorest of the poor, but information about him is thin on the ground. Most people in this area couldn't afford a doctor at all, but attendance after a death would have been mandatory. He may have been attached to the police station in some way. He may have been working for a charitable concern, a young medic who served the poor for a small sum of money.

The inquest was scheduled for Tuesday, 27 December 1881, with the Leeds Borough coroner, Mr Malcolm, presiding. Elizabeth Manley was summoned to tell her story. She said that she had formally identified the body as that of her brother, John Manley, for the police and the surgeon. She confirmed that she had been with her brother in the tavern and that John Ross had come in. Although he had sat down close to her brother and his friend, the landlord had 'refused to fill Ross beer because he said he had come into the house to create a row'. She also confirmed that her brother never spoke after he fell, which suggests that she must have run back and crouched down beside him. She added that, as far as she could tell, Ross himself had not been much the worse for drink, and that both she and her brother had known him for years.

Others gave evidence, too. Mary Ann Burke confirmed that she had been in the pub when the quarrel began. Michael Kelly told how he had helped to carry Manley home after the blow was struck and Ross had run away. John Fee had been passing the public house, although he had not been a customer, but he had witnessed the blow struck by Ross and had seen the blood. Along with Elizabeth, he seems to have been greatly struck by the volume of blood. Ellen Connor claimed to have seen the stabbing and called out, 'He has killed him.'

Harral's evidence served to elaborate on the aftermath of the crime. He had measured the depths of the wound. Although it was very narrow, it was a catastrophic three and a quarter inches deep. One artery and two veins were wounded, and the cause of death was haemorrhage from these blood vessels. He was confident that a light blow could not have caused such a wound, so there was a certain amount of angry intent. The coroner, at this point, directed the inquest jury that the case was certainly one of 'wilful murder; given that there had been no provocation, which might have reduced the charge to manslaughter'. The full charge was that 'One John Ross did feloniously, wilfully and of his malice aforethought, kill and murder the said John Manley.' When the inquest was reported in the newspapers on 28 December, Ross had not been traced, but the manhunt had already been extended well beyond the city.

At the end of the inquest, Harral, who was still clearly upset by the events of the previous day, complained to the coroner that he had been 'very much obstructed' while he was attempting to make the post mortem examination at the Manley home in Brussels Street. Word had clearly got about during the intervening hours. He reported that a large crowd had gathered near the house, and that people 'shrieked and howled disgracefully' while trying to kick the door in. I wonder if at least some of those people who were shrieking and howling disgracefully might have been the McDonalds, about whom Ross, Rooks and Manley had been quarrelling in the Railway Hotel, but perhaps it was a more general disturbance. It does, however, seem to have marked the beginning of an inexplicable groundswell of feeling against the Manleys and in favour of Ross, now perceived to be the underdog.

It's almost impossible to imagine the horror of these events for the murdered man's young sister, with her brother lying dead, in or immediately next door to this tiny dwelling, and the mob at the door. Bear in mind that her parents were dead, too, and that her elder brother, twenty-five-year-old Thomas, seems to have been absent at this point. We don't even know for certain whether Bridget was present or not. Mary was living nearby and she and her husband would have offered shocked assistance. Certainly Bridget was not called to give any evidence and nor was Mary. Elizabeth must have felt very much alone and utterly panic-stricken.

Harral described how he had managed to secure the help of two police constables, with one stationed inside and one outside the door. The policeman standing at the door took fright at the mob and fainted, whereupon the crowd became frightened in turn, and started to shout that he too had been murdered. They became even more unruly, burst through the door and crowded into the room, which was, we must remember, very small. They actually prevented Harral from continuing with his examination for a little while. He too must have been scared, but he at least managed to exert some authority to the extent that they backed off.

The officers at Millbank Police Station, meanwhile, had

got wind of the unrest and sent a further five policemen to deal with the situation. They evicted the troublemakers and held back the crowd until Harral had finished his post mortem. At the inquest, Harral seems to have been seeking some assurance from the coroner that the situation had been unlawful and would not occur again. The coroner agreed that such behaviour was unacceptable and should be punished, but asked specifically if anyone had used force against him personally, to which the surgeon replied that they had not, but he had been compelled to halt his examination for a time. There had been some reluctance on the part of the crowd to directly challenge his authority, perhaps because they knew this would be open to severe punishment. Harral added that it was unpleasant enough to have to make such an examination in these circumstances, without the additional annoyance of the mob raging outside. Normally, a post mortem would have been carried out in a hospital or other official building, whereas this was a much more ad hoc, not to say bloody, affair, undertaken in cramped and dirty surroundings, under threat from a howling mob, and in the presence of distraught family members or with an awareness of their close proximity. Given that no actual force had been used against the surgeon, the coroner pointed out that the fainting policeman must have played some part in inflaming the crowd, and let the matter drop. But where was Elizabeth while all this was going on? Had her sister given her shelter? And in the middle of all her grief, how dreadful her situation must have been.

Attempting to unpick these events from a present-day perspective, and in spite of later judgments to the contrary, we find that there had been intermittent tensions between the Irish and English communities in Leeds for years, but these were political rather than sectarian. The issue of Home Rule for Ireland had inflamed feelings and the 1860s had seen occasional flare-ups of civil disorder. However, the mob seeking to challenge the post mortem and the police presence in Brussels Street had confused motives. They don't seem to have been on the side of the murdered man and his family at first but, given that the fainting policeman is immediately assumed to be another murder victim, perhaps some of them were. Of all those who gave evidence, none spoke of any previous hostility between the murderer and his victim. The conversations between Manley, Rooks and Ross in the pub suggest tensions, but only such tensions as often arise between young men who have had too much to drink. Fights were commonplace and generally harmless, with the participants sustaining nothing more serious than cuts and bruises. Some kind of territorial dispute seems more likely, but even those were uncommon in Leeds. I'm forced to the conclusion that the community – disturbed by the events unfolding, along with the usual rumour and misinformation – had a general feeling that the authorities were not on their side and that whatever had really happened, somebody would be falsely accused. They got their retaliation in first, as it were. This goes some way towards explaining subsequent events, ill feeling generated by the trial, and the resentful and persisting sense in the Manley family, something even passed on to me by my grandmother, that the murderer had 'got away with' something.

In view of Harral's complaint, Superintendent Ball told

the coroner that two policemen had already been sent to Brussels Street, instead of the one requested, and that when one of those had fainted, still more had been sent. The coroner pointed out, with some truth, that the police were not to blame for any of this, but he repeated that if anyone could be named as having hindered the post mortem, that person would be prosecuted. When no names seemed to be forthcoming – Harral probably didn't know them – the matter was dropped. The police carried on hunting for the murderer. It would be some weeks before they finally caught up with him and even then his arrest had something of the ridiculous about it.

6. *Rogues and Vagabonds*

On 27 December, the police are still frantically searching for the murderer. 'Vigorously', the newspapers term it. They report his various aliases: John Cross, John Cunningham and Martin Lofthouse, and point out that he is already well known to the police for his previous life of crime, although many of those crimes have been fairly minor. The *Post* is at pains to point out that the police are being hampered in their investigations by 'friends' of Ross, many of them eyewitnesses to the murder, who have assisted him in his escape and who are now reluctant to inform on him. This seems very strange, in view of the testimony given by those friends of Manley who were in the Railway Hotel that night. It's worth pointing out that this word 'friend' is sometimes used to describe relatives or extended family, so it may well be that Ross had siblings and cousins who were shielding him from the police. The maze of small, crumbling houses in which the Irish population of Leeds lived would have made it reasonably easy to hide a wanted man from the authorities, but because these were such close communities, it would also have been impossible to hide John Ross for long. Some of the people who knew him were friends of the Manleys. They knew that he was being hunted and they may not have been quite so well disposed towards him as his own friends and relatives.

There is some evidence that other members of the Ross family were known to be 'troublesome' and this in itself may have made people in the immediate area reluctant to get involved. When it came down to a choice between shielding the murderer from the forces of law and order or delivering him to them, many must have decided on the former course of action or at least on turning a blind eye to his escape in the interests of community cohesion. Leeds in winter is a chilly place, and any freezing temperatures would have driven the smoke down and made the pollution much harder to bear, but this was not a particularly cold winter, which helps to explain how Ross managed to evade capture for a few weeks, make his way out of the city and head south towards the Midlands. It is this part of the story – that the murderer 'escaped with the help of his friends' – that was handed down in my family. Succeeding events were never mentioned and in fact the story told was that he had 'gone to Canada'. This was fantasy. The truth was somewhat different.

Ross was well known to the police; they knew his various aliases and he already had a criminal record, as did at least one of his brothers at that time. Patrick Ross, two years John's junior and sometimes calling himself Patrick Lofthouse, had already been convicted of stealing lead piping and 'frequenting the streets with intent' as well as more minor offences such as assault, drunkenness and being a 'rogue and vagabond': a specific offence at that time, encompassing all kinds of idle and disorderly behaviour. In later years, he would go on to have convictions for house breaking, stealing a watch and assaulting the police, among a string of more or less grave offences. Like his elder brother, he was sentenced to several terms of imprisonment, depending upon the seriousness of the crime. The brothers seemed to constitute an intermittent but persistent two-man crime wave in that part of Leeds, and this may help to explain why people were reluctant to give Ross away to the police after Manley's murder. The family had relatives in nearby Bradford and at least some of the crimes were committed there.

After the trial, newspaper reports describe John Ross as a 'hawker', which helps to explain some of his previous petty thefts. He had needed items to sell and couldn't afford to buy them. Like his victim, John Ross had known little else but grinding poverty. In 1861, twenty years before the murder, we find four-year-old John Ross living at 10 Cawood Court, with his father, forty-eight-year-old Philip Ross, a bricklayer, born in Ireland, and his thirty-three-year-old mother, Mary, also Irish born. He has, at that time, a seven-year-old sister called Ann, a two-year-old brother called Patrick, who will play an important part in his story, and a baby sister Maria, who doesn't survive infancy. John will also have a sister called Catherine or Kate who – if anything – is even more important to his eventual survival than Patrick, and a younger brother called Henry, born in 1865, who is also destined for a troubled life. In 1868, Philip Ross is in the over-optimistically named House of Recovery, where victims of contagious diseases were sent in extremis. Most didn't recover at all. Poor Philip died at the age of fifty-five of a terrible combination of typhus fever and bronchitis. An attendant from the house, Mary Edmonds, made her mark, but could not sign her name. His death was registered on 27 August, and his 'rank or profession' was unknown. By that time, he probably had none.

A few years later, in 1871, the family, minus Philip, is living at 8 Riley Court. Mary is now described as the head of the household and is working in a flour mill, alongside her sixteen-year-old daughter, Ann. This flour mill was, in all probability, the monumental, looming group of buildings on the stretch of land on the bank of the Aire, known as the 'Isle of Cinder', like something from a dystopian fantasy. This whole area was created by original goits or waterways that had once served the old King's Mill on the site. A medieval dam on the River Aire had diverted water into man-made streams and channels, which then acted as mill races or lades, providing power to drive the corn mills and discharging water back into the river. This engineered landscape had formed an island. The huge mill complex, impressively high, founded by one Roger Shackleton in 1846, survived until 1907, when at least some of the buildings were demolished. In the 1870s Mary and Ann Ross are working there. Fourteen-year-old John, meanwhile, has found some work in a paper mill alongside twelve-year-old Patrick. Eight-year-old Kate and six-year-old Henry are termed 'scholars', which, as we have seen, means very little in terms of real scholarship. Still, Kate would prove to be a bright spark.

In April 1871, when John Ross was almost fifteen years old, he was brought up on a charge of felony, a serious crime. He was examined and discharged, perhaps because of his youth, but later that year he was again arrested, this time on a charge of 'stealing five ballads', for which he was sentenced to five months imprisonment. Broadside ballads, also known as broadsheets, were hawked about the city and Ross must have intended to sell his ballads on the street. These would be printed on one side of a sheet of cheap paper and contained poems and songs both traditional and contemporary, sometimes the news of the day, often attractively illustrated with woodcut images. There would be songs of lost love and bloody murder. There might even be Irish rebel songs. Genuine dealers would string them up in lines, perform extracts to entice buyers in, and sell them at a halfpence each or three for a penny. It's doubtful if John could even read what he was stealing and selling. We know that some of these ballads were printed in Leeds. Like matches and brushes, they might be legitimately acquired in small quantities and sold on by hawkers. The ballads were popular, and people who could afford them would use them to decorate their rooms. They must also have been reasonably easy to pocket, which maybe explains why court cases of the time so often have people, especially young people, brought up before the magistrates on a charge of 'stealing ballads'.

Hawking was one of the few ways in which elderly or sickly men, women of all ages and children who might be unfit for heavy work could make an honest, if very meagre and inadequate living. Ross, however, seems to have been a strong young man, so he might have found a steadier job. Perhaps he had already proved himself untrustworthy, or perhaps his family connections had done him no favours when it came to finding work. After all, employers could pick and choose easily enough. The workhouse was a constant, hideous threat for people who were picked up on charges of vagrancy or destitution. Perhaps he was simply inadequate. He comes across as curiously vulnerable and maybe he was.

In 1872, still foolishly opportunist rather than determinedly criminal, Ross had stolen three sacks, for which he was imprisoned for two months, and then not long after, purloined a silver fork, for which he received a more draconian six months. A little while after his release, his occupation is given as 'paper stainer', which may have meant colouring wallpaper, a job that seems to have been going out of fashion even then and in all likelihood was not at all well paid. Still only sixteen, he was then charged with stealing from the dwelling house of one Edward Ogden. There was a man named Edward Ogden who was a 'whitesmith' or tinsmith and machine maker, living in the commercial heart of the city, and he may have been the victim on this occasion. John took a coat, two books, a bank note for the payment of five pounds and four orders for the payment of twenty-three pounds. After his previous small-time criminality this was certainly an escalation to the big time.

Ogden seems to have been fairly affluent and, on this occasion, Ross had overstepped the mark. He was tried for larceny at Leeds on 2 February 1873 and found guilty. He was sentenced to ten months hard labour in the House of Correction because this act of larceny was committed so soon after the earlier theft of the silver fork, and a further six months with hard labour on account of this more recent and much more serious theft, but even so, the authorities were reasonably lenient. These sentences must have run concurrently, because on 23 May 1874, the following year, he was out for long enough to be given seven days in prison or a fine of eighteen shillings for playing at pitch and toss in the street. In October of that same year, John and Patrick, presumably working in concert, were found guilty of stealing five yards of lead piping, for which Patrick was sentenced to ten months while John, the elder of the two, was given a hefty eighteen months imprisonment for what was judged to be a serious crime. This kept him out of mischief for a little while, but not long after his release, in July 1876, he was charged with being a 'rogue and vagabond' and sent back to prison for a further three months. On 4 September 1878, he was up in court yet again on a charge of being drunk, and fined eleven shillings and sixpence or three days imprisonment. He must have been so used to being imprisoned that it seemed like a second home and, in all honesty, conditions couldn't have been much worse than the environment in which he spent most of his time. But the term 'recidivist' does come readily to mind. As it does for his brother. For John, at least, alcohol induced a kind of recklessness that was to do him no favours. Some whisky drinkers grow maudlin, but some turn wild and aggressive. John Ross was one of the latter.

After that, there followed a short interval of honesty for John, or perhaps he just didn't get caught. He was living with his widowed mother, Mary Ross, in Leeds, just off St Peter's Square, a little way to the west of Brussels Street, so maybe she and his sister Kate managed to keep him out of trouble for a while. The peaceful interval didn't last too long and when it broke, it was in a big way. By 1881, only John and eighteen-year-old Kate are left at home with their mother. Early in 1882, John Ross, alias Cunningham, alias Lofthouse, labourer, is at Leeds Crown Court, having been indicted on a charge of wilful murder. Mr Barker and Mr Walton are prosecuting while Mr Lockwood speaks for the defence. Ross pleads not guilty, which is hardly surprising, since if found guilty, he will be sentenced to death.

Young Kate cared enough about him to be present at his trial and to do what she could to help him. There was a groundswell of popular opinion in his favour locally, but I think this had more to do with the looming death penalty than any personal popularity. On the whole, the poor didn't approve of the death penalty, which so often seemed to target the desperate and needy. They didn't want him to hang. Did he have a girlfriend? Seemingly not. Could he even read the ballads he stole to hawk about the streets? Probably not. Could he sing? Play the whistle? He liked to fight. Did he fight for money, with bare knuckles, in some yard, or back court somewhere? Was that why he taunted John Manley? Because John Manley had refused to fight for sixpence, and said that he would rather fight for fun? Did John Ross, in his far from sober state of mind, see this as some kind of challenge to his masculinity?

7. Very Questionable Statements

What became of Ross after he had stabbed John Manley and run away in a panic down York Street? Directly after the coroner's inquest, the next reference we can find to him is in the *Police Gazette* for Friday, 30 December, five days after the murder. Under the heading 'Informations' we find the following report. It is quite precise and fleshes out more of the physical details of the man.

> Wanted on a charge of murder, John Ross, Alias Cunningham, Alias Lofthouse, about twenty-seven years of age [*he was probably younger – more likely twenty-five*], 5 feet 5 or 6 inches high, dark brown hair, dark eyes, fresh complexion, prominent forehead, dark eyebrows, sunken eyes, slight moustache, mole on left shoulder [*who gave that information, I wonder, or was it already in police records?*], and squints; is a hawker, born at Leeds, but of Irish descent; dressed in a pair of dark cord trousers, bell bottoms, slightly frayed, shabby black coat and vest, Turkey red plaid scarf, dirty shirt, old shoes [another description speaks of clogs, which seems more likely], rough bully cap with knob at top. Has aunts who go by the name of Ross, residing near Chain Street, White Abbey, Bradford; has been several times convicted of felony and

> other offences, and is supposed to be well known to the police at Bradford and the West Riding generally. Information to Chief Inspector Nortcliffe, Leeds – Bow Street, 28 December.

We know that he lost his cap at the scene of the crime, but perhaps somebody who was also in the street on that dreadful night returned it to him. Ross's use of aliases was, no doubt, related to his and his brother's previous criminal activities, although it must only have served to confirm his guilt. Cunningham was his mother's name but he was said to be 'well known to the police'. One version says Ross was a 'labourer' while another declares that he had no visible means of subsistence and lived with his mother in Somerset Street. He was described as a 'well-known thief' and as we have seen, he had several previous convictions. He had been a hawker, had worked in a cloth mill and as the aforementioned paper stainer, but latterly had 'relinquished all regular employment'.

Somerset Street, where Ross lived with Mary Ross and his sister Kate, was, if anything, even more miserable than Brussels Street. There is a photograph in existence of Hobson's Court, a yard just around the corner from Back Somerset Street. A low, tumbledown house is utterly dwarfed by the factory building behind it. Elsewhere, tiny terraced houses have again been built in the shadow of some vast industrial building.

This appeal for information about the fugitive is fascinating for several reasons, not least because the crime was so serious that Bow Street had taken an interest and circulated the description via the *Police Gazette*. At the same time, this confirms that Ross had relatives in nearby Bradford, and he may have headed in that direction in his efforts to escape arrest. Ross himself, however, was born in Leeds. His birth certificate details him as John Edward, born on 23 July 1856, at 6 Cawoods Yard, Marsh Lane, to Mary Ross, formerly Cunningham, and Philip Ross, bricklayer's labourer. This would make him only twenty-five years old instead of the estimated twenty-seven on the police report. His mother didn't get round to registering the birth until 2 September, and then she could only make her 'mark'.

The *Leeds Times* of Saturday, 28 January 1882 describes the eventual capture of Ross in great detail. It reports that 'after many false arrests' John Ross was captured at Wolverhampton. He had managed to evade arrest for almost a month. The *Times* relates again how Manley 'bled profusely and died in minutes'. Ross, it goes on, 'decamped instantly and could not be found, although strenuous exertions were made by Chief-detective Nortcliffe of Leeds and his staff. It was believed for some time that the murderer was hiding on the Bank, at Leeds, a low quarter of the borough, and that some of the people in that classic neighbourhood were screening him.'

There may have been some truth in this for at least a few days after the crime was committed, but as Ross could not be found and time was passing, representations were made to the Home Office and a reward of £100 was offered. This was a huge sum, bearing in mind that a middle-class family could live in reasonable comfort on £150 a year. From that moment, everyone must have been on the lookout for Ross. The police must have grown weary of fielding reports of sightings. Or, as the newspaper report puts it, 'This stimulated the efforts of persons in various parts of the country and several men were arrested on suspicion but none of the captured men proved to be the right man.' Pity the poor suspects – all those smallish, darkish young men who must have been detained by enthusiastic members of the public on suspicion of being a murderer.

Eventually, Ross's arrest was brought about by the vigilance of a civilian and it happened a hundred miles away from Leeds. Some four weeks had elapsed since the murder and Ross had headed south. How had he managed the journey? It's doubtful that he or any of those close to him would have had enough money for the train journey, so he must have gone on foot, sleeping in barns or under bridges, possibly cadging the occasional lift from a carter or farmer, but even that seems doubtful, given his fear of discovery. Certainly he had the right idea in heading for a populous place, where he might stand a chance of blending in, and there was a large Irish population in Wolverhampton, so perhaps he had friends or relatives there. No one came forward to help him, though.

On that Saturday evening at the end of January 1882, Ross was loitering about the town, when a file cutter named John Goodhead of North Street, Wolverhampton, went to the police station, described the man he had seen in a local pub, and asked the police to detain him on suspicion of being the Leeds murderer. Police Sergeant Evans, the officer on duty in the charge room at the time, was apparently incredulous and refused to comply with the request. He believed that the prisoner's supposed resemblance to the official description of the Leeds murderer was 'not sufficiently close to warrant such a step'. There had been too many erroneous sightings already and the reward must have prompted even more tiresome potential identifications.

A short time afterwards, however, another officer, Police Sergeant Hendrick, hearing of the encounter, asked about the last sighting of the stranger. Goodhead had related that the man was at Snow Hill, quite a busy street, being followed by a crowd of people, all of them anxious not to let him give them the slip. When asked to describe the arrest later, Hendrick said, 'I found the prisoner in a crowd of men and youths around the Agricultural Hall, where a dog show was held on Saturday night.' Ross must have been very nervous by this time because Goodhead was still on his tail. Goodhead himself, sure that he was on the right track, had been joined by a friend who, no doubt, hoped for a share of the reward. They had carried on following the supposed murderer as others began to tag along behind.

When Police Sergeant Hendrick came along, he found Ross standing on the footpath, complaining bitterly that 'two men were following him about the town, claiming that he was Ross and should be arrested'.

This was nothing less than the truth, but – in his panic – Ross had decided to brave it out for the moment and deny that he was any such person.

In the enquiry that followed, to allow Ross to be taken back to Leeds, Mr Loveridge, the magistrate, asked, 'Who wanted him to be arrested?'

Hendrick replied, 'He complained that two men were following him about the town.'

'They wanted this man to be arrested as Ross?' noted the magistrate.

'Yes,' said Hendrick. 'I said to him, I'm a policeman. If you'll come with me, I'll see about it. I have a description of the man.'

Ross turned round and pointed to one of the men who had been following him around and said, 'This is one of them!' (that is, one of the men who had been dogging his footsteps), whereupon one of the witnesses threatened to give the prisoner a blow on the mouth.

Not surprisingly, Hendrick intervened and said to the prisoner, 'You had better come quietly with me to the station and I'll see about it.'

He took hold of Ross and asked him where he lived, to which, as he later reported, the prisoner 'gave me very questionable statements'. He continued:

> I told him he must go to the police station with me and I would give him a description of the man who was wanted. He then became very timorous and wanted to go away, but I again took hold of him by the arm. I brought him to the police station and charged him with having committed the murder at Leeds on the 25th December. I read to him the bill giving a description of the missing man. I also took his shirt off and found a mole on the left shoulder, similar to the one described on the murderer, as mentioned in the bill.

As well as this, in the safety of the police station, the prisoner's features were again compared with the portrait of the murderer and were found to correspond in every particular. He was therefore charged with the murder of John Manley, but refused to make any reply, nor would he give any account of how he had spent Christmas evening.

Irish emigrants leaving after the famine (1851, Illustrated London News).

Leeds, painted by JMW Turner in 1816, as the city was expanding with the industrial revolution.

Below: The author's great-grandfather, James Flynn, (seated, hands on knees, fourth from right).

Bottom: Marshall's flax mill, Leeds, c. 1880.

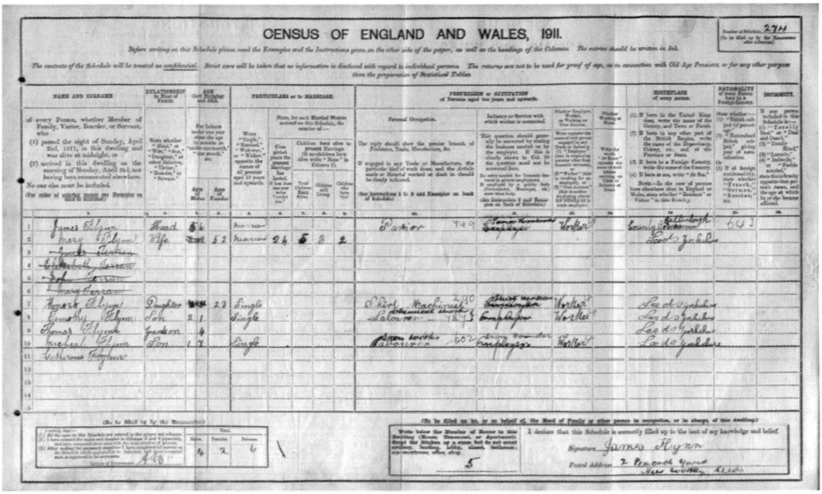

CENSUS OF ENGLAND AND WALES, 1911.

Name and Surname	Relationship to Head of Family	Age (Males)	Age (Females)	Particulars as to Marriage	Completed years the present Marriage has lasted	Total Children Born Alive	Children still Living	Children who have Died	Personal Occupation	Industry or Service	Whether Employer, Worker, or Working on Own Account	Birthplace	Nationality
James Flynn	Head	56		Married					Pavior	Employed	Worker	County Roscommon	
Mary Flynn	Wife		52	Married	24	5	3	2				Leeds Yorkshire	
~~Jacob Terran~~													
~~Elizabeth Terran~~													
~~John Terran~~													
~~Mary Terran~~													
Honora Flynn	Daughter		22	Single					Shirt Machinist		Worker	Leeds Yorkshire	
Timothy Flynn	Son	21		Single					Labourer	Employed	Worker	Leeds Yorkshire	
Thomas Flynn	Grandson	4										Leeds Yorkshire	
Michael Flynn	Son	17		Single					Labourer	Employed	Worker	Leeds Yorkshire	
~~Catherine Flynn~~													

Signature James Flynn

Above: The census return described in Chapter 17, completed by the 'Head of Family', James Flynn. The 'Profession or Occupation' column relates to 'Persons aged ten years and upwards'.

Left: Mary Manley's curly-haired grandson, the author's uncle, George Sunter, 1920.

Left: Catherine, skipping; and *opposite, top*: with Honora, her grandmother, both outside 32 Whitehall Road. *Below*, Catherine inside the house at Whitehall Road.

Opposite, below: Catherine, her grandfather Joe Sunter (Honora's husband) and Aunty Vera on holiday in Scarborough.

STANDEVEN'S CAFE

Right: Julian Czerkawski, late 1940.

Opposite, top: Kathleen Sunter looking timeless, c. 1948.

Opposite, bottom: Vera, George and Kathleen Sunter, c. 1935

Below: Julian, Catherine and Kathleen Czerkawski, Wallis's holiday camp, Cayton Bay, early 1950s.

Overleaf, top: Julian Czerkawski with his parents, Wladyslaw and Lucja, at Dziedzilow, Poland, c. 1930. *Below*: Vera and Kathleen Sunter flanked by friends on holiday in Douglas, Isle of Man.

ALL PHOTOS: AUTHOR'S COLLECTION

During the afternoon of Monday, 30 January, Detective Easby of the Leeds force arrived in Wolverhampton in answer to a telegram that had been sent to the Leeds Chief Constable. The prisoner was paraded in one of the corridors and, on seeing Easby approach him, he began to tremble. As the newspapers reported, 'On being asked several questions by the officer, he replied in a low tone, and appeared very nervous. Easby quickly identified him as John Ross, the murderer, whom he had known for several years.'

Obviously, Easby was very familiar with Ross from his previous police record and there was no way in which he could dissemble now.

Ross was doomed.

*

On Monday morning, 30 January, at a very crowded Wolverhampton Police Court, John Ross with his 'several aliases' was charged on suspicion of the wilful murder of John Manley of Brussels Street, York Street, Leeds, on Christmas night.

The magistrate's clerk asked the prisoner, 'Have you anything to say for yourself, as to why you should not be remanded?' to which the prisoner replied, 'No sir.'

Hendrick pointed out that he had already charged the prisoner with the murder that morning, but he had made no reply, at which point the magistrate remanded Ross until the following morning.

The prisoner was taken back to his cell, after which the court emptied. People had only come in for a sight of the murderer. On Tuesday, 31 January, the prisoner was again brought before the Wolverhampton bench to obtain permission for his removal to Leeds. The courtroom was again full. The landlord of the inn where Goodhead the file cutter had first recognised Ross, as well as Goodhead himself, were in court.

The court was told that the prisoner's appearance corresponded with the portrait published in the official announcement, offering £100 reward for his capture. It was alleged at this point – strangely – that the 'cast' in his eye was not altogether a physical defect, which makes us wonder what else it could have been other than some kind of physical 'tic'. Ross seemed to have been quite resigned to his fate at this time.

> From the moment he entered the dock until he left it, he stared fixedly at the bench, standing in an attitude of sullen defiance and answering the few questions put to him in a thick, deep voice.

The magistrate's clerk read over the charge of wilfully murdering John Manley, at the Railway Hotel, York Street, Leeds on 25 December 1881.

To this the prisoner made no reply.

Detective Easby of Leeds was sworn in and said that he knew and could identify the prisoner as John Ross, and that he asked for him to be remanded to Leeds, in his custody.

The Chief Magistrate then asked the prisoner if he had any questions for Easby, to which he replied that he did not.

'Have you any cause to show why you should not be removed to Leeds in the custody of the officer?'

The prisoner didn't reply; the magistrate then said that he would be remanded to Leeds and Ross was immediately taken below. This was, incidentally, rather more opportunity for questions than the prisoner was given at his later trial, something which probably had some bearing on events that followed.

Chief Inspector Nortcliffe had travelled to Wolverhampton on that same Tuesday and by lunchtime on the same day, John Ross has been handed over to him by the chief constable. Mr Nortcliffe left Wolverhampton with Ross under his charge by the one o'clock London and North Western train. Special permission was given for the guard to stop the train at Wortley Station, outside Leeds city centre, on the south side of the River Aire. A cab was waiting there, in which the prisoner was swiftly conveyed to Leeds Town Hall for the magisterial hearing. A large crowd had collected at the Leeds Joint Station to meet the train, people who may not have been quite as hostile to John Ross as the crowd in Wolverhampton, but they were disappointed not to catch a glimpse of him.

'This device succeeded so well,' reported the newspapers, 'that the prisoner was quietly conveyed to the Leeds Town Hall and Nortcliffe had his prisoner safe and sound in the cells by a quarter to seven, when the train they had travelled by reached the Joint Station.'

Ross was back on home territory again, but there is one more mystery.

The *Leeds Mercury* reports on the same day, Tuesday, 31 January 1882, with feelings in the community no doubt running high, that a woman called Hannah Conway had been up before Mr Bruce, the stipendiary magistrate at the Leeds Borough Court, 'yesterday', that is, 30 January, charged with assaulting Elizabeth Manley, whose address is now given as 'Brick Street', Leeds. This street, another grim little row of crumbling brick houses, ran at right angles to Brussels Street and beneath the railway line. Elizabeth had understandably found it necessary to move away from the room in Brussels Street in which the body of her brother had lain, but had not managed to go very far. She was to find no peace from the move. Mr Child appeared for the defence. He would later appear for the defence of John Ross, too. Elizabeth was described as the 'prosecutrix' and the 'sister of John Manley who was murdered in York Street on Christmas Day'. After leaving the court on 'Thursday last', which would have been 26 January, the court was told that Hannah Conway met Elizabeth in Dyer Street. This is inexplicably described in the newspaper as the 'day of the committal of Ross', but Ross certainly wasn't brought back to Leeds until 31 January – that is, the very day of this report in the *Leeds Mercury*. We are left to decide whether on 26 January some decision had been made to commit Ross to trial, whenever he could be apprehended. None of this is clear. What is clear is that this woman named Hannah Conway – one of John Ross's supporters – accused Elizabeth Manley of committing perjury in some way and resorted to attacking her in the street. She struck Elizabeth on the mouth, cutting her lip. Hannah Conway was sent to gaol for one month for the assault. The scar from the blow remained with Elizabeth until the day she died.

8. A Downcast, Dogged Look

On Wednesday, 1 February, as might be expected, there was great interest in the magisterial examination of the prisoner before Mr Bruce at the Leeds Town Hall. This was a pre-trial hearing and was conducted before the same magistrate who had sentenced Hannah Conway to a month in prison only a day or two earlier for her assault on Elizabeth Manley, so he must have been well aware of the feelings roused by the case. Once again, the local press took a great interest in the proceedings and reported that:

> Crowds of people assembled in the corridors and the court was speedily crammed. Thanks to the precautions of Chief Constable Bower, a staff of constables keeping the corridors free, access to the court was not impeded, but hundreds of people had to be refused admission and the heat and smell in the court was fearful.

In the absence of other free entertainment, court cases like this one attracted a great deal of public attention. The Irish community in Leeds were following events with interest, and seem to have taken sides more passionately than usual. The smell in a warm court can only be imagined, but dirty clothes tend to smell even worse than dirty bodies.

The magistrate and the court officials were in an unenviable situation.

John Ross is again described as being twenty-seven years old, of bad character, well known to the police, and a man who has assumed various aliases in the past. The court reporter notes that he is comparatively slim and also that when he is placed in the dock, he has a 'downcast, dogged look'. He either kept his hands in his trousers pocket or placed them on the bar of the dock. When he was formally charged with wilful murder, he made no reply, and when asked if he wished for a remand so that he could obtain the services of a solicitor, he said that he did not. The case for the prosecution was conducted by Mr Morrison, the town clerk, who appeared at the request of the Chief Constable, but the prisoner wasn't represented by counsel at all at this stage. Affording one must have been a major hurdle for such a family, but it appears that Ross didn't even realise that he needed representation.

The depositions at this point are recorded in some detail, and again tell the sorry tale of events in the Railway Hotel on Christmas Night, including the assertion that Manley had said that if he had been there when Anthony McDonald had hit Rory Brannagan, he (Manley) would have hit *him* (McDonald), to which Ross replied that he could not have done it. During the ensuing childish war of words, Ross had declared that he could slug the pair of them, Manley and Rooks both. Manley said he was not a fighting man, and didn't want to fight. Ross and Rooks then began to 'fratch' about fighting and Ross and Manley each produced sixpence, the latter offering to back Rooks to fight Ross in the morning for the money laid down – or for a larger sum.

Ross seems to have replied, 'Blind me, I could pay you in one hit.' It's at this hearing that the court first hears the word 'fratching' used to describe the quarrel. And the expletive 'blind me' may seem harmless enough, but at a time when swearing in mixed company was unacceptable, it must have been somewhat shocking. It was certainly indicative of the escalation of the quarrel. Outside the pub, the fratching continued, with Ross telling Rooks, 'You talk about fighting me! I could pay you in two minutes.'

There were depositions from Rooks and from John Hardaker, who said that both Ross and Manley were in the habit of coming into his establishment, but Manley more often than Ross, who lived further away and came only occasionally. The court heard from Elizabeth Manley, who testified that when she was outside the pub, she had heard somebody cry out, 'Oh, John, are you dead?' and then she saw the prisoner without his cap, running away. She went towards her brother and found him lying dead in a pool of blood.

Mary Ann Burke deposed that the only blow struck was the fatal one. There was no previous fight, only talk about fighting. After Edward Kilvington's evidence had been heard, the court adjourned for luncheon. During this lunch break, Kate Ross, John's younger sister, who seems to have become acutely aware of the predicament in which her brother found himself, and of the need for some kind of expert help, whatever the cost, went in search of a solicitor. The morning's proceedings and the sheer gravity of the charge had been brought home to the family, and

Kate engaged Mr Alfred Watson. The state would provide a defence lawyer for the accused in the case of a murder trial, but Kate wanted to secure the advice of a solicitor at this stage. Heaven knows how she managed this and with what resources, but perhaps some other family members had come to her assistance, financially, at any rate.

When the hearing resumed after lunch, Alfred Watson, solicitor, said that he had been instructed by Kate Ross, sister of the prisoner, to appear on his behalf. He had offices at 68 Great George Street, Leeds, and was more used to handling bankruptcy cases than murders, but he must have been the only person Kate could find in the time available. He told the magistrate that, because he had not yet had an opportunity to hear the evidence that had already been given on behalf of the prosecution, he intended to apply for a remand. This was a case of such importance that he needed time to read over the depositions and decide what line of defence he should pursue. There were no objections to this. He must have been well known to the court, and the presence of a defending solicitor was desirable. The prisoner was therefore remanded until Thursday, 2 February. During the afternoon, the records state that a photograph was taken of the prisoner, but I have not been able to find it. At the end of this hearing, predictably, and in spite of the presence of a solicitor, Ross was committed for trial, before the Honourable Mr Justice Cave, on a charge of murder, and the trial itself took place at Leeds Assizes on 10 February.

Since this was a case of national importance, even the *Aberdare Times* for 18 February reports the trial in some detail:

> John Ross, alias Cunningham, alias Lofthouse, was charged with the wilful murder of John Manley at Leeds on 25th December 1881. Mr Barker and Mr J L Walton appeared on behalf of the prosecution; the prisoner was defended by Mr Lockwood.

In less serious cases, as now, the poor seldom had access to a lawyer, although travelling solicitors would take on a case for payment of a guinea. Even this payment was beyond the means of most working people. However, this was a capital case; and the state paid Mr Lockwood to conduct the defence, instructed by Alfred Watson. The transcripts of the whole case are available, but they vary very little from all of the other enquiries, including the inquest, the magistrate's enquiry in Wolverhampton and the magisterial enquiry in Leeds, at which Watson had represented the prisoner.

The story told is pretty much exactly the same as that related previously. It never varies. There was a quarrel in the pub that was instigated largely by Ross, Ross threatened Manley and Rooks, becoming ever more aggressive, and – once the party were outside the pub – pulled out a tobacco knife and stabbed Manley in the neck. Michael Kelly was called to court as witness, but was not questioned on this occasion. Dr Harral testified as to the nature of the wound, and James Nortcliffe spoke of the arrest in Wolverhampton.

All the same, there are a few anomalies, largely to do with Mr Lockwood, who was representing the prisoner, and with the testimony, or lack of it, from the prisoner himself. When a defence lawyer was available, it was normal for the prisoner not to speak on his own behalf, probably for fear of an inarticulate person incriminating him or herself. (From this practice, the notion of the right to remain silent developed.) Lockwood did his job, up to a point. As can be seen from the transcripts of the trial, there was a certain amount of cross-examination and re-examination of witnesses, but all of this seemed rather vague and fruitless, serving only to confirm the guilt of the prisoner, rather than to cast any doubts on what happened. The fact of the stabbing, and the identity of its perpetrator, are unarguable and there is never any proof of real provocation, nor is there any suggestion that others were involved in the murder.

Ross was the culprit. The only possible argument or enquiry that might have helped the prisoner would have been to establish whether or not Ross intended to kill Manley at the moment when he struck the blow. The fact that the young men had known each other for so long, and that even friends and relatives of the victim were prepared to say they had been 'friends' for many years, might have been used in extenuation, but it hardly seems to have occurred to Lockwood to put this forward. His defence of Ross seems half-hearted at best. Proving these extenuating circumstances, however, would have involved putting his client on the witness stand and he was reluctant to do so, perhaps with good reason. Ross wasn't exactly articulate.

The newspaper account describes how:

> After the close of the case for the prosecution, Mr Lockwood asked that, before he addressed the jury, the prisoner might be allowed to make a statement. His

> Lordship intimated that the request should have been made earlier, but if the prisoner did so, the learned counsel for the prosecution would have the right to reply, as it would be a statement of fresh facts, which the jury would be asked to believe.

This was to be a last roll of the dice, but as soon as it became clear that Ross would be cross-examined by the prosecutors, Lockwood yielded and gave his own final address to the jury, with the intention of reducing the crime to manslaughter. He did his best.

We are never really given Ross's version of events in his own words, neither at the trial, nor during any of the previous enquiries. All of the reports of Ross's behaviour, before and after the crime, suggest that he was a man of few words. If a question is asked, he gives a one- or two-word answer, and seems to have been quite incapable of realising the gravity of his situation, until the very end of the trial. In the pub, on that Christmas Night, both Manley and Rooks first brush off the suggestion of a fight, and then make plans to fight the following day, seemingly in an effort to distract Ross. There may be some suggestion that they are humouring him, especially when Manley says that he would 'rather fight for fun' than for sixpence. They don't even want to take his money.

There are various possible explanations. Ross may simply be the kind of man in whom alcohol triggers aggression and reckless behaviour and we have plenty of evidence of this in his previous criminal record. On the other hand, his demeanour at the enquiries and the trial, when he must have been stone-cold sober, seems to suggest an individual who is not particularly bright, and who may have been very easily led. This struck me only after I had read accounts of the trial and the various enquiries beforehand, in all of which Ross says almost nothing, as he would have been advised. He was a habitual criminal, he may have been naturally taciturn, but, with some exceptions, many of his crimes had been petty acts of theft, gambling, drunkenness: nuisances rather than anything more serious. Those crimes that were more serious, such as burglary, may have involved the agency of other people. Ross seems vulnerable. The stabbing was impulsive and the wound couldn't have been anything but fatal, given where the knife landed, but it's surprising that Lockwood didn't raise doubts as to whether Ross intended to strike his victim in the neck. From the statements of some witnesses, it's possible that John Manley may have been in the act of turning away. There's a chance that Ross was aiming for his shoulder. It's also surprising how often reports of non-fatal knife crimes at this time involve stabbing in the arm or shoulder, with heavy jackets protecting the victims from serious injuries. I doubt if Ross had thought about the consequences of his actions. I wonder if he was even capable of such foresight, and then I also wonder if this vague perception that Ross might not have been entirely responsible informed everything that followed, in the behaviour, not just of the community, but of those officials who were or who became involved with the case, from the jury, to the judge, right up to the Home Secretary himself.

Given that Ross was not allowed to speak on his own

behalf, Lockwood did what he could in his final submission:

> To think that on this day of all others, Christmas Day, these men were spending their time in that public house, drinking and talking about fighting, inflaming their minds with strong drink and their passions with talk about a quarrel and a fight in another public house. The pitch of excitement into which the men had worked themselves really rendered them hardly responsible for their actions.

Quite apart from the fact that Lockwood is trying to throw the blame for the crime on all parties for a commonplace quarrel (the members of the jury were not fooled), it seems to have been quite beyond the collective imagination of the Victorian middle classes to perceive the Christmas Day alternative for these young men and women: overcrowded and poverty-stricken domestic surroundings. Even Bob Cratchit with his small goose and his plum pudding would have had a more comfortable Christmas.

Lockwood went on to say that, although drink was no excuse for serious crime, the witnesses might be untrustworthy and that Ross's immediate reaction demonstrated the impulsive nature of the stabbing. 'Sufficient time did not elapse to allow of the inflamed blood of Ross cooling. Directly he struck the blow he was brought to himself.'

This is true enough.

The jury retired at half past twelve to consider their verdict and, returning to court after an absence of around one and three-quarter hours, found the prisoner guilty of wilful murder. The foreman of the jury said he had been asked by some members of the jury that mercy should be extended to the prisoner if possible. His Lordship said he would take care that 'the recommendation should be forwarded to the proper quarter'.

'John Ross,' he said, 'you have been found guilty of the wilful murder of John Manley and those who have heard the evidence which has been given must feel that the jury had no alternative in following the law but to return the verdict which they found. My duty is simply to pass upon you the sentence which the law directs.'

The learned judge then assumed the black cap and passed sentence of death upon Ross. Until that moment, he seems to have remained calm, but the sentence was 'received with much agitation on the part of the prisoner who wept audibly as he was led from the dock'.

9. The Mercy of the Crown

John Ross was taken to Armley Gaol to await execution: a grim, soot-blackened, castellated place, which I used to pass every day on my way from our house in Whitehall Road to Holy Family Primary School. My school was quite a distance from my house, the reason being that my parents and grandparents had judged the nearer school, St Francis's, to be too big and too rough for their precious infant, and perhaps they were right. Holy Family was smaller, with a strict headmistress and an excellent, motherly infant teacher, Winifred Burgess. The classroom had an open fire with a big fireguard, over which we dried our hats and woolly mittens in winter. In the infant classes, we wrote on slates with old-fashioned slate pencils, so that mistakes could all be rubbed clean.

My mother didn't mind the time involved in taking me there. Sometimes we caught a bus for part of the way, sometimes we walked. It was over a mile, along Wellington Road, up Bruce Street and Hall Lane. It was even further when we moved across the city to Bellevue Road, but again we would take a bus part of the way and walk the rest. The school was small, heavily populated by people of Irish descent, and as we grew a little older, we would have to walk down the hill at lunchtimes to the dinner hall, next to Holy Family Church, where school dinners that have given me an abiding loathing for mashed potatoes were served. Every day, we would see the high wall of a big cemetery on one side, and Armley Gaol on the other, and wonder about it.

I always thought of the prison (now known officially as HM Prison Leeds, but still called Armley Gaol by a significant majority of the locals) as a castle, before I ever knew what it really was. My friends and I would make up stories about it. A little later, when I read *The Wind in the Willows*, I visualised Armley Gaol as the place where poor Mr Toad was imprisoned. Ross would have served his previous sentences here but, were he to hang, the authorities would have anticipated popular unrest, and unrest there certainly would have been. Feelings in the Bank area of the city were running high. The death sentence was widely thought to be unfair.

Almost immediately, the community, the local press and various interested officials began the process of requesting that the death sentence be commuted to one of life imprisonment instead. The speed and vigour with which this was supported by everyone except the immediate friends and family of the murdered man suggest there was a definite groundswell of opinion regarding Ross's responsibility. There was no disputing that he had stabbed John Manley, but whether he had intended to kill his friend was another matter. The lobbying seemed to involve all classes, from the judge himself to friends and relatives of the Ross family, some of them with their own criminal records.

As we've seen, the family were known to be 'troublesome' and even after his brother's imprisonment, Ross's younger brother Patrick carried on engaging in criminal behaviour for many a long year. I doubt if anybody was genuinely afraid of testifying against Ross, certainly not the men who had known him well, although poor Elizabeth had already been attacked, and Bridget wouldn't escape unscathed. All the same, the Ross family were relatively powerless in the grand scheme of things and John Ross was no folk hero in the making. He was taciturn, resentful and had proved to be dangerous, although in the past he had fought mainly with his fists. He carried a knife, but only for cutting tobacco. He aroused a modicum of sympathy among the jurors, as well as the officials and politicians who were lobbied on his behalf. He wasn't very likeable, although his family obviously cared about him. All we are left with is a sense of pity, a feeling that he didn't deserve to hang, because he might not have intended to murder John Manley in the way that, for example, a poisoner would intend to kill. It was rare for such a drunken weekend scrap between friends to end in death. The devastating effects were the same, and the Manley family couldn't be expected to agree with this groundswell of pity. I've found it hard enough to agree with it myself, at this distance in time. But the fact remains that there was an air of hopeless susceptibility about Ross that seems to have elicited some pity where none would normally be shown. While never bringing any evidence to show that John Manley had provoked the assault – quite the opposite, in fact – people still didn't believe that Ross was guilty of a capital offence, and the fact that he had been sentenced to death somehow risked bringing the system under which he had been sentenced into disrepute.

First of all, a 'memorial in favour of a commutation of the sentence of death' was prepared by Mr Albert Watson, the Leeds solicitor retained by Kate Ross. The memorial was signed by the mayor and 'other prominent gentlemen in the city'. After that it was 'deposited for signature at the Victoria Hotel behind the Town Hall'. I still wonder, uneasily, what it was about John Ross that made so many prominent gentlemen feel so well disposed towards him and where the money to pay the solicitor came from. How on earth did Kate Ross manage it? Was Patrick Ross involved? As with everything about this case, from the night of the murder onwards, events moved with astonishing speed. Anyone today, making comparisons with the law's glacial speed even in the matter of a minor traffic offence, will be amazed by how much was accomplished in such a short time.

On 11 February, writing from Judges' Lodgings in Leeds, Lord Justice Lewis W Cave forwarded his personal notes on the evidence in the case to the Right Honourable Sir William Vernon Harcourt, MP, Secretary of State at the 'Home Department'. The various documents and reports still exist, with all their fascinating handwritten notes and annotations. By 13 February, Harcourt will have been made aware of the nature of the case, which is described succinctly as a 'reckless stabbing by a drunken man after some verbal quarrelling. The blow was given in the neck behind the ear and the natural and probable consequence of it was certain death. Some of the jury recommended mercy.' Harcourt, although a Liberal, was a stickler for law and order, and no supporter of the Irish Home Rule movement, so the case must have genuinely interested him.

On 14 February, Valentine's Day, Harcourt asks when the judge is likely to be in London. If not for some time, he says that he would like to ascertain his opinion on aspects of the case, and would also like to read one of the newspaper reports. He asks to see a copy of the *Leeds Mercury*, or 'any other having a report of the trial'. On the same day, one of Harcourt's minions sends a telegram to the judge and Cave immediately responds: 'Shall reach London tomorrow afternoon about two. Will come to Home Office about three if convenient.'

At the same time, there is a message from Dr Orange, of Broadmoor, also to the Secretary of State. Harcourt has requested his expert opinion about the state of mind of Ross and several others for whom commutation is sought. This consultation is with regard to a group of four prisoners who had been sentenced to death, with some debate as to how sane they may have been. These capital cases were reconsidered by Harcourt at the same time: Ross and Snell, Nulty and Stebbings. Of these, both Ross and Snell have been found guilty of a similar kind of drunken assault, ending in death, while Nulty and Stebbings have been judged insane, and it is recommended that they be removed to Broadmoor. It was not always the case that insanity guaranteed an escape from the gallows. People were hanged who might today have been judged to be of unsound mind. But then again, many – some say a majority – of people filling our prisons here in the UK today have significant mental health problems. Certainly, in this case, the authorities moved expeditiously.

The report of the trial from the *Leeds Mercury* is swiftly sent to Harcourt.

On 18 February, a wordy and rather convoluted letter is also sent to Harcourt by Mr Bruce, the stipendiary magistrate who held the pre-trial enquiry in Leeds.

> Sir, I have the honour to write to you in reference to the case of John Ross who was convicted of Murder at the assizes at Leeds and who now lies under sentence of death. I was requested to sign a memorial to you begging that the mercy of the Crown might be extended to the convict, but I have declined to do so.

He doesn't think it fitting for a man in his position, and with his intimate knowledge of the case, to sign such a memorial, but he hastens to explain himself further. He goes on to say that Harcourt himself:

> would have before you the notes of Mr Justice Cave, his report upon the case and the memoranda here of the jury to mercy.

The point of this verbose letter quickly becomes apparent when he goes on to say:

> I hope you will not think me superfluous in joining in the prayer . . . that the mercy of the Crown may be extended to the convict. I was the stipendiary magistrate in the case and . . . I brought the charge of murder as described by the criminal law. And yet it appeared to me that taking all the circumstances into consideration, and I do not specify them because you will have them all before you in the judge's report, the case seems one which might be appropriately redirected to . . . murder in the second degree.

This appeal from the stipendiary magistrate finally swayed Harcourt, along with the direct recommendation of the judge, Mr Cave. For, on 20 February, Harcourt writes that:

> the magistrate joins in the petition on behalf of those praying for rejection of the extreme sentence. I have seen the judge on this case who recommends the commutation of the capital sentence. Therefore commute and sentenced to life.

On 23 February, we find:

> Received from the Secretary of State's Office, Home Department, a letter said to contain a respite addressed to the governor of HM Prison, Leeds.

This was an intermediate stay of execution, so that the full commutation could be confirmed later. On Friday, 24 February 1882, the governor of HM Prison Leeds received notice that the sentence of death had been 'respited with a view to its ultimate commutation'. A fuller account of this is to be found in the much-favoured *Leeds Mercury* for that date, which relates how:

> The Home Secretary, in advising the Queen to grant a respite in the case of John Ross, sentenced to death at the Leeds Assizes, has really given effect to the general feeling of the public in the district where the crime was committed . . . the circumstances under which the crime was committed fairly raised the question whether the quarrelling both in the public house and outside, which preceded the actual crime, did not reduce the offence to one of manslaughter. No-one will regret that the Home Secretary has felt himself justified in advising Her Majesty to comply with it.

No one, except perhaps John's grieving family. I know they regretted it.

Meanwhile, the *Yorkshire Post* more or less tells the same tale, adding that the prisoner is to be 'detained until further signification of Her Majesty's pleasure'. Ross did not serve out his sentence in Leeds. Maybe it was thought inadvisable to keep him so close to home. At some point, John Ross was transferred to Portland Prison in the South of England, to serve out the rest of his life sentence with hard labour, far away from family and friends. He was lucky that he did not find himself the subject of a broadside ballad, but perhaps he did. Not all of them survived.

The regime at Portland was harsh, and some prisoners did not survive. Ross fared better than many. The prison had seen some distinguished Irish Republican inmates in its previous history, notably Jeremiah O'Donovan Rossa. Rossa hailed from Skibbereen in County Cork and had seen some of the most dramatic and terrible effects of the Great Hunger at first hand. He and several others were convicted of the crime of Treason Felony in Dublin in 1865 and sentenced to penal servitude for life. Sent to England in late 1865, he arrived at Portland in Dorset in May 1866, where the 'Fenian' prisoners were housed together, with extra-strict guards patrolling them. Rossa noted in his diaries that he had started his sentence with the intention of keeping to the rules of the prison, but that his treatment there made it impossible, given that he didn't even recognise the validity of the regime under which he had been sentenced. Rossa and his colleagues began a programme of deliberate insubordination and while they were treated harshly, it was also clear that the authorities were cautious of the political fall-out from external scrutiny by sympathisers in Ireland and elsewhere, including America. In 1868 he was manacled after throwing a chamber pot at the governor. He was released from gaol in 1871, after a good deal of political pressure, and immediately went to America.

John Ross would not have expected to be treated so circumspectly. Nevertheless, he decided to keep his head down and get on with his sentence, which involved bad food in uncomfortable and frequently verminous surroundings, and unrelenting hard work in a local stone quarry – although not, so far as we know, being manacled in a punishment cell. I have a sneaking suspicion that the bad prison food and uncomfortable surroundings may have been better than John Ross was used to at home in Leeds, although he probably missed his pipe and his drink. Perhaps even the pipe was allowed. At any rate, there he stayed for the next twelve years, giving very little trouble to his gaolers, and there we must leave him for the time being.

*

Fate had not yet finished with poor Mary Ross, who was to be beset by even more cares. Henry, John's younger brother proved himself equally troublesome during the next few years. Whatever lay at the root of their misbehaviour, they were a very challenging family, and Henry, like John and Patrick before him, already had a record for petty criminality. While only twelve years old, in 1877, he had been given a beating of 'twelve strokes' for stealing threepence halfpenny and a four-pound weight. However, early in 1881, the year of the murder, we find him, aged sixteen, as a private in the York and Lancaster Militia, which he has joined in August 1880. From there, on 30 March 1882, not long after his brother's trial, he applies to join the South

Yorkshire Regiment, or, as the official letter states, he is 'desirous of enlisting into Her Majesty's Regular Forces and has applied . . . for a Conditional Discharge' from the militia so that he can join the South Yorkshire Regiment.

Perhaps he had some hopes of escaping Leeds and his family's murky reputation. At the time of his enlistment in the South Yorks Regiment, he is described as five foot five inches tall, with fair physical development and some scars on his body, perhaps from previous beatings and not just the twelve strokes he had received for theft. I sometimes wonder if his father may have been responsible. It might help to explain the problematic and frequently reckless behaviour of all three sons. His next of kin is his mother, Mary, still living in Somerset Street. We first find him in training at the barracks at the Curragh, County Kildare, in 1882. This extensive plain had been viewed by the British as a good place to train the soldiery from the time of Queen Elizabeth onwards, but its military associations go back even further. The ancient kings of Ireland had staged their battles there. The actual Curragh Camp was built in 1855 and it was, during Queen Victoria's reign, in constant use as a training ground for the British army. She and Albert had even visited it, back in 1861.

The camp had a particular problem with prostitution; commonplace everywhere, but such an obvious gathering of large numbers of young men, with money to spend, would be a particular attraction to a starving and poverty-stricken population. The high incidence of disease among the soldiery had been a factor in the passing of the Contagious Disease Acts by the British parliament, which allowed for the arrest and detention of women suspected of prostitution. As usual, there was no acknowledgement or even comprehension that the men might be passing diseases onto the women. It's all one-way traffic as far as the law is concerned. Henry Ross was making a determined attempt to escape a troubled background, but would turn out to be all too easily distracted and on as short a fuse as his brother.

Meanwhile, in 1882, it was Bridget's turn to be victimised by some of her neighbours in Leeds. It was reported in the ubiquitous *Leeds Mercury* as 'A charge arising out of the Leeds Murder Case'. At the Burgh Police Court, again before Mr Bruce, John Edward Kelly, cloth dresser, of Brussels Street, Marsh Lane (therefore a near neighbour of the Manleys at the time of the murder), was brought up on a charge of assaulting Bridget Manley of Brick Street. Bridget and Elizabeth had moved around the corner together. The prosecutrix, said the reporter, was 'one of the sisters of John Manley who was murdered on Christmas Night last year'. The case was still something of a cause célèbre. Bridget said that late on Saturday night last, that would be 4 March, soon after the commutation of the death penalty would have become common knowledge in Leeds, she was going home with two other young women. They were met in Brussels Street by Kelly, who jeered, 'Well, you have not hanged Ross yet!' to which taunt Bridget is said to have replied, 'I'll make you pay for this.' Whatever 'this' was – the taunt itself or some other action of Kelly's – is unclear. The prisoner, Kelly, then said, 'I have done one five years and I will do another for you,' seconding his words, according to the paper, by punching Bridget in the face and also kicking her on the leg.

Bridget's statement was corroborated by her female

companions. Kelly denied the assault, alleging that Manley was the aggressor. Witnesses were called for the defence but their evidence was, not surprisingly, conflicting. In sharp contrast to the sentence handed down to Elizabeth's female attacker only a month previously, Bruce ordered Kelly only to 'enter into his own recognisances at £40 and to find two sureties [i.e. guarantors] of £20 to keep the peace for six months'. Once again, where he found the money is all unclear. Kelly may or may not have been a relative of Michael Kelly, who was a witness to the murder and called to give evidence at the magisterial hearing, although not at the trial. Kelly was a common enough name, and by his own admission, John Edward Kelly had already spent five years in prison. Sentences of this length tended to be handed down for serious crimes such as larceny, which again raises the question of whether John Ross had been encouraged in his thieving by a gang of more experienced burglars.

One other sad little tale belongs to those few weeks following on from the trial and around the time of the commutation, while the Manley murder was still 'news', with stories making a connection, however tenuous. On Saturday, 4 March, the day on which Bridget was punched and kicked by Edward Kelly, the *Leeds Times* was reporting the trial of an 'unfortunate waif' called Patrick Manley of whom it was said that he was related to John Manley, the murder victim. When John Manley senior came over from Ireland in the late 1840s, he had lived with members of an extended Manley family, and it is possible that this 'waif' might have been a cousin of the younger Manleys.

He had been up in court on the preceding Tuesday,

charged with the 'high crime and misdemeanour' as the newspaper ironically termed it, of 'sleeping out'. Sleeping on the streets was not allowed. The boy is described as a 'thorough specimen of his class'. His growth was stunted, and he was so diminutive that he was only just visible in the dock. His clothes were ragged, his hair shaggy and uncombed, and 'in short he looked like a poor, lost creature'. The report, which puts us vividly in mind of Oliver Twist, goes on to call him a 'street arab'. Seemingly, he had been an inmate of an industrial school. These unfriendly institutions were aimed at inculcating the virtues of hard work into those judged to be the undeserving poor. He had a mother and sister in the school. His father was in prison. His mother took no interest in him at all and didn't even come to court to see what became of him. Mr Bruce was very much exercised as to what he could possibly do with this 'tiny specimen of humanity' with nobody to take responsibility for him, so he remanded the lad for further enquiries, when at least he would be kept off the streets. Eventually, the magistrate forced Patrick's mother to come to court and take charge of him. We don't know whether or not he returned to the school in the company of his mother and his sister, whether some other family member came forward to look after him or whether his father, upon leaving prison, took responsibility for him.

He was just ten years old.

10. Three Sisters

I began this book with the aim of telling the story of John Manley's murder, but soon found myself drawn into another equally dramatic and tragic tale, that of his young sister, Elizabeth, who witnessed the murder, or at least its preamble, and gave testimony in its immediate aftermath. The two are inextricably linked. When I was describing this project to a friend, he remarked that it must be like 'throwing a stone into a pool. The ripples spread further and further out.' Elizabeth's fate seems to have been bound up in, provoked by, and a consequence of the death of her brother. We can't know for sure what might have become of her if John Ross hadn't put his hand in his pocket and pulled out a tobacco knife on that Christmas Eve in 1881, but we can be fairly certain that some of what befell her was a result of the experience of seeing her brother bleeding and dying before her eyes.

In both of these instances, the murder and Elizabeth's story, I began with twenty-first-century expectations about prejudice, about incompetence or malice on the part of the authorities. All of those things were present in some measure, as they would certainly be now, but as I found myself reading further into the background to this story, it became clear that Elizabeth's dreadful fate seems to have been the result of a failure of imagination, a state-sponsored complacency and a lack of care, sustained by the inability of people in authority, even those whose intentions may have been good, to put themselves in another's shoes. This is something that also persists to this day, with only a little less savagery.

Another thought struck me as I trawled through records and pieced together the facts with a little speculation. That failure of imagination, that complacency, didn't, ultimately, apply to the murderer. There, and with justification, they made allowances. John Ross survived, although he was certainly punished for his crime. Few allowances were made for Elizabeth, and it killed her. If to know all isn't quite to forgive all, it certainly causes the historian to revise and refine her opinions. Time and again, I became aware of the belief, running through all official pronouncements, through newspaper reports, commentary and opinion, that the poor were responsible for their own situation. The plight of the 'undeserving poor' in particular, young, old and every age in between, was too often seen as something that must be sternly and strictly punished and controlled by those confident Victorian authorities, rather than addressed more sympathetically. It emerged as a battle against some fearful chaos, just waiting to swamp the triumphant middle classes. Sympathy and imagination existed, of course, as we can see from the extensive work of Henry Mayhew, but it was always easier to repress and punish than to improve conditions. There were sympathetic people, but they were seldom in positions of power, and even when their intentions were good, their influence was limited. The widespread belief that the Irish in mainland Britain were prepared – even happy – to accept a much lower standard of living than their English- or Scottish-born neighbours persisted long after various attempts at slum clearance in places such as Leeds and Glasgow, to which city the story makes a surprising and still largely unexplained shift. This is also a belief that persists to this day, generally with regard to a different set of incomers but certainly springing from the same innate sense not just of our difference, but of our superiority.

When in trouble, blame the stranger, the incomer, the immigrant.

Or the victim.

There is an air of raw and, at times, unbearable misery about this story, and it has made the process of research and writing uniquely difficult and harrowing. It was like attempting to do a complicated jigsaw, with no picture to guide me and no edge pieces at all, and finding out that the emerging image was one of unrelenting horror. I didn't set out to write a misery memoir. My post-war childhood was far from affluent, and I was seriously unwell for a large part of it, but I was loved, and although money was frequently in short supply, we were, as a family, clean, well clothed and well fed. We were not exactly prosperous, but we were doing all right. Those four cheerful young women, marching into the future, symbolised everything we had gained, everything that I would benefit from in the way of education and encouragement, from the free cod liver oil and malt at the baby clinic to the free night school my Polish refugee father attended, cycling there straight from work, several evenings a week. This would eventually result in him studying for his BSc and PhD. I did not know or meet most of these earlier, struggling people, but I heard about them;

we are of the same blood, the same background, and that matters. It has occurred to me before that the difference between the historian and the writer of historical fiction is that the historian asks who, how, when, where and why and so does the novelist. But the novelist also asks herself, 'What did that feel like?' Well, with a subject as close to my heart as this one, I too must ask, what did that feel like? For Mary, for Bridget, and above all, for Elizabeth.

I was aiming to ferret out as much of the truth of those long-ago events as I could, but because the tale involves members of my family, I couldn't help but ask myself what it must have felt like to be these people. The possible answers to that question came thick and fast, with each new discovery adding to the stomach-churning horror of what became of those young siblings who must have set out jovially enough for a Christmas Day drink in 1881. These discoveries have made me uncomfortable, sad, but above all angry. And yet, for all that this is a sad story, I have reason to believe that the young Manley children were as much loved as I was, that John and Mary were loving parents, placed in an impossible position. The clues, inexpressibly sad, are all part of Elizabeth's story.

We must now move forward to 1884, which for various reasons seems to have been another significant year in the life of the three Manley sisters. John Ross is safely in Portland Prison and the community anger and unrest have died down. Patrick Ross is keeping out of trouble too – at least for a while – although their younger brother Henry's escape into military service has been short-lived. In 1883, Henry goes from the Curragh to Cork, from where he is sent to Dinapore, now Danapur in Bihar State in India. That same year also sees him treated for gonorrhoea – no doubt as a result of his stay at the Curragh – and tonsillitis. In May 1884, his brief military career comes to a sudden end when he is discharged on medical grounds with a diagnosis of 'mania'. The medical officer rejects the idea that the illness was caused by his army service, and instead decides that it is a 'hereditary tendency, aggravated by intemperance, the latter possibly a phase of the disease'. He doesn't expect a cure any time soon. When young Henry is discharged, it is with the single-word description on his discharge papers under 'character on being discharged': 'bad'. Significantly, he is not placed in an asylum, but he is returned home, probably to his long-suffering mother and sister.

The murder of their brother would not by any means have been forgotten by the Manleys, especially perhaps by Elizabeth, who had seen him lying covered in blood in the seconds before he died. Bridget is living at 32 Off Street, and that is probably where Elizabeth is living too. She is working as a mill hand, putting in long hours for low wages in a flax mill. Bridget is courting again: a young man called John Castle, who lives, if not next door, then just along the road, at 23 Off Street. John is younger than Bridget, and he has a decent job as a mechanic. They plan to marry.

At the turn of the year, in January 1884, Mary Terran is living nearby, at 33 Little Off Street, with her husband Charles, and her surviving children, nine-year-old James, three-year-old Elizabeth, and baby John Thomas, born after the murder. He will be two years old later in the year. But all is not well in that household. Charles, who has worked as a 'puddler', is now reaping the dubious rewards in terms of ill health. The poisonous fumes have taken their inevitable toll on this young man. He isn't fit enough to undertake heavy work. Still he struggles on. In January 1884 he is described as a 'soap boiler'. It is likely that he was working for Joseph Watson and Sons at the Whitehall Soap Works. This business was founded in the 1830s, in Horsforth, by Watson's grandfather, thence moving to Woodhouse Lane. In 1861 the business had expanded still further, and moved to a site between the city centre end of Whitehall Road and the river. We passed the soap works whenever we went into town. It had become one of the largest soap factories in England, employing some 750 people in its heyday and making six hundred tons of soap a week. I remember it well. You could smell it for miles around, a pungent but not unpleasant smell, compared to so much round about. It was always known as 'Soapy Joe's'. They imported oil, resin and tallow, some of which they stored in the Dark Arches, below the railway. (These materials were hugely inflammable, and were to cause a disastrous fire in 1892.) Later, they also made glycerine for dynamite manufacture, and dealt in not nearly so pleasant hides and skins. In Charles Terran's day, they were well known for products with names such as Watson's Matchless Cleanser, otherwise known as the 'housewife's friend'. Reproduction metal advertising signs for this product can still be bought on eBay, with an endless trail of pretty young housemaids leading off into the distance, dressed in frilly aprons. They look like young women who have never blacked a range or scrubbed a floor in their lives, all of them holding baskets of soap in one hand and brandishing individual bars like weapons in the other. I'm quite sure my grandmother must have used it.

It would have been here that Charles Terran worked

during the last years or months of his short life, while the family were living at 33 Off Street. On 15 January 1884, he died of heart disease at their home address, leaving Mary alone with three young children. Mary still couldn't write, and made her mark on the death certificate. She was, not to put too fine a point on it, in desperate straits. What work could she possibly undertake, alone in the world, with few skills and three young children to care for? The only means of earning a living open to Mary was hawking, and that is what she found herself doing, probably selling brushes or matches or something similar. In all likelihood, she would have had to leave her younger children at home in the precarious care of her ten-year-old son, James, while she went out, but if this wasn't possible, hawkers who were widowed like Mary sometimes took their children with them in all weathers, or secured the services of a frail elderly neighbour, for the few pennies they could ill afford.

It has proved difficult to find many references to the surviving brother of the family, Thomas Manley, throughout these years. He would have been twenty-eight years old by this time, younger than Mary and Bridget, older than Elizabeth, but he is notable by his absence. Back in 1871, he was living in Brussels Street and working as a cloth dresser, but there is little other information about him during succeeding years and he is never mentioned at the time of the murder. From time to time, an unmarried Thomas Manley of the right age crops up, working as a labourer and living in Leeds. In 1911, we find him in his fifties, a single man still, and a boarder in a lodging house run by an Italian called Pietro Pacitto and his wife Antonia in Shannon Street, a stone's throw from Brussels Street and a place where a small Italian community seems to have been living among the Irish migrants. Like the Irish, nineteenth-century Italian migrants were often fleeing extremes of poverty, although there were far fewer of them in these northern cities. Thomas didn't move very far from home in all this time and he will die, still in Leeds, in 1923. None of which is to assume that he didn't keep in touch with his sisters Bridget and Mary and their families, didn't sometimes visit them.

In view of Elizabeth's next destination, however, it is interesting to find one Thomas Manley living in Glasgow in what appears to be some kind of lodging house. In 1885, this Thomas was lodging in William Street, at the edge of Glasgow Green, in a house crammed with people. His housemates are labourers, painters, a shoemaker. Poor people. And he is only of interest as the most tenuous of connections, the most unlikely of explanations for what Elizabeth did next. It is just possible that Thomas went to Glasgow in search of work, and from a desire to get out of the city that had seen so much heartache. It is possible, but not likely, that he stayed there for a while and that Elizabeth followed him. It is much more likely, however, that this is a different Thomas Manley altogether, since the name is not uncommon. It is even more likely that Elizabeth followed or went with somebody quite different, that she was enticed north by a man, perhaps with the offer of work, a change of scene, the possibility of some improvement in her life. The possibility of adventure. There is an impulsive streak in my family and Elizabeth, unmarried, without children, free as her sisters were not, may have been encouraged to try something new.

Whatever the reason, she went to Glasgow.

By the end of that year, on 27 November 1884, Mary's sister Bridget has married John Castle. She is working as a cloth filler, a skilled occupation that involved the craft of thickening cloth by adding in extra threads. Bridget's new father-in-law, Richard Castle, makes brushes for a living. He may even have kept her widowed sister Mary supplied with the brushes that she now has to hawk around the town, but life must still have been indescribably hard. Both Bridget and John are able to sign their names at this wedding, so Bridget has been learning how to write, perhaps from her husband-to-be. Their witnesses are William Castle, probably John's brother, and Sarah Jane Wilson, and they too sign their own names, a hint of progress, however small.

Mary Terran, meanwhile, is pregnant again. The child, another Mary, will be born in March 1885, which means that she cannot possibly be Charles Terran's child. He died in January 1884. No father is named on the birth certificate. Nor does she seem to be my great-grandfather James Flynn's child, either, since James was one of those warm-hearted men who loved children and was reluctant to deny any child a home. He would no doubt have given her his name if he had been on the scene at that time, but I don't think he was.

Some time between Charles Terran's death, early in the year, and Bridget's marriage late in the year, and while Mary is making the unwelcome discovery of another pregnancy, Elizabeth travels all the way to Glasgow. She may have gone there to work as a servant, but for whom and by whom she was engaged, there is no indication, neither officially, nor in family stories. We know her occupation only from the documents in which she will be described as a servant, two years later, but there are no details of who might have employed her, and Elizabeth herself never makes it clear.

How did she get there? The cost of a train fare would have been well beyond her means. She could have walked but that would be a perilous undertaking indeed for a young woman alone and in her reduced circumstances. Glasgow is an arduous journey of more than two hundred miles from Leeds, along turnpike roads, through some of the most wild and inhospitable countryside in England, across the Pennines, through the Lake District and the wild Borders country of Scotland. What possible explanation can there be for a very young woman, traumatised only a couple of years earlier, with almost no resources and certainly no money, to set off on the long journey to Glasgow, a city of which she has no knowledge. The two most likely explanations are that she went to stay with a relative, possibly even her brother, but there is virtually no evidence of that in the history of subsequent events and certainly no family member offers to take responsibility for her in the city when she needs help. The simplest explanation is that she was taken there by somebody on the promise of something. A good job. A better life. A new beginning. Maybe even the possibility of the longer and much more perilous but thrilling journey taken by so many Irish exiles, across the sea to America.

11. *Spoutmouth*

At some point in this project, one of my Leeds cousins, David Watson, another of Mary Manley's descendants, sent me a vivid picture of present-day Brussels Street, a part of Leeds with which I was unfamiliar, both as a child and in more recent years during which there have been massive changes to the city I used to know well. It arrived when I was trying to find out more about Elizabeth's time in Glasgow, when her last address was 32 Spoutmouth, just off the Gallowgate in that city, blending with Molendinar Street at its north end. I was immediately struck by the uncanny similarity between the two places now and the thought that back then, in 1886, when Elizabeth was living here, there must have been a certain grim similarity as well. Both streets run alongside the railway, both have now been cleared of houses – the ancient, crumbling houses where Elizabeth found lodgings – and the tenements that succeeded them when the slums they had become were cleared, only to be cleared again in their turn. At present there are car parks, with a handful of business premises beneath the railway and a number of hopeful patches of green here and there, grass and trees that seem to be making a determined attempt to return to something that had once been another part of St Kentigern's 'dear green place' as surely as the traditional site where Glasgow's magnificent cathedral sits.

Of the Loch Erne pub that once sat on the corner of Spoutmouth and the Gallowgate, and that Elizabeth must surely have known, there is not a sign. The notion that pubs were purely male domains is more recent than you might think, although some taverns and inns were always thought more 'respectable' than others. Further to the east, along the Gallowgate, Little Dove Hill still leads up to Bell Street, with Great Dove Hill beyond it. A Polish supermarket sits where the old Saracen's Head Inn used to be, although the newer pub with the same name, keeper of its history in all kinds of ways, can be found further east still, beyond the Saracen Head Road.

The name Molendinar – *Mellingdenor* in Jocelin's *Life of Kentigern* – may have some connection with an ancient mill, since water-powered milling came to this island with the Romans; the burn may be named after the mill, rather than vice versa, but there are other possibilities. Of the Molendinar, the stream that defined this place and indeed the whole city, for many hundreds of years, there is also no sign. Like the poor themselves, it has gradually been driven underground, although I'm told it is far cleaner now in its variety of tunnels, old and new, than it was in Elizabeth Manley's time in Glasgow, from 1884 to 1886. For a long time, 'The Spoutmouth', as it was called when it had visible springs of water, was one of the few places where the burn remained uncovered, after the lands round about were built over and streets formed across the old College Lands, but now, the only surviving sign of it is in the street names and documentary evidence. The railway is – and was – a dominating presence in both places. Elizabeth went from one of the poorest, filthiest and most deprived areas of Leeds to live in one of the poorest, filthiest and most deprived areas of Glasgow. Nevertheless, she also found herself residing in one of the oldest and most interesting streets in the city.

Spoutmouth has a fascinating history. Writing about it in his *History of Glasgow* in 1737, John McUre describes it in terms of its wonderful wells and springs, calling it 'the Spout-wynd, which reaches north from the Gallowgate, and is one hundred and twenty ells long and six ells wide, in which are the four cisterns of very fine, sweet water'. An ell is an old measurement meaning the length of a man's arm from elbow to the tip of the middle finger, and is deemed to be about eighteen inches, so at some nine feet, this was not at that time a wide street and the description of it as a wynd is accurate. On the other hand, when McUre was writing, it seems to have been built up on one side only, with the burn flowing freely along the other. A map from 1778 shows the street narrowing to the north, where it veers away from the burn, and where a veritable wynd passes between buildings.

The Molendinar, in its old, free-flowing course, would have tumbled south past the site of the cathedral – said to be the location of St Mungo's original church – across the eastern side of the Old College lands, not far from the physic or medicinal garden, and then touching the Spoutmouth Wynd, before curving more or less along the course of the present-day Molendinar Street to find its way eventually into the Clyde. There are eighteenth-century maps that show the original course of the burn in some detail. Mungo, or Kentigern, the much-loved patron saint of Glasgow, was one of those robust early Celtic saints, when the language spoken here would have been a variety of Brittonic Welsh rather than Scots Gaelic. He was the son of a princess named Teneu, possibly of what was the old northern kingdom of Gododdin, and he may have been conceived as the result of rape, or perhaps simply an illicit affair. Learning of her pregnancy, her savage father had her thrown from Traprain Law, in the Lothians, but she survived, only to be put in a coracle and floated out into the Forth. A determined survivor, she washed up at Culross, where the monks took her in, and where she gave birth to Kentigern. The boy was brought up by St Serf, who was attempting to convert the Picts of Fife, and it was he who gave him the name of Mungo, or 'dear one', although his baptismal name was Kentigern.

At the age of twenty-five, Mungo took himself off to the west coast, to the house of a Holy Man named Fergus. Fergus died the night he arrived and Mungo placed his body on a cart yoked by two bulls, commanding them to carry it to the 'place ordained by the Lord'. The Lord obligingly halted the bulls at a fertile and sheltered spot called Cathures, the ancient name for Glasgow. Fergus was duly buried there, and then Mungo established a small church. Mungo referred to this spot as 'Glasgu', or the beloved green place. Dates are a bit of a moveable feast, but Mungo probably flourished during the late 500s and very early 600s. His was a robust and ascetic form of Christianity, although miracles and legends accumulated around his name. After some years on the banks of the Molendinar, he was forced to leave the district by a king of Strathclyde who was hostile to Christianity. He travelled to Wales and allegedly to Rome, although that seems very doubtful. The Welsh connection, however, is credible enough. Later still, a new king of Strathclyde, Rhydderch Hael, turned out to be much better disposed towards these early Christian holy men and their useful fusion of Christian and Celtic beliefs, and invited him to come back. He may or may not have spent some time in Galloway, but without a doubt, he returned to his beloved Green Place, where he built up a sizeable community before succumbing to age and extreme frailty, collapsing at a baptismal service. As is so often the case with these stories, there is a seed of truth somewhere, overlain by centuries of subsequent embroidery.

Kentigern's shrine at the cathedral was a great place of pilgrimage until the Scottish Reformation, but there is also a connection with the area close to Spoutmouth. Only a little way east of Spoutmouth, also running to the north of the Gallowgate, we find two streets named Little Dovehill and Great Dovehill. Dove probably had nothing to do with birds, since the place name Dowhill crops up frequently in Scotland, and may derive from the word *dubh* in Scots Gaelic, or *du* in its British form, both meaning dark or black. These may have been the 'dark hills', in that they were well watered by burns and therefore thickly wooded. Tradition has it that Mungo used to take the air on the Little Dovehill after bathing in the Molendinar, and where else might he have bathed than at the confluence of the burn with Spoutmouth? There are tales that Christian converts met Kentigern near this spot when he came back from Wales, and that he also had a meeting with St Columba here, where they exchanged their holy staves, although other sites are, of course, available. Whatever the truth of that meeting, during the mediaeval period, a chapel called Little St Mungo's was founded here, surrounded by a burial ground, on the north side of the Gallowgate, just beyond the old port or gate. There was a well or spring dedicated to Kentigern, as well as a small wood known as the Trees of Kentigern, or Trees of St Mungo, all of which suggests a strong traditional association between the saint and this once beautiful area close to the Molendinar.

In his 1896 book on *Bygone Glasgow*, David Small tells us more about the Spoutmouth in the olden days. He describes:

> the narrow lane which led from the Gallowgate to the Old Vennel, crossing the Molendinar Burn by a bridge at the point where the two roads met. A little way north from the Gallowgate, the Spoutmouth broadened out towards the east, forming a triangular plot, and here in ancient times there were four famous springs, known as the Four Sisters. The waters from these wells were received by four cisterns, with a spout or stone channel that served to supply the citizens in the neighbourhood with what was described long ago as very fine sweet water. In some of the old charters relating to this locality the road was variously designated as the Spout Vennel, Spout Wynd, the Gait to the Spout, and the Road to the Spout Wells.

McUre, writing in the previous century, tells darker stories of a burial ground on the left bank of the Molendinar, situated in the Spoutmouth, in which there were three tiled or thatched houses, used as a 'sort of hospital' where persons employed as plague searchers or cleansers lived. These were mostly women, hired by each parish to inspect corpses and determine the cause of death – in other words, whether it was plague-related or not. The bodies of those who had died of the plague were buried behind these three houses in Spoutmouth. We know that plague came to Glasgow on several occasions during the 1500s, which is the likely date for our plague hospice, although plague again struck the city in the 1600s.

The Spoutmouth must have been a pleasant place, in spite of the plague hospital, and there were, by the eastern side of the Molendinar Burn, several houses that were said to be the 'town mansions of leading citizens'. In 1669, James Brome was describing Glasgow as notable for 'pleasantness of sight, sweetness of air and delightfulness of its gardens and orchards, enriched with the most delicious fruits'. In *Glasgow Delineated*, written in 1826, the unknown author tells of 'white houses' surrounded by elm trees, old buildings in quadrangular shape at the east end of the Gallowgate, which were the 'principle inns of the city' back in the 1600s.

To the west, the Gallowgate Bridge that crossed the Molendinar below the Spoutmouth ran only half the breadth of the street, leaving the north side as a ford for ease of watering horses, for those parties riding into and out of the city. In the eighteenth century, the Wells of the Four Sisters at the Spoutmouth were – in good Presbyterian fashion – locked on a Saturday night, but people who wanted water on a Sunday could go to the Spout of Stone at the edge of the Molendinar, from where the water from these wells could be drawn, even on the Sabbath day. Who were the Four Sisters? Nobody knows, although there is a long tradition of dedicating springs and wells to female deities, later transformed into holy women. The more prosaic, but much more likely, explanation may be a conflation of the old word 'cistern' with 'sister' in popular usage.

Towards the middle of the seventeenth century, a number of small bark mills and saw mills had already been erected along the west side of the Molendinar, to take advantage of the good flow of water. Bark mills processed not just bark, but roots and branches into a powder known as tanbark, used in the leather-tanning process, which again suggests a wooded area round about. This was a small domestic industry, and nothing like the later industrial concerns. Since the Spoutmouth formed the most direct access to the Gallowgate, several private bridges had been built across the burn. David Small, in his *Bygone Glasgow*, points to an old plan, dated 1750, which was used in a 'protracted litigation regarding the pollution of the Molendinar Burn'. It shows a wide bridge crossing the burn immediately opposite the Spout, leading from the yard of the tannery company, while farther up the burn are two more bridges from tanyards with the Gallowgate Brig crossing the Molendinar a little to the west of the Spoutmouth. The process of industrialisation was well under way.

In November 1785, over a hundred years before Elizabeth Manley's arrival in Glasgow, torrential rain caused the Spoutmouth to flood. The low bridges acted as dams within the narrows, and the water flooded the houses along the banks to a depth of six feet or more. Some of those living on the upper floors had to cut holes in their wooden floorboards to drag occupants of lower rooms to safety, but miraculously there were no deaths. Before the beginning of the nineteenth century, most but not all of these small tanneries seem to have been removed, and instead the warren of ancient houses to the east, presumably with additions, were as thickly populated with working people as the Bank area of Leeds where Elizabeth Manley had grown up.

Meanwhile, in 1755, a new inn called the Saracen's Head had been built. This too was not far from the Spoutmouth, on the old site of the Little St Mungo's Chapel, with a fine spring of water dedicated to the saint in the garden behind. T C F Brotchie in his *Tramway Guide to the Borderlands of Glasgow* describes how the inn was host to the first mail coach to arrive in the city from London on 7 July 1788. In its heyday, this beautiful and imposing building boasted thirty-six rooms, stabling for sixty horses, and an elegant ballroom or assembly room at the back. The assembly room had a gallery, where the celebrated fiddler Neil Gow is said to have played. The inn possessed a five-gallon blue and white punch bowl decorated with Mungo's legendary bird, fish and tree, his saintly bell for calling the people to prayer, and the inscription 'Success to the town of Glasgow'. Much mended over the years, this has survived and is in the People's Palace.

The Saracen's Head Inn stood just outside the city, beyond the East Port, a massive oaken gate that was locked at sunset to keep undesirables out, or in, depending on your perspective. At its opening, the inn was described in glowing terms as having beds that were 'clean and free from bugs', a highly desirable quality that Robert Burns himself, who stayed here, would have appreciated. Elizabeth Manley and her siblings would have appreciated beds that were clean and free from bugs, too. William Wordsworth and his sister Dorothy lodged here for two days on their travels through Scotland. Among other luminaries, the inn also played host to Dr Johnson and James Boswell when they were returning from their tour of the Hebrides in 1773, with distinguished professors walking down the green lane from the Old College of Glasgow to converse with the great man. Johnson, in typically acid fashion, is said to have put a leg up on each side of the grate and said, 'There am I, an Englishman, sitting by a coal fire' – as opposed, presumably, to the peat fires of the Highlands and Islands that he disliked, as he seems to have disapproved of so much else about the country.

Time passed and slowly but surely industry changed the face of this part of Glasgow forever. The City Union Railway acquired some of the houses at the north end of what had once been the Spoutmouth and the railway and Gallowgate Station sliced diagonally across the street and the city, just as the railway had sliced through the more impoverished parts of Leeds. In some city plans and maps from the late 1800s, even the street name Spoutmouth seems to have disappeared altogether, as surely as the old springs had been driven underground, but the street itself was still there. By 1861, Glasgow was accommodating five times as many people as it had in 1775. The population density was a thousand people per acre and many of those were Irish immigrants drawn across the water, like Elizabeth's parents to Leeds, in the hope of escaping famine and privation in one country, only to find themselves in hardly less disastrous circumstances in another. The city was in the midst of a vast population boom. The influx of migrants, mainly from Ireland and the Highlands, caused the demand for housing to increase exponentially. Unfortunately, as in Leeds, most good new housing was built in the suburbs and richer areas in the West End, while the working people were crammed into the crowded City Parish. There were two main types of working-class housing in this area. 'Made-down houses' were the old town houses of the middle classes from which their former occupants had decamped 'above the smoke', haphazardly adapted to cram in as many tenants as possible. Among them, we find cheaply and quickly built tenements, insanitary and equally prone to overcrowding. Neither of them could cope with the vast increase in population.

The Improvements Act of the mid-1860s, acknowledging the 'moral and physical evils' of the living conditions of so many people, meant the purchase and demolition of swathes of ancient houses in the city centre, but the process was a slow one. We can see from the official ownership of many of the properties in Spoutmouth, during the time when Elizabeth Manley was living there, that she had the misfortune to be there at a time when properties had been bought for demolition and improvement, but the demand for land had collapsed. Financial problems meant that the housing project slowed and the Improvement Trust effectively became landlord to large numbers of people who had nowhere else to go and no hope of betterment. In places like Spoutmouth, the process of clearing the houses prior to demolition seemed to be going on, perhaps deliberately, and perhaps by a natural process of attrition. In the valuation rolls for 1885 we can see that there were empty lodgings in parts of the street, but overcrowding in others.

For some idea of the conditions in which people were living, of the Glasgow to which Elizabeth had come, we have the extraordinary images of Thomas Annan, who photographed the old closes and streets of central Glasgow in 1868 and 1877. The fascinating nature of his images should not blind us to the shocking, squalid, inescapable poverty they record. By the late 1800s, industries had come and gone, but Spoutmouth was forever changed and the Molendinar, once so pure and sweet that the people of Bridgegate were accustomed to use it in brewing their ale, could be described in 1890 as giving 'neither fragrance nor beauty to the district'.

12. A Ruinous and Dangerous State

If we assume that twenty-year-old Elizabeth Manley, diminutive, illiterate, feisty but vulnerable, lived in Spoutmouth, her last known address, during the two years that she was in the city, let's try to imagine the appearance of the street where she spent at least some of her time. Wells, fields and trees are long gone, but it seems that the later, much less squalid tenements are not yet built either, although they will soon be coming. A photograph of this area from the early twentieth century shows us solidly built tenement houses of the type that are still to be found in many parts of Glasgow. Demolished in their turn here, they were nevertheless far less wretched than the housing that Elizabeth would have found. With a large part of it sliced through by the railway, this was still an area where, as in Leeds, industrialisation sat cheek by jowl with overcrowded housing. It would have seemed all too familiar to her, perhaps disappointingly so.

A look at the Dean of Guild Reports for Glasgow in 1848 and 1849 shows us that even at that date, changes were very much afoot, but the Irish were inevitably blamed for the poor living conditions in which they found themselves, even though they were not the owners of these properties, but the exploited tenants. In November 1848:

The individual and collective proprietors of no fewer than thirty distinct tenements were charged, at the instance of the Procurator Fiscal, with having their properties in a ruinous and dangerous state . . . These properties are principally situated in Main Street, Rutherglen Loan, Gorbals, and on the east side of High Street, the Spoutmouth, the Old and New Wynds, and some other of the densely populated localities in the city. . . . We may instance the tenement belonging to the community of the village of Gorbals, well known as the Community's Land, and situated at the corner of Main Street and Kirk Street. This case furnishes a striking instance of the frail condition of many of the dwellings occupied by not a few of the poorer classes. For the last forty years the Community's Land has remained in its present rickety condition hanging together rather from old attachment than from solid cohesion; but it so happened last week that a decent Paddy had died in the premises at a green old age, and out of respect to his virtues it was resolved by his friends that he should have a Christian wake and burial. Accordingly a large number of sympathisers assembled in the apartment in which the body lay, which, by the way, was so confined that a dancing-dog might have complained of want of elbow-room therein to exhibit his antics. Of course there was an unusual weight accumulated on one portion of the tenement and, when the whisky began to speak, there was the usual amount of boisterous merriment, relieved and varied by occasional Celtic howls, in the midst of which the entire inmates were alarmed by the wall fronting Main Street suddenly becoming

> rent, and the whole fabric evincing symptoms of speedy dissolution. The building was immediately . . . propped up by beams, and temporarily rendered secure, in which condition it at present remains. . . . The defunct cause of all this tipsy gathering lay in a corner of the apartment, with a Bible and plate of salt on his breast, and a number of candles placed around the body – the living and the dead together.

Notable for its habitual patronising humour at the expense of the Irish community (although it does bear a striking resemblance to the song 'Finnegan's Wake' in all but the resurrection of the corpse), this report at least acknowledges the precarious position in which so many working people find themselves. In December 1848, 'at the instance of the Procurator-Fiscal . . . a number of these houses, which are principally situated in the High Street, the Old Wynd, and Spoutmouth, were either ordered to be taken down, or the matter was remitted to competent tradesmen to inspect and report to next meeting of the Court'. Perhaps some of the Spoutmouth properties were inspected, subjected to repair and left intact for a while at least.

Again, with regard to the Gallowgate, and at about the same time, we read:

> In this street, there are some good fragments of a bygone time. The Saracen's Head Inn, on the north side, at the Great Dovehill, where the Laird of McNab held high jinks when he visited the city, where the Lords of Justiciary, after holding dread state at the Cross Court-House during the day, treated the bailies

> and freeholders to a poor man, alias shoulder-blade of mutton, and oceans of claret at night, the Old Saracen's Head . . . still stands as fresh externally as ever. But internally it is now packed as full of decent people, with their shops and dwellings, as it will hold and, on the whole, this sort of city landmark is in fine preservation. On the same side [*of the Gallowgate*], near the Spoutmouth, there is a most picturesque cluster of small possessions. On one of these is still to be seen a dial plate, with the date 1708: the domicile, doubtless, of some scientific citizen who prided himself on being able to tell the hours on sunshiny days, independent of the horologes at the Cross or Laigh Kirk.

By 1849, though, they are reporting that:

> The Gallowgate, by the action of the Improvement Trust and the Union Railway, has been entirely changed. The Cutler's Close and the old dial plate, near to Spoutmouth, have disappeared, but the Saracen's Head Inn, over whose interesting associations of bygone days the genial Pagan delighted to linger, yet remains.

What we don't know, however, is how long the old buildings in the Spoutmouth lingered, or how densely they were intermingled with newer constructions. Some industries had departed, but some of the tanneries certainly remained. A photograph in the Burrell Collection, from 1895, long after Elizabeth had been taken back to Yorkshire, shows an old tannery at Spoutmouth, with a ramshackle collection of stone buildings with broken windows, as well as premises with wooden louvred walls on the upper floors (for drying).

Four workman and a lad in breeches are holding up a cured fleece for the photographer. Health and safety does not look as though it was uppermost in their minds. This tannery must still, even at this date, have been making use of water from the heavily polluted Molendinar, as stinking as the goits Elizabeth had left behind in Leeds.

Whatever jumble of surviving, rebuilt or made-down properties characterised the remains of Spoutmouth in 1884, it could not have been much of an improvement on Off Street in terms of overcrowding, dirt and discomfort. Old town houses had become places of multiple occupancy, with businesses, stores, workshops and warehouses beneath them, as well as beneath the railway. Valuation rolls from 1885 show a sack maker, a tailor, a printing office and engine shop, a rag store and even a coal-ree: a house where coal was bought by a small-time merchant, stored and sold off in small quantities to the nearby residents for their coal fires or ranges. Spoutmouth would have had many more actual occupants, in all likelihood, than are listed as official tenants. Further along the Gallowgate, the Saracen's Head was still standing, but it had lost much of its grandeur as the buildings round about it encroached and swallowed it and as various parts of the premises themselves were slowly but surely rented out for other purposes. The old inn was finally demolished in 1905, as carelessly as with so much urban heritage, to be replaced by tenements, although a new Saracen's Head is sited further along the Gallowgate, preserving memories of a fine old inn.

It has been hard to determine precisely what kind of place Elizabeth Manley came to in 1884, or even whether she came first to Spoutmouth at all, but that was the address she gave in 1886: 32 Spoutmouth. There is no Elizabeth Manley as tenant here in the Valuation Rolls for 1885, but that doesn't mean that she wasn't living here. In fact, number 32 Spoutmouth is a warehouse at that date, belonging to Thomson McMullan, wholesale cask and bag merchant. Given that Elizabeth is described as a 'servant', I wondered if she had been working for Thomson McMullan in some capacity. The McMullan family had a big house on fashionable Monteith Row, by Glasgow Green, but Elizabeth isn't named among the servants there. Perhaps she worked and slept in the warehouse.

The nature of the valuation rolls for the street during Elizabeth's time suggests that the older buildings had not yet been demolished but their function had certainly changed. When an old house was 'made-down', each room would be let separately to one or more tenants, with the individual rooms often being subdivided by flimsy wooden partitions. Precarious staircases might be tacked on to the back of the building to allow access to upper floors. There would be little or no sanitation and, at Spoutmouth, no internal water supply, since when originally built, these houses would have had access to the fresh water of the Four Sisters Wells and the Molendinar. Plans from the 1880s often show an undifferentiated mass of buildings here. There was very little limit to the number of people who could be accommodated – much like the 'dancing-dogs' of the above account. Cellars would be used as living spaces, as they had been in Leeds; substandard tenements might have been built between older houses, and the result would be yet another unhealthy labyrinth of dwellings. The sun never shone into these closes and wynds. The overall impression is of an area in a state of transition, a jumble of industrial, commercial and residential premises, dominated by the railway, and with more empty lodgings than might be expected.

It's possible that when Elizabeth came north, she used an alias, much as John Ross had used various aliases to disguise his identity. His were for criminal reasons, but Elizabeth was no criminal. Did she become ashamed to use her own name for some reason connected with her time in Glasgow, or did she want to escape the connection with a murder that had become notorious in the public imagination, and might still be provoking some kind of reaction? One name we definitely know that she used was Ann Smith, with the name Ann presumably recalling her dead sister. There is also a hint, no more, that she may at one time have called herself Isabella, but the reasons why she travelled to Glasgow in the first place remain a mystery.

It was not uncommon at this time for servants to travel about with the families by whom they were employed. Had Elizabeth been working as a domestic servant in Leeds, it would be reasonable to assume that the family had moved north, taking her with them. But in Leeds she was only ever described as a mill hand. We know from later documentation that her sister, Mary, knew that she was going north, so there is no suggestion that she had run away. As we shall see, in 1886, Mary writes, or more accurately dictates, a letter expressing 'surprise' that Elizabeth is in trouble. But since Elizabeth can't write either, she has no way of communicating with her family once she is in Glasgow. The only conclusion we can draw is that somebody offered her a job, somebody must have paid the fare for her to travel north, almost certainly by train, and that somebody may even have accompanied her on the journey. Today, we read plenty of stories of young women being tempted away from home on the promise of a good job and a nice place to live, only to find themselves sold into prostitution. How much worse at a time when young, single women were even more vulnerable, and communications were so difficult?

Other than as a servant or governess, for marriage or under the protection of a male relative, it was rare for a young woman, some twenty years old, to travel all by herself to a strange city where she had no known relatives or connections of any kind. As we have seen, it's remotely possible that her brother Thomas was working there, but, if so, he didn't come to her aid when she badly needed help. Even the Irish fleeing famine, in her parents' day, had tended to come in family or friendship groups if they possibly could. Like Henry Mayhew's young Irish woman who had been quite unable to find her brother in London, even those who were summoned by a sibling might come to grief in a big city. We have a few tantalising scraps of information about what became of Elizabeth and what may have led to the tragedy that was to follow. As a novelist, I can invent a dozen stories accounting for what follows. All of them are possible, but I suspect that the true explanation is the most commonplace one.

In the absence of any evidence to the contrary, I think Elizabeth was exploited. I suspect she was brought to Glasgow by a man who promised much and then betrayed her. I don't know precisely when she headed north. I can find nothing about her during the two years or thereabouts between the time when she left Leeds and the shocking events of the late afternoon of 5 August 1886, when she was picked up by the police on Castle Street and declared to be insane, a danger to herself and others.

13. Found in Castle Street

A sustained hunt through the available valuation rolls for Spoutmouth, or indeed various other streets in this area for 1885, the year before Elizabeth's arrest, reveals nobody by the name of Elizabeth Manley; but there is an Isabella Smith living with a man called John Brown at 58 Spoutmouth. No occupations are described for them but Smith and Brown were fairly common aliases used by those who wanted to disguise their true identity. From the records we can see that this was a house, or more likely a jumble of rooms, above a 'coal-ree', with Peter McInnes described as a 'merchant, coal dealer'. Nearby is a rag store, with part of the building housing another store, said to be empty. The landlords are the Trustees under the Glasgow Improvements Act, 1866. These trustees have become, in effect and however unintentionally, slum landlords. The properties have been bought with demolition and renewal in mind but finances have dictated a halt in proceedings.

Also rented from these same trustees, 30 Spoutmouth, which must have been very close to, or even a part of, the address of 32 Spoutmouth given by Elizabeth at her arrest in 1886, is a house heavily tenanted with working men, with names such as Murphy, O'Neil and Burke indicating an Irish origin. As we have already seen, Thomson McMullen, cask and bag merchant, is the overall tenant of a cask store, associated workshops and a bag store, probably on the ground floor, with the lodgers living above.

Was Isabella Smith our Elizabeth under an assumed name, living with a man, also under an assumed name? It's a possibility, but a remote one. More likely is that she had been lured north and had simply disappeared into the dangerous labyrinth of this part of Glasgow, with no real home to call her own and nobody to rescue her from the monsters inside. At home, in Leeds, Elizabeth had an extended family and friends nearby. However bad life might have become, she would have had resources, support, people to cry out to in time of need. She would also have had people who knew and understood what had happened to her, who remembered what had happened to her brother. If that had caused problems for her in the past with some members of the community, it would also, in other situations, have been the saving of her. Here, in Glasgow, there was nobody to remember, and no such support.

My heart aches for her.

Two things seem relevant to the events of that summer of 1886. In 1870, the district of Calton, in and around Spoutmouth and Gallowgate, was supposed to have had some 200 houses of ill fame and 150 shebeens, or illegal drinking dens. There is, in Carl MacDougall's tour de force of Glasgow people's history, *The Words and the Stones*, a description of the nineteenth-century city's shebeens, at a time when pubs had been forced to close at eleven o'clock and all day on Sunday. Much like the area of Leeds that Elizabeth had left, there were numerous pubs in this part of Glasgow, but the enforcement of licensing hours and the predictable failure of the temperance movement meant that the numbers of shebeens increased through the second half of the 1800s. MacDougall quotes from an anonymous nineteenth-century pamphlet, 'Doings of a Notorious Glasgow Shebeener', in which a shebeen in the Saltmarket was also a dance hall. The drink served consisted of 'five gallons of water and one gallon of raw grain whisky, sixpence worth of meths and a pint of raspberry vinegar'. This hellish brew was served to the dancers between sets. Shebeens could be very lucrative for those who owned them, but possibly deadly for those who frequented them. Elizabeth had been used to drinking in Leeds, but the pubs she had visited with her sisters and friends were, like the Railway Hotel, well run and with a certain amount of supervision. A shebeen would be a different matter entirely.

The 'houses of ill fame' were, in fact, brothels, and it would have been all too easy for a young woman like Elizabeth to be sucked into the kind of life they offered: one of exploitation and misery. There is another, more dangerous aspect to all of this. By the 1880s, the so-called Glasgow System would have been in full force. Linda Mahood explores this in some detail in a fine piece of research. In England, attempts had been made to contain prostitution by means of the Contagious Diseases Act. In Glasgow, Chief Constable Alexander McCall had made it his life's work to eliminate prostitution, seeing it as nothing less than a sexual threat to the establishment itself. Prostitution had been flourishing in these packed and poverty-stricken areas for years, but McCall's 'solution' was the 1886 Police Act, which allowed working-class women to be classified as prostitutes on the flimsiest of evidence and to be fined or imprisoned. Some women were released from prison only on condition that they accepted treatment at the Lock Hospital – a place for the treatment of venereal diseases so shameful, the treatment of women and even young female children so cruel, the premise on which it was based so misogynistic, that for many years Glasgow seemed to prefer to forget about its very existence.

The Glasgow System of draconian repression and incarceration did, according to McCall, reduce the number of prostitutes in the city, although the harsh truth was that such an approach reduced only the number of brothels. Besides that, unemployed, unmarried or homeless women were often arbitrarily identified as prostitutes. The definition had expanded to include any woman who might be living with a man outside marriage. The onus of blame was all on the women for tempting men from the straight and narrow. In what amounted to a witch hunt, the Glasgow police had assumed the power to denounce almost any working-class woman of even slightly 'irregular' – that is, unconventional – habits as a prostitute, with disastrous consequences for the woman concerned. This would mean, for example, that wherever that woman lived could then be condemned as a brothel. There was no escape from the consequences of the system. The aim was to drive prostitutes off the streets and into institutions where they could be controlled, but, unsurprisingly, nothing was done to address the poverty that had caused and propagated the exploitation in the first place. It criminalised women, and institutionalised the double standards involved in blaming them. It may be that Elizabeth fell foul of that law, too.

At 5.10pm, on 5 August 1886 – not even late at night – Elizabeth was found in a distraught state in Castle Street,

Glasgow, and taken to St Rollox Police Office. Then, as now, people tended to be afraid of other people who were audibly and visibly agitated in public places, possibly using foul language and behaving oddly, especially women. Once the police officers had assured themselves that she wasn't simply drunk, the presumption that she was mad would be immediate and damning. From there she was transferred to the city parochial asylum for assessment. This would have been the big Glasgow City Poorhouse, with its complicated history, nearby.

In 1810, with some recognition that those with mental health problems should be treated more professionally and kindly than previously, the foundation stone of a new city-centre asylum had been laid and the new asylum itself was opened four years later, in 1814. Ten years after that, with a royal charter granted, it became the Glasgow Royal Asylum for Lunatics. This building was a large and impressive institution, standing on Parliamentary Road, on a site that, on modern maps, would be quite close to the present-day Buchanan Street Bus Station. The asylum provided separate wings for male and female patients, but until the building of a new asylum at Gartnavel outside the city, later in the century, the inmates of the Royal Asylum would also be separated by class. Treatments were bizarre. In 1817, an officer of the asylum invented 'a leather muff which is better, and much less irksome than a strait waistcoat', while in 1819, a whirling chair that caused patients to rotate, presumably until they were too dizzy to do more than stagger about, was reported to have a 'wonderfully good effect'. By the 1840s, attitudes were changing again and new asylums were built to facilitate supposedly more enlightened treatments. Gartnavel Hospital, some three miles outside the city, opened in 1843, standing amid sixty acres of 'pleasure grounds'. This hospital too provided for both higher- and lower-class patients, although the genuine, honest-to-God, poor immigrants from Ireland and the Highlands would still have been destined for the poorhouse. It would be true to say that for most of its history until the formation of the NHS in 1948, the hospital at Gartnavel housed mainly private patients.

In 1845, the year that the Scottish Poor Law Act was passed, the large Glasgow Asylum building on Parliamentary Road became known as the Glasgow City Poorhouse, housing both the destitute poor and those unfortunates detained for suffering from insanity as well. It had swollen in size to 1,500 beds and was one of the largest institutions in Britain, but doctors who were appointed to conduct an enquiry after 1887 found 'poor sanitary arrangements and bathing facilities with badly lit and ventilated rooms'. The fact that it was near the North British Goods Station can't have helped, but it didn't close as a poorhouse till 1905.

In 1888, a couple of years after Elizabeth's detention, a report outlined provision for those suffering from the twin ills of insanity and poverty in Scotland. The majority were in dedicated asylums, with some of the more 'harmless' insane in ordinary poorhouses. It seems as though many patients lived at home with their own relatives, while a significant number were 'boarded in specially licensed private houses, but not more than four under one guardian'. This system was called the Scottish boarding-out system, and was unique to the country.

The first we learn of any details about Elizabeth's case

is in an application for poor relief number 85082, which has to be filed before any procedure to help her can begin. The poor law officer, Thomas Morton, visits at 10am the following morning, 6 August, in order to expedite the application. Her place of birth is immediately noted as Brussels Street, in Leeds, so she must have been lucid enough to be able to give him some details about herself. The entry on the handwritten form has the name Isabella, crossed out, followed by Elizabeth Manley or Ann Smith. This might mean that she was so incoherent that she couldn't say Elizabeth properly – or it might mean that she had been calling herself Isabella. Ann Smith, though, seems to have been a definite alias. Further details are that she was 'found in Castle Street'. Her occupation is declared to be 'servant etc.'. There is a wealth of insinuation in that little 'etc.'. Her religion is Roman Catholic, and she is 'insane'. She is described as the daughter of 'John Manley, a brushmaker, who died in Brussels Street, Leeds, on 3 July 1874 , and Mary Hepron (sic) who died in Brussels Street, Leeds, on 5 February 1879'. While accurate as to month and year, these are not correct on the date of death. John had died on 6 July and Mary on 9 February, but Elizabeth must have been at least lucid enough to remember something of these dates and her parents. The alternative explanation is that some unnamed person, who knew something of her background, accompanied her and gave the information, but this is never confirmed. The report states that she has two sisters, although it does not name them at this point, says that this is the first application on her behalf, with the comment 'settlement in England' (to which she will be returned in due course, given that they don't want her to be a drain on local funds) and under 'remarks' adds, 'had a brother stabbed four years ago and the man was sentenced to penal servitude'. This is perhaps some indication of a more than usually insightful poor law officer, but, sadly, it seems to be the only time in which the circumstance of this young woman having witnessed the violent death of a close relative is seen as being in any way relevant to her condition.

Further reports and assessments follow, all of which were later copied into various record books. First of all, on 7 August 1886, comes the Petition to the Sheriff to grant an order for the reception of a patient into an asylum:

> *Unto the Honourable Sheriff of the Shire of Lanark, the petition of Archibald Dempster, Inspector of Poor, City Parish, Glasgow, humbly sheweth that it appears from the subjoined statement and accompanying medical certificate, that Elizabeth Manley or Ann Smith from Rollox Police Office, previously residing at 32 Spoutmouth, Glasgow, is at present in a state of mental derangement and a proper person for treatment in an asylum for the insane. May it therefore please your lordship to authorise the transmission of the said Elizabeth Manley or Ann Smith to the City Parochial Asylum, Glasgow and to sanction her admission into the said asylum.* Signed: *A Dempster.*

The 'subjoined statement', also dated 7 August, fills in a little more information, some of it damning:

> *Elizabeth Manley or Ann Smith.*
> *Female, 22 years, single.*
> Condition of life: *Supposed of loose character.*

Castle Street may well have been the haunt of prostitutes, but the only evidence for Elizabeth's 'loose character' at this time seems to have been the fact that she was out and about on her own, in a confused state. The assumption of her character may have been more a sign of current beliefs than any more concrete proof. Or it may have been the truth.

Religious persuasion: *Roman Catholic.*
Previous abode: *32 Spoutmouth, Glasgow.*
Place where found and examined: *318 Parliamentary Road, at City Parochial Asylum, Glasgow.*
Length of time insane: *A few days.*
Whether first attack: *Unknown.*
Age: 22, *so far as known.*
When and where previously examined: *Not previously, so far as known.*
Duration of existing attack: *A few days.*
Supposed cause: *Unknown.*
Subject to epilepsy: *No.*
Suicidal: *No.*

This is untrue, since she was very clearly suicidal if some of what follows is to be believed.

Dangerous to others: *Yes.*

This is written without elaboration as to exactly what danger she constitutes. Was she violent? Had she been fighting? All we know is that she was very distressed and that the people around her, and the police who were on hand, had become alarmed by her behaviour.

Parish or Union to which the lunatic, if a pauper, is chargeable: *City Parish, Glasgow.*
Date of becoming chargeable: *5 August 1886*
No relatives known, unknown if insanity in family.

Archibald Dempster certifies this as true to the best of his knowledge on 7 August 1886. There follows an Intimation of a Pauper Lunatic, which more or less repeats the foregoing information. Certificates of lunacy are signed on 9 August by Drs Todd and Wilson, with said lunatic being received formally into the City Parochial Asylum in the charge of Andrew S Day and Helen Watson. Being designated a pauper was one thing, but being described as a pauper lunatic of loose character would have sealed her fate. Elizabeth was on a deadly carousel from which descending would now be almost impossible. There was, as we shall see, one last possible means of escape, but that too failed her.

Of interest are the two medical certificates of lunacy that accompanied her admission, because they at least give us a little more indication of her condition.

Medical Certificate Number 1

I the undersigned, George Bell Todd, MB & CM, being a graduate in Medicine of Glasgow University, do certify that I have this day at No 318 Parliamentary Road visited and examined Elizabeth Manley or Ann Smith and that said person is a person of unsound mind. Facts indicating insanity: She is very excited and cries out for someone to kill her. Talks incoherently, and refuses to answer questions. She is dangerous to herself and others.

Other facts: *Shown letter from Lieutenant of St Rollox Police Chambers.*

This directly contradicts the judgment of Archibald Dempster, who had no medical knowledge, that she was not suicidal, but also contradicts the notion that she was dangerous to others. I would very much like to have been able to find the letter that accompanied her from the police station, because it would undoubtedly have given more details of her arrest, exactly where in Castle Street she was picked up and what her behaviour was at that time, but it has long ago been destroyed. There follows:

Medical Certificate Number 2

I the undersigned, Hon Macknight Wilson, MD & CM, Graduate in Medicine and Surgery, Glasgow University, physician and surgeon, have this day visited and examined Elizabeth Manley, late of the Police Office, Rollox, Glasgow and that the said Elizabeth is a person of unsound mind and a proper person to be detained under care and treatment.

Facts indicating insanity: *When visited, she was sullen and morose, would scarcely answer a question. She wishes that anyone would only end her existence. She is dangerous.*

Other facts: *(Information from James Paton, Attendant) She implores the Blessed Virgin to come and destroy her as she is tired of her existence; cries out at times, maniacally, and threatens to put an end to herself. William Macnight Wilson. 30 Grafton Square, 6th Day of August 1886.*

I find this second certificate particularly heartrending. They have in their care a young woman in a state of extreme anguish, a Roman Catholic who is praying to the Blessed Virgin to end her existence. She is crying out for help and comfort, and instead they declare her sullen, morose, insane and dangerous. But I am thinking thoughts that Todd and Wilson could never and would never have thought. It was not in their experience to think anything of the kind. A similar judgment might well be made today and probably is made every day in our courts, where troubled people, women especially, are committed to prison for lack of any other means of treating them and of preventing them from becoming a nuisance to their community. How much more so, then, in an era when the only concept of 'care in the community' was that families should be responsible for and look after their own members as best they could.

After that comes a stamped notice of admission to the City Parochial Asylum:

I hereby give notice that Elizabeth Manley or Ann Smith was received into this house as a pauper patient on the 5th day of August, 1886, and I hereby transmit a copy of the order and medical certificate and statement on which she was received. Subjoined is a report with respect to the mental and bodily conditions of the above named patient. M Laing, Superintendent. Signed 18 August 1886.

The report is short and to the point.

> *With respect to her mental state, on admission she was excitable and talked incoherently. With respect to her bodily health and condition, they are good.*

The single word 'mania' is handwritten at the bottom. This was something of a catch-all diagnosis and could be used for all kinds of symptoms. Later, in Glasgow's Mitchell Library, I managed to see the original poor law application, copied into the records, but this time with later handwritten annotations. That's when it became even more interesting but also tragic. I am looking at the application made by inspector Thomas Morton on the morning of 6 August, but this time we can see that Elizabeth's birthday has been inserted, in red ink, as 15 August 1864, after the authorities have received a letter from her sister Mary Terran, or Manley, perhaps with additional information from another source. In fact, it is this birth date that – in the absence of any formal registration – I have decided to use throughout, even though Elizabeth's age varies from record to record. I elected to assume that Mary, her elder sister, must have been well aware of it and, once again, I find myself wondering if Mary was, in fact, Elizabeth's mother. Mary seems also to have reported to whoever was helping her with the letter that Elizabeth 'only went to Glasgow about two years ago'. Appended to this report is a copy of Mary Terran's letter, sent from Leeds on 14 August 1886.

Given that Mary has been, until this point, illiterate, and still will not be able to sign her own name on the occasion of her second marriage, the letter is unusually articulate. I realised that it must have been written for rather than by her. The person to whom she would have gone for help may have been her parish priest, and it does have the ring of clerical formality about it: a letter written by a sympathetic pastor, who, given the extreme nature of his parish, the demands of the utter poverty in which people are living, has no real help to give except to write an explanation, including details of Elizabeth's birth date and the duration of her time in Glasgow as an aside.

> *I received yours of this morning and was both surprised and very sorry to hear the news it contained. You ask if I am disposed to take her home or come to Glasgow to see her. I should be very glad to do either, if I was in circumstances to do either. But I am not. I am a widow, left with three children, and I have nothing coming in, only what I can earn by hawking. So you see it is utterly impossible for me to either send for her or come to Glasgow. Signed, Mrs Mary Terns (or Terrans), 33 Off Street, Leeds.*

This letter intrigued me for various reasons. One was Mary's own expression of 'surprise'. She must have believed or persuaded herself that Elizabeth was getting on well in Glasgow. There is no evidence that Elizabeth wasn't of sound mind when she was in Leeds, so the news of her detention must have come as a great shock. But around two years had passed. Had Mary received any news of her at all? If so, who had brought it? Had she known and trusted the person who had encouraged her sister to travel north? Might it have been somebody Elizabeth met at work? Perhaps McMullan's sacks and barrels were transported to Leeds for some practical purpose and a personable young man, employed by the company, enticed Elizabeth to come north with him on the promise of work in the warehouse in Spoutmouth. The other puzzle is Mary Terran's reference to three young children. We know for certain that her eldest, James, the young Elizabeth Terran, and the second John, John Thomas, born the year after the murder, all survived. But by this time, another little Mary would be toddling about, aged some seventeen months, a child born to an unknown father, well after Charles Terran had died. So why was her mother speaking of three children and not four? Baby Mary seems to have been ignored by whoever was helping Mary Terran to write her letter to Glasgow. The child was baptised and it is not likely that a priest would ignore her existence. It was too commonplace an occurrence and although he may not have approved, he would probably have accepted her. Perhaps Mary no longer thought of her firstborn, James, as a child. But there are all kinds of questions about Mary as well as Elizabeth during these years following the murder, most of which will never be answered.

The other touching aspect of this letter is that it obviously comes in reply to an enquiry sent from the hospital to Mary Terran in Off Street. Once again, like everything to do with this story, it undercut my first assumptions about the case. Initially, it seemed as though, once committed to the asylum, there would have been no way out for Elizabeth. But that was not the case. Somebody had a conscience about her. Or was it, less humanely, that they didn't want to have to go to the trouble and expense of transporting her back to the English asylum where they believed she belonged, so as not to be a drain on parish funds in Glasgow? Well, either explanation is possible, and the truth may lie – as it so often does – somewhere in between.

In Scotland, at least, some form of care in the community existed. They would prefer not to keep her in hospital. The fact remains that somebody, in all probability the poor law officer, took it upon himself to write to Elizabeth's sister, telling her of the young woman's plight and asking if she could possibly come to Glasgow, and 'take her home'. So the detention wasn't irrevocable after all. Had Mary had the resources, had she come from a middle- or upper-class family, she – or more likely her husband or brother – would have been able to travel to Glasgow, obtain Elizabeth's release and bring her home to Leeds, where the effects of whatever had precipitated her breakdown might just possibly have been alleviated by kindly treatment. It didn't always happen, even in middle-class households, even where the resources to provide care were available. But there is something about the nature of the response, even if written by Mary with the help of somebody else, which suggests that the enquiry sent to her is hoping for such a way out.

We are left with the puzzle of what had happened to Elizabeth to cause such a catastrophic breakdown? I admit to lying awake at night wondering about it. One potential explanation is that she had been abandoned by whoever had enticed her north, and then been driven to prostitution. Alcohol must surely have played a part. Possibly violence, too. I wondered if she had been not so much manic as drunk when picked up by the police in Castle Street. The date was just after the Glasgow Fair fortnight, when a great deal of drinking and associated bad behaviour, ranging from minor mischief to delinquency, would have gone on. But there is no official record of drunkenness, and the police would surely have recognised the symptoms and given her time to sober up. Her behaviour must have been more extreme, more alarming, albeit of short duration. She has not come to the attention of the authorities before, and the documents reiterate that her current 'mania' has lasted for a few days only.

I also wondered if she had given birth to a child and was now suffering from postnatal problems. Certainly, there are vague hints about this in later documentation. Perhaps most significant of all are her reiterated and heart-rending pleas for somebody, including the Blessed Virgin Mary, the model of kindly maternal intervention for most young Catholic women of the time, to end her life, her very existence, which has become unbearable to her. These suggest an overwhelming sense of guilt about something: some monumental conflict between her upbringing, and the situation in which she has found herself.

It's also possible that she was suffering from post-traumatic stress disorder, resulting from the murder of her brother, her presence beside him as he bled to death that night, and the subsequent trauma of the trial. There had been so much trouble: the violence of the popular reaction to the verdict, the harassment by Ross's friends, followed so quickly by the bereavements suffered by both of her sisters. Perhaps she had been enticed to Glasgow as a way of escaping to begin a new life, only to find that that too had turned to ashes, her promised fairy gold all transformed into a few dry leaves. As we shall see, there are tantalising hints later on in other official records: not enough to be certain of anything, but enough to make us suspect that Elizabeth felt sad, desperate and guilty, but not insane. In other circumstances, at another time, in another place, she could have recovered, just as her sisters recovered from their own terrible experiences.

For now, though, Mary Terran was a widow, with young children and no obvious means of support other than what she could obtain for herself through whatever piecemeal work she was managing to do. She was hawking brushes about the streets of Leeds. In her desperate state, she herself may have been in relationships with more than one brutal or exploitative man. The possibility of her going to Glasgow to fetch Elizabeth was about as remote as the possibility of her flying to the moon.

14. *A State of General Exaltation*

Elizabeth was taken south by train, a 'big locomotive' she called it later, accompanied by an attendant, to the South Yorkshire Asylum, also known as Wadsley Asylum near Sheffield, where she would spend the next four years of her short life. The journey itself would have presented some problems. There was a Victorian phenomenon known as 'railway madness'. Writing about it for *Atlas Obscura*, Joseph Hayes describes how:

> In the 1860s and 70s, reports began emerging of bizarre passenger behaviour on the railways. When seemingly sedate people boarded trains, they suddenly began behaving in socially unacceptable ways.

Predictably, the media, in the shape of newspapers, whipped up a perfect frenzy over this madness, with horrifying tales of lunatics riding the railways.

From the Victorian era onwards, well into the twentieth century, there seems to have been a fear not just of madmen on trains but of 'escaped lunatics' rampaging across the countryside and leaving a trail of devastation in their wake. The convenience of train travel and the speed with which it was possible to move across country fed into this myth. Such escapees even figure, less terrifyingly, in Richmal Crompton's twentieth-century *Just William* stories.

But this was a little different. Otherwise sane people would be seized with a sudden and inexplicable mania and the only common denominator seemed to be the environment of the train itself. Even George Eliot, when travelling by train and seeing an odd-looking person (who turned out to be a perfectly ordinary clergyman), was, much to her own amusement, reminded of 'all the horrible stories of madmen' in trains. There must have been something alarming about the sheer size and monstrosity of the steam engine, the noise of the train, the previously unheard-of and never-before-experienced speed. In retrospect, people may have been suffering from panic attacks, such as even now passengers sometimes experience on aeroplanes. Elizabeth, when talking about her journey later on, seems struck by the size of the engine. One of the precautions taken with 'known lunatics' when travelling was the provision of an individual carriage for patient and attendant, so Elizabeth probably travelled south in splendid isolation. Such provisions didn't, however, do much to solve the problem of ordinary people, usually men, in whom the train journey was said to trigger a sudden mania, but the phenomenon of train madness disappeared with the century, as people became more familiar with this mode of transport.

Elizabeth was admitted to the asylum outside Sheffield on 30 September 1886, and her given age is the right one of twenty-two years. Records of her time at Wadsley are virtually non-existent, although they would have been kept, but unlike the very full records of the West Yorkshire Asylum, otherwise known as Stanley Royd at Wakefield, they were destroyed or are at least unavailable. We know the barest facts of her admission and discharge. She is described as a 'mill hand' this time, rather than a servant, reverting to her Leeds persona, and the cause of her insanity is 'not known'. The circumstances of her brother's murder have been completely forgotten or ignored, at least by the hospital authorities, if not by Elizabeth herself, even though they were known and noted in Glasgow.

No relative had accompanied her on her journey south, and no one visited her in the hospital. Her own speech was often recorded in her patient notes, at least during her last two years in a different hospital, and in all likelihood during her time at Wadsley as well, but the words she said are consistently and frustratingly dismissed as the ravings of a maniac, clinically and coldly recorded, with no very obvious attempt to deduce anything from them. There was no way of linking her past experiences with her present condition. Perhaps no connection would have been made anyway. Psychiatry was in its infancy; it was a rare and imaginative doctor who might make these kind of connections, and those that were made were often of the most obvious kind. Although, for example, low mood and a 'despondent state' might be linked with the after-effects of childbirth, which seems unusually enlightened. People would be admitted who had attempted self-harm or who suffered from epilepsy; children who might be judged unmanageable were also detained. Since many of the treatments had a moral basis, young women who were thought to be in 'moral danger' might also be committed to an asylum, and so they were, in ever greater numbers. This practice continued well into the twentieth century, with some women becoming so institutionalised that they could never leave. Housewives, who were clearly the victims of domestic violence and were suffering in consequence, might themselves be sent to the asylum, rather than the husband who was inflicting the violence.

Building on the hospital site began in 1869, and it opened in 1872, with Dr Samuel Mitchell moving from the West Yorkshire Asylum in Wakefield to take up the position of superintendent. The hospital had originally been built to relieve overcrowding in Wakefield, and was thought to be vastly superior in design to any previous asylum in the country. The press described it as a 'most imposing' structure, although it must have been intimidating for Elizabeth. This was a time of huge change in the approach to treating mentally ill people, with some aspects of it better than others in terms of patient care. People were certainly treated with less cruelty than had once been the case. The motives for change were good, especially given the inhuman treatment of those who had been declared insane in the preceding centuries. Coping with a distressed mind still seems to be immensely problematic even in the present day, let alone in a nineteenth-century pauper asylum, but as Mark Stevens says in his book on *Life in the Victorian Asylum*, throughout the mid-1800s every county in England 'experienced an unplanned increase in its number of admissions'. They should perhaps have been asking themselves why this was the case, instead of extending asylum provision. As Stevens goes on to say, since asylums had been created to look after people who were helpless, this criterion of helplessness was soon extended to mean the 'disabled, the anti-social and the habitually criminal'. Any unusual or eccentric behaviour, anything that was seen as some kind of threat to the stability of society and the existing social order, might be judged insane. There is a sense therefore in which asylums were seen as providing relief to society in general as much as to the patients themselves.

The history of the Bethlem hospital in London – St Mary Bethlehem, or 'Bedlam' as it was popularly called – from the fourteenth century onwards, serves to illustrate something of the changing attitudes towards insanity. Bethlem has been a psychiatric hospital for 600 years, but its history reflects the dramatic changes in treatment of those suffering with mental ill health. In the sixteenth- and seventeenth-century hospital, dangerous or disturbing inmates – with the emphasis very much on those whose behaviour was disturbing to others as much as themselves – might be kept in chains and might become a source of amusement for a public hungry for entertainment. Public executions and lunatics were both rich sources of diversion for the masses. The Victorian insane asylum was quite different in its attitudes, but even when Elizabeth Manley was being assessed in the Glasgow asylum, this diminutive and distressed young woman was said to be 'dangerous to others'.

In Bethlem and other hospitals, during the sixteenth and seventeenth centuries and even later, patients were kept on a very meagre diet in the belief that rationing the mad would help to restore balance to the body. Although the reasons for this, the old belief in 'humours', and particular kinds of temperament that had to be regulated, had fallen out of fashion, a plain diet persisted into the nineteenth century, especially for pauper patients. Value for money was and would remain an issue, particularly where the poor were concerned. When we come to look at the ways in which Elizabeth is assessed, her appearance, her physique and her appetite, the notion that temperament is reflected in, for example, physiognomy, and that there is some link between this and insanity, still persists.

In the eighteenth century, the water cure – bathing in chilly water, sea water if possible – was very much in vogue, and was a routine treatment for the sick and the worried well, for all who could withstand it, and many who could not, including the insane. Following the fashions of the time, in the mid-1700s, Bethlem physician John Monro, for example, advocated cold bathing for his patients for its 'excellent effect'. In addition, patients were bled and blistered and purged into near oblivion.

The state of care at Bethlem had been and remained for some time entrenched in the old ways, but those ways were becoming unacceptable. Edward Wakefield, Quaker and reformer, visited Bethlem in 1814, inspected it, and found the treatment of inmates to be inadequate at best, horrific at worst. James Norris, an American patient, had been detained in the hospital since 1800 and restrained for many years in conditions that would have been unacceptable for an animal.

> *A stout iron ring was riveted about his neck, from which a short chain passed to a ring made to slide upwards and downwards on an upright massive iron bar, more than six feet high, inserted into the wall. Round his body a strong iron bar about two inches wide was riveted; on each side of the bar was a circular projection, which being fashioned to and enclosing each of his arms, pinioned them close to his sides. This waist bar was secured by two similar iron bars which, passing over*

> *his shoulders, were riveted to the waist both before and behind. The iron ring about his neck was connected to the bars on his shoulders by a double link. From each of these bars another short chain passed to the ring on the upright bar. . . . He had remained thus encaged and chained more than twelve years.*

Throughout the nineteenth century, treatments certainly became more humane at most of the major insane asylums in Britain. For the very poor of the great industrial towns and cities, with few resources, caring for a relative who might be incapable of looking after him or herself was never going to be possible. At the same time, new attitudes towards the treatment of those judged insane emerged as the century progressed, with physical restraint giving way to a form of 'moral management' that focused on systems of reward and punishment, aimed at instilling self-discipline in patients. The problem with 'moral management' was that any deviation from accepted social norms might be seen as insanity. The Victorian era had seen the rise of the huge public asylum, remote from centres of population, the very epitome of Victorian values. There have been histories praising and histories damning these institutions in equal measure. Writing in his thought-provoking 2012 thesis, *The West Riding Lunatic Asylum and the Making of the Modern Brain Sciences in the Nineteenth Century*, Michael Anthony Finn says, 'Like the fear of being buried alive, worries that sane individuals – especially women – might be unjustly incarcerated preoccupied many Victorian minds.'

To some extent the worries were well founded.

The great increase in admissions to asylums during the

nineteenth century put a strain not just on the staff, but on the buildings themselves and the facilities they contained, pauper asylums like the one where Elizabeth was housed in particular. Then as now, finance was always a problem for these hospitals and parsimony was a virtue. Those who were paying for the institutions, the pauper institutions especially, set up as philanthropic projects, needed to know that they were getting value for money, although they themselves might also fall foul of the system. Even the middle and upper classes might run the risk of being declared insane for unconventional or aberrant behaviour. A woman judged to be immoral might be even more at risk. Those with some wealth could be looked after by paid nurses at home, unless their relatives wanted to be rid of them, but often they were an embarrassment at best or – in the most extreme cases – a shameful secret to be hidden away.

Charlotte Brontë, in *Jane Eyre*, displays little sympathy for the plight of the madwoman in the attic, the first Mrs Rochester. But perhaps we can't expect her to do so, since she would have perceived the lunatic in the contemporary light: a frightening, demonic person. There are hints of a belief in possession, even in the hospital notes of some mental patients at this time; even, as we shall see, in those concerning poor little Elizabeth Manley. Charlotte was writing her novel many years before Elizabeth was detained, but just as the asylum population was inexorably on the rise. Any understanding of Bertha Mason, the first Mrs Rochester, was left for the Caribbean-born Jean Rhys, writing in another century and from quite a different perspective, in *The Wide Sargasso Sea*.

In *Wuthering Heights*, on the other hand, Emily Brontë's

extraordinary portrayal of what would certainly, in the Victorian era, have amounted to insanity in both Heathcliff and Cathy is at once more impartially, but more sympathetically (because less judgmentally), drawn than her sister's depiction of Bertha Mason, locked in an attic for ten years by her husband. 'Don't torture me till I'm as mad as yourself,' cries Heathcliff, when he sees Cathy for the last time, while sensible but partial Ellen Dean recollects that:

> the two . . . made a strange and fearful picture. Well might Catherine deem that heaven would be a land of exile to her, unless with her mortal body she cast away her moral character also. Her present countenance had a wild vindictiveness in its white cheek, and a bloodless lip and scintillating eye; and she retained in her closed fingers a portion of the locks she had been grasping. As to her companion, while raising himself with one hand, he had taken her arm with the other; and so inadequate was his stock of gentleness to the requirements of her condition, that on his letting go I saw four distinct impressions left blue in the colourless skin.

For a less original writer than Emily, both Cathy and Heathcliff would have been candidates for detention in the nearest insane asylum. In a scene that seems to mirror the above, poor, mad Bertha Mason has been reduced to something less than a beast, not just by her sickness, but by her erstwhile lover, her voice turned to animal rantings – and Jane concurs.

> What it was, whether beast or human being, one could not at first sight tell: it grovelled, seemingly, on

> all fours. It snatched and growled like some strange wild animal: but it was covered with clothing, and a quantity of dark, grizzled hair, wild as a mane, hid its head and face.

And a little later:

> the lunatic sprang and grappled his throat viciously, and laid her teeth to his cheek . . .

Having subdued her 'convulsive plunges' by means of a rope, Rochester compares her resentfully to his Jane.

> 'That is . . . the sole conjugal embrace I am ever to know!' he says. 'And this is what I wished to have, this young girl who stands so grave and quiet at the mouth of hell.'

Both are fine pieces of writing, but Charlotte's attitude to the prevailing belief in the 'moral' nature of madness and its treatment seems quite different from her sister's more nuanced approach, the voice of seeming 'normality' always filtered through a narrator who is clearly *not* the author, so that various perspectives can be seen at once: the conventional judgment of Victorian society about morality and the need for control of degeneracy, the lack of self-control that excludes the madwoman from heaven, and the nature of an emotion so elemental that it overrides all other concerns.

It is worth noting here that the Irish background of the Brontës, at a time when the migrant Irish were routinely described as lazy, foolish and filthy in their habits, 'but little above the savage', was consistently played down by Charlotte. Yet Patrick Brunty, their father, came from a poor background. He had known prejudice, and the family still contended with fiercely anti-Irish sentiment. In *Wuthering Heights*, Mr Earnshaw's discovery of Heathcliff, the dark, fey creature abandoned on the streets of Liverpool, babbling in a foreign tongue, may be Emily's nod to her family's past, since that city was the port of entry for many of the starving Irish who were so despised by their unwilling hosts, not least because some of them spoke Gaelic.

'We crowded round, and over Miss Cathy's head I had a peep at a dirty, ragged, black-haired child; big enough both to walk and talk: indeed, its face looked older than Catherine's; yet when it was set on its feet, it only stared round, and repeated over and over again some gibberish that nobody could understand.'

As the century progressed, the moral approach to madness became the norm, and can clearly be seen in the way in which Elizabeth Manley was treated, or at least in what we know of her treatment after she left Wadsley. There were many like her. The expansion of asylum populations was blamed on the asylums themselves, with next to nothing being done to tackle the root causes. We could say the same thing about our burgeoning prison populations today. Wakefield was, in fact, becoming an international centre for scientific research in the discipline of neurology, although it was still commonly accepted that the causes of insanity were chiefly moral. The corollary of this was that the doctor must be a gentle, but all-powerful, figure in the lives of his patients, the Victorian paterfamilias in a hospital setting. Cures were rare. Fewer than eight people per hundred were discharged as cured, and even those statistics – if we take Elizabeth Manley as an example – may not have been accurate.

Mental diseases were categorised in various ways: idiocy, imbecility and cretinism, dementia, delusional insanity, emotional insanity and mania, which was Elizabeth's original diagnosis. This was described as a 'state of general mental excitement or exaltation'. Facial features of patients were observed, as we can see from Elizabeth's later notes, when she was moved from Sheffield to Wakefield. These were thought to reflect underlying conditions and to help in diagnoses. An orderly environment was desirable. As with John Ross in prison, the surroundings for some people may have been no worse and possibly a little better than the places in which they had lived. At Wakefield, as Finn details:

> Crafts, farming, church, manual labour, gentle exercise and regular entertainments, all had their use not only in healing patients, but in the upkeep of the Asylum.

One thing is inescapable: with the asylum population growing, the popular press reflected public concern that an epidemic of insanity was sweeping the nation, something that they, and a significant majority of the medical men too, saw as a sign of the increasing degeneracy of the population. The press blamed it on the rise of the cities and the concomitant moral decay of the working populations. As we've already seen, the concept of 'moral decay' tended to be blamed on immigrants rather than natives and on women rather more than on men. Women were, and still to a large extent are, judged to be the keepers of the moral compass, except when it suits men to decide otherwise. When debauchery and depravity were blamed for an increase in lunacy, society at large was thrown into a panic. The madwoman might refuse to remain in the attic. She might, in fact, burn the whole house down. Something had to be done. This may help to explain the incarceration of so many women over so many years on somewhat flimsy pretexts.

To this more general increase in asylum populations, we might add the fact that throughout the nineteenth century, Irish migrants were portrayed in the press as a particular burden on the system. Engels would no doubt have agreed with them. The Irish were a necessary evil: useful pairs of hands when controlled, terrifying when not. While there had initially been some sympathy for those fleeing famine, the native population resented the incoming Irish, especially when so many of them were dependent on the poor law for their survival. How could it be otherwise, when most of them were in dreadful health on arrival, and were then given the most menial, insecure and physically difficult jobs, on the lowest pay, while living in the worst possible housing? Ratepayers, however, objected strongly to having to support 'Irish paupers'. One of the additional expenses was provision for those Irish people, either incoming or second-generation, who were increasingly falling victim to mental illnesses. It was one thing to be poor, mad and English; quite another, and a much more culpable fate, to be poor, mad and Irish. Rates of admission to asylums among Irish migrants were much higher than average. The Irish were believed to be prone to problems associated with drink, to 'general paralysis of the insane' (as a result of syphilis) and a range of behavioural problems often diagnosed, as in Elizabeth's case, as 'mania'. Irish patients had a reputation for being especially unmanageable. Their case records, as we shall see from Elizabeth's, laid much emphasis on their excitability and unruliness, all stereotypically Irish. Newspaper reports of the time contributed to a sense that the Irish were dangerously disruptive, prone to manic and criminal behaviour.

Writing in *'A Burden on the County': Madness, Institutions of Confinement and the Irish Patient in Victorian Lancashire*, Catherine Cox and Hilary Marland point out that in Rainhill Asylum, in the second half of the nineteenth century, over half of all male and female Irish patients were diagnosed with mania, as opposed to some 20 per cent of non-Irish patients. Mania was associated with energy and strength, even in a slight person like Elizabeth. This meant that those who were in poor bodily health, weak and sickly, were still deemed frightening and dangerous to others. If we add to that the fact that many Irish people were solitary, isolated from friends and family, who were often without the means to visit them, or to communicate with them in any way, we can see how a situation arose in which the very people who were most at risk were also those most blamed for the plight in which they found themselves.

As far as many asylums were concerned, increasing overcrowding was sometimes the chief problem that interfered with what might have become a helpful and hygienic regime. The Wadsley Asylum soon became equally overcrowded, as ever more people from the industrial conurbations nearby were diagnosed with insanity. The name of the hospital became synonymous with mental illness, although throughout its history, it was more than just a mental hospital. During Elizabeth's day, it would also have housed those elderly, sick and destitute paupers who were in need of medical care, although there is some evidence that the workhouses were reluctant to refer such patients except in extreme cases. Patients were accommodated in large wards in two three-storey blocks, with men and women being completely separated, as was usual in Victorian institutions. The asylum had its own bakery and brewery in the grounds and there were workshops for upholstery, carpentry, plumbing, book-binding and other skills, few of which, except perhaps baking and book-binding, would have been thought suitable for female patients back then. Elizabeth was, according to the records, discharged as 'relieved' four years later, on 5 December 1890, but this was an official lie, although by accident or design it's hard to tell. Sheffield is thirty-five miles away from Leeds, so the chances of anyone from her impoverished family being able to visit Elizabeth during her detention were slim to none, especially since visits were permitted only monthly.

The hospital, renamed Middlewood Hospital, closed only in 1998 and the site now contains a residential development. The Kingswood block has been listed and converted into apartments. There are, of course, ghost stories told about the old buildings, most of them involving sounds; the walls are said to exude spooky footsteps, whispering, moaning and other manifestations of suffering, but such ghosts as choose to inhabit it don't seem to favour the renovated parts, which is perhaps just as well. About Elizabeth's four years in this place, the records are disappointingly silent. We don't know whether she experienced spells of recovery, we don't know what she said or did, or what, if any, treatment she received. But we can guess. Because the next time we hear from her, is the very full account given of her when – as a hopelessly sick and institutionalised young woman – she is transferred to the West Yorkshire Asylum at Stanley Royd near Wakefield, much closer to home in Leeds.

Once again, nobody visits her, although in Wakefield, only ten miles from Leeds, visits might just conceivably have been possible for a determined relative. It's as though those intervening four years have caused everyone to forget about her. It's hard to place any blame on those who didn't visit her. Their own lives were so hard, so circumscribed, that concern for Elizabeth must have been the last thing on their minds. Nevertheless, she must have felt utterly abandoned. She *did* feel abandoned as we know from the accounts of those charged with looking after her, although they seemed to find nothing strange or pitiful in her distress. What else could be expected from one Irish madwoman among so many others?

15. A Large Institution or a Small Cabbage

On 5 December 1890, four years after she was detained, suffering from 'mania' in Glasgow, Elizabeth Manley, still only twenty-six years old, was transferred from the asylum in Sheffield to Stanley Royd in Wakefield. Very full notes on her condition and treatment are still in existence, and they are enlightening, if deeply depressing.

Once again, it is noted that she is single and a Roman Catholic. Curiously, the document lists her previous place of confinement as the grim and inhospitable Leeds Union Infirmary in Beckett Street, which suggests that she may have become physically as well as mentally ill and have been sent to the infirmary before being discharged from the Sheffield Asylum as 'relieved', only to be transferred immediately to the Stanley Royd Asylum. The answer to most questions on her admission is 'not known', but this time she is described as definitely suicidal. Her nearest relative is still given as Mary Manley, sister, 33 Off Street, York Street, Leeds, and J Radcliffe is the relieving officer, although since Mary is now married to James Flynn, and has moved to Hound Street with her new husband and family, the hospital's own details are out of date.

There follow a series of 'facts observed by Dr James Allan, Leeds Union Infirmary'.

He was the medical superintendent and we must assume

he has some knowledge of her condition, although all of these observations that will follow are disturbing in their impartiality. He tells us that:

> *She is depressed in mind and has delusions. Communes with persons she imagines to be present. Thinks also her food is drugged, gets excited at times, and when asked what is the matter, is very reticent, and either gives no answer, or says 'you know'.*

This last observation is hardly surprising and, looked at from a modern perspective, Elizabeth seems to display a certain amount of spirit, even at this late stage in what she saw as her abandonment or, worse, imprisonment. Her food may have been 'drugged' as she saw it, since she was sporadically medicated. Although she may have been hearing voices, many of us commune with persons we imagine to be present, and when she is constantly being asked what the matter is, 'you know' is the answer of somebody who has been questioned too many times to be bothered to answer yet again. 'Miss Benzie', who must have been a nursing attendant, says – again with somewhat horrifying calmness – that the patient 'has tried to commit suicide by jumping through a window'. This report is written and signed by J Hudson.

We then move on to three pages of handwritten, dated notes, detailing Elizabeth's condition and treatment over the next two years, following on from the date of her admission.

> *The patient is transferred from Wadsley Asylum, and was taken thereto from Glasgow in September or*

October 1886. She has not been visited by relatives or friends while in Wadsley. Said to be very angry at times. Seldom violent, attentive to the calls of nature.

In other words, Elizabeth seems to be reasonably calm, coping, but justifiably angry at her confinement, and resentful that she has been left alone.

Family history: Not known.

This is surprising and disappointing, since in Glasgow her family history was noted, but perhaps they didn't consider the murder and especially the time of year to be relevant to her current condition.

Only a few days later, though, Elizabeth seems much worse. The transfer has disturbed her very much.

December 8, 1890: Patient on many occasions has been very excited and worse since admission, using very foul language, struggling, spitting, etc. Last night she was so extremely troublesome that half a gram of hyoscyamine was given. Patient became quiet and slept from 1.30 till 6am. She has been clean as regards her evacuations. Bowels have moved daily. Taken food well and passed water. On admission, when asked her name, replied, they call me Sarah Floss. No [indecipherable] was discovered.

Who calls her Sarah Floss and where was she given the name? She was never, as far as I know, called Sarah in Leeds. Floss is a kind of silk braid used in millinery, and in the nineteenth century, the profession was often associated with prostitution. This may be a clue – albeit a nebulous one – to events in Glasgow.

Later the same day, which suggests they are keeping a close watch over her at this stage, comes the following report, at once intriguing, desperately sad, and worthy of Ophelia herself.

> *Present mental state: Patient is much excited. She rattles profusely, most incoherently and uses the filthiest language. Often starts up and tries to get out of bed and to expose herself. Her memory is greatly impaired. She is unable to converse sensibly, is too inattentive and deranged to properly understand much of the discourse addressed to her. Remarks, partly through the suggestions afforded by queries, and partly spontaneously, 'If you knew where you came from, sir,' and 'a Tommy Burns. That is just the . . . fool! What you call your person in bed.'*

It's not hard to imagine that the question to which she answers 'If you knew where you came from, sir' has probably been the often repeated, 'Where do you come from?' To which, 'If *you* knew where you came from, sir' is a reply at once clever, mischievous and exasperated. Here it is disregarded as the maunderings of a madwoman. 'Tommy Burns' is surely a joke name for a penis, perhaps a private name used between her and a man or men. She says as much. 'What you call your person in bed', but the doctor doesn't notice. Perhaps she is calling *him* a 'fool'. It can be a woeful business, making jokes to doctors, even today. How much more precarious, then, when you're an inmate of an asylum? The only Tommy Burns I can find any reference to at that time, one who might have been referred to as 'a Tommy Burns', was a young Liverpool-born athlete who at a youthful age was adept at diving, swimming, walking, running and boxing among other things. In 1886 he would already have achieved a certain fame if not notoriety. And since some of his feats were part of various variety shows, it's just possible that he might have visited one of the Glasgow music halls, the Britannia perhaps, in 1885 or 1886, while Elizabeth was in that city. His exploits would certainly have been well known, and an athletic or daring man might have been termed a 'Tommy Burns', much as we might describe somebody in terms of a famous footballer or other sportsman today.

She goes on, still perhaps trying to explain where she has been, where she comes from, still trying to answer the endless questions:

> *I've only been home. I've been in the bed, you know, the old asylum, what do you call it, and I said six rubies and £6 a dozen for every milliners. I've been in, you came in the biggest of these locomotive engines. I've been here fifty years, ah, I call it the prison, in Wakefield. After many repetitions of the question, patient replies that she has lived in Wadsley Asylum for ninety years. Further remarks that no man takes part of the baby, and no man ever did. I had it in the beautiful? Ah! Right side. That's just . . . America.*

What are we to make of this?

She is aware that she has been in another asylum, and is also aware that she is in Wakefield. She feels as though she is in prison – and indeed she is in prison, as surely as John Ross, but with no hope of release. Fifty years, ninety years, impatiently she tells them that she has been in this state for what feels like forever. The 'six rubies and £6 a dozen for every milliners' seems to be harking back to an earlier time, perhaps her time in Glasgow, especially since she remarks immediately on the locomotive engines: 'you came in the biggest of these locomotive engines'. £6 a dozen is a high price, a retail price rather than anything paid to the workers in millinery sweatshops, who were paid very little. The memory of the journey from Glasgow to Yorkshire, and perhaps also her original journey from Leeds to Glasgow, both of which would undoubtedly have involved one of the big steam engines, has stayed with her all this time. The sorrowful 'no man takes part of the baby and no man ever did' is intriguing. It suggests pregnancy and betrayal. In fact, it sounds very much like a line from a broadside ballad. Maybe it's a reference to the Punch and Judy shows that were such popular public entertainments at the time and that she would certainly have seen on Glasgow Green during her stay in the city. Mr Punch beats the baby entrusted to him by Judy. But 'no man takes part of the baby'. Elizabeth follows this quickly with 'I had it in the beautiful . . .' Had she, in fact, given birth in Glasgow? If so, what had become of the baby? And why the reference to America? I wonder if promises had been made that were destined never to be fulfilled, if she had fallen pregnant and been abandoned, and lost the baby. Had it all become too much for her, that day on a late afternoon in Castle Street?

> *When not talking, patient is laughing noisily and uncontrollably. Her flow of* [discourse?] *frequently is broken by these outbursts. She is not hostile or violent, just mad. Does not display any hallucinations.*

The doctor then goes on to describe her physical condition in some detail. Record keeping was something that Stanley Royd was good at, even if they were not always adept at interpreting what they were hearing and seeing.

> Physical Condition: *Hair brown, irises grey and pupils dilated from hyoscyamine.*

This is a drug frequently prescribed in those days to calm down manic patients. It is still used to treat intestinal conditions, but has side effects including dizziness, blurred vision and nausea.

> *On admission a small, old scar on left cheek and on right side of lower lip were seen.*

These were probably the scars of the assault on her by one of John Ross's supporters, just after the trial.

> *Also a small wart, just below left* [indecipherable]. *Bodily condition: Fairly good. Height: 5ft 3 inches. Weight: 118 lbs. Complexion pale, expression demented and maniacal.*

The doctors set great store by facial features at the time and expressions such as 'demented and maniacal' would be recorded as evidence of insanity.

> Respiratory system: *Quite normal as far as can be ascertained.*

> Circulatory system: *Heart sounds normal as far as can be ascertained. Pulse 88, regular, of fair strength.*

> Digestive system: *Teeth irregular, tongue large, pale*

and healthy, abdominal digestive organs appear to be normal.

Genito-urinary system: *Possibly alkaline, but fairly clear, no sugar or albumen.*

Diagnosis: *Dementia with excitement.*

Causation: *Unknown.*

Prognosis: *Bad.*

Treatment: *Deferred.*

It's worth noting that her condition has now moved from a diagnosis of mania to one of dementia, another catch-all term for cognitive impairment or some kind of intellectual deficiency. Once again, this is bad news for Elizabeth, and any chance of a cure would now have been remote. The possibility of syphilis can't be dismissed, but all the indications at this point seem to be that she is in reasonably good physical health and that although profoundly distressed, she also seems to have moments of intense clarity. So much of her behaviour might be the result of something like post-traumatic stress disorder or postnatal psychosis, or some deadly combination of both, coupled with the sheer frustration of her situation, what she sees quite clearly as her imprisonment, as surely as her brother's murderer has been imprisoned with more justification.

December 9th 1890: *Patient is so noisy, excited, restless and violent as requires a safe room at night.* [This would be a padded room, intended only for very short-term use.]

She is destructive and impulsive. Ordered 1/12 grain of hyoscyamine daily.

December 15th 1890: *Patient is no better. She is very wild this morning, jumps about, throws her arms about and raves loudly. The hyoscyamine has brief calmative effect.*

December 22nd 1890: *Has required to be in bed most of the time since last report because of the excitement and violence. Is now quieter. Takes food fairly well.*

December 29th 1890: *Patient remains an excited, chronic dement.*

December through to February would have been a very bad time for Elizabeth. The days leading up to, and after, the anniversary of her brother's murder and the trial that followed – had the medical staff taken note of them or even realised the connection – might have been significant in the worsening of her condition.

January 5th 1891: *Was maniacal: noisy last night until 3am, whisky was taken then slept. Prances about laughing, shouting, putting her fists in a fighting attitude. Continue this sedative.*

This again seems very much like post-traumatic stress disorder, given the date. It's interesting that whisky was given for its calmative properties.

February 19th 1891: *Requires to be in bed much of her time because of her violence. Is always excited when awake. Walks about naked to attract others. Remains weak and feeble, though takes food well enough.*

March 14th 1891: *Patient chatters incoherently but is too deranged to give sensible answers to queries. Is a wild, violent dement, dirty in her habits.*

March 17th 1891: *Has a patch of erythema on part of her right leg. Plumb Lact was applied.*

This would have been redness and swelling, which, had they realised it, was also an indication of tuberculosis. Instead they used something called Plumb Lact, a topical cream or plaster containing lead and lactic acid that was used to treat excoriated surfaces. There is a cream, diachylon, with these ingredients, that was often used at this time. People occasionally poisoned themselves by overusing it, and pills containing these ingredients were sometimes used to procure a miscarriage.

April 15th 1891: *Erythema greatly subsided. Patient requires to be in constant charge when up because of her violence and impetuous destructive propensities.*

May 19th 1891: *Patient requires to be in bed most of the time because of her turbulence. When up she requires the attention of a special nurse, to prevent her smashing, fighting and tearing. Never converses sensibly, is incoherent and foul and always excited.*

Sedation was stopped some weeks ago on account of her debility.

It's clear from this that Elizabeth is not really receiving any treatment at this time, not even to alleviate her symptoms, and that she is, moreover, in a state of great physical debilitation. In short, she is now in the final stages of the tuberculosis that she may have contracted years earlier, or – more likely – in the crowded, confined spaces of her previous place of incarceration.

> June 6th 1891: *In a most troublesome, demonic mania. Very noisy at times and violent. Dirty and destructive.*
>
> July 14th 1891: *There is no change in the state of this patient.*

The use of the term 'demonic' seems significant too. The moral dimension to this diagnosis is never very far from the surface, with implications of possession. In August, September and part of October, however, there is some small improvement in her mental state, albeit not physically. This is temporary, but it is a respite of sorts, although by the end of October, she is again sliding into acute anxiety.

> October 31st 1891: *Patient has been more excited lately. For several weeks was quieter and able to be up. She remains very thin and weakly.*
>
> November 6th 1891: *Says she has bad pain in her left side and shoulder for three weeks past. Does not know the name of this place. Insists that she 'has been here 6 years'.* [Her tormentors are still, relentlessly, asking her how long she has been here.] *She came here from Liverpool: is only 16 years old.* [She may well have been thinking about her mother at this point. Mary Manley senior would have arrived in Liverpool at a young age.] *Patient is pallid and thin as usual. All parts of the lungs are resonant.* No *cardiac arrhythmia. Abdomen*

apparently normal. Anorexia. Is supplied with milk and a light diet.

It's clear by now that she is losing weight fast, is in pain and is unable to eat.

December 22nd 1891: *Patient is remarkably quiet as a rule, never swears loudly as she used to do, much depressed, does not know where she is, does not know if it is a large institution or a small cabbage. Does not know how long she has been here, nor how long she was at Wadsley. Is clean now, more emaciated. Temperature continues high in spite of the quinine she is taking. There are signs of phthisis at both apices, more marked on the right side. R S Earl.*

Even in extremis like this, she can make an exasperated joke out of the endless questions. No, she does not know where she is, nor does she care. I keep thinking about her dreadful loneliness during these years, the terrible absence of love from her life. The one thing these families had, amid the poverty and privation, wasn't so much the mutual support, beloved of storytellers, although they had that too. It was the physical closeness, the affection, the laughter that allowed them to survive through thick and thin. We were a physically close family. My grandmother nursed me on her lap. My aunt would tell me how her grandfather, James Flynn, would dandle her on his knee and sing to her. Young women linked arms when they walked down the street. Young girls huddled together, confided secrets. Young lads play-wrestled in the streets. Like any social animal kept confined and starved of human touch, Elizabeth would have been driven mad anyway. She doesn't know whether this is a 'large institution or a small cabbage' and nor does she care. But phthisis is TB and they are now well aware that she has it and that she has not long to live. The name R S Earl is a new one in these records, so a new doctor has begun with the questions again, although he seems to be the one to finally diagnose the tuberculosis that is consuming her.

> February 15th 1892: *Secondary dementia. Has been very excited, violent and filthy, has auditory hallucinations, asserts that she heard her parents last night. Emaciated and phthisical.*

Maybe she did hear her parents. Maybe she has wanted them all along.

> May 6th 1892: *Mind is much clearer. Emaciation and debility much increased.*

Her mind seems to grow clearer as her physical condition deteriorates and as she finally stops fighting against her detention.

> May 25th 1891: *A note made on the 18th inst has been inserted in the Chronic Case Book.*
>
>> Chronic Case Book No 1 p642: *Patient is sinking, hardly will swallow, has whisky and lemonade. Can barely articulate, unable to talk other than in a faint, hoarse whisper. Pulse barely perceptible.*
>
> May 26th 1892: *Slowly sank. Death occurred at 10.05 this morning.*

Included in all these documents, explicit and horrifying, are copies of the graphs taken of her pulse; the last, a dreadful zigzag across the page, with a downward leap and the single word 'died'.

Her death certificate, giving her age accurately as twenty-seven – she had not yet reached her twenty-eighth birthday – names 'tubercular phthisis' as the cause certified by Edward Birt. The death was registered by F St John Bullen, Resident Medical Officer, Lunatic Asylum, Stanley. Elizabeth was buried in Beckett Street Cemetery, in a grave that is known, but unmarked, among the rows and rows of pauper graves. There may be as many as nine people in one grave and the register of burials gets her age wrong. She is in what is labelled as the 'unconsecrated' side, but, like so much else about this story, it isn't as it first appears. It means only that this is the side of the cemetery reserved for Roman Catholics as opposed to the part where those people who were of the 'established' church can be buried. It seems that she had a Catholic funeral with Father George Edward O'Machelly officiating, although it's hard to read the cramped writing on the list. Along with several others, she is buried in the same grave as Mary's father-in-law, James Terran, who, conveniently enough, died in the workhouse on the same day, aged 65 years, his useful days, like Elizabeth's, being all behind him.

16. Excitable, Fiery and Generous to a Fault

Elizabeth died in 1892, aged twenty-seven. It was not unusual for the poor to die young at this time, but Elizabeth seems to have drawn a particularly short and tragic straw. In 1893, meanwhile, John Ross had served eleven years hard labour, quarrying and dressing stones in Portland Prison, and the time was coming when he might be considered for release, on licence. He had kept his head down, kept quiet, behaved himself – an exemplary prisoner, in fact. Perhaps the strict routine suited him. He managed to stay in good health, too. In 1893, John's younger brother Patrick, who had, and would continue to have, a criminal career of persistent if not particularly serious proportions, nevertheless managed to send a letter to Mr Asquith, QC, on 30 June, bringing his brother's case to his attention, and asking if John's release could now be considered. Asquith was a Liberal politician who was appointed Home Secretary in 1892, in Gladstone's fourth ministry, remaining in post until the Liberals lost the 1895 election. The letter looks and reads as though it has been written by Patrick himself, rather than on his behalf. This may have been the case. For all his less than law-abiding character, Patrick seems to have been as bright a spark as his sister Kate.

26 Brewery Street, Regent Street,
Leeds,
30th June 1893

To Mr Asquith, QC

Sir, trusting you will excuse this liberty taken by a stranger to you of writing you on so grave a subject, it is with reference to a brother of mine, who was tried and convicted of murder in February 1882 before Mr Justice Cave and who was defended by Mr Lockwood, J C, to whom I now refer you. Re as considering of the case again as it is now close upon twelve years ago, he has written me from Portland asking me to petition you and I now write you to ask the opinion of Mr Lockwood and the courts who tried him. I remain yours etc.
Patrick Ross.

My brother to whom I refer is John Ross.

Perhaps John Ross too had learned to write during his years in prison. This letter certainly implies as much, and has a very business-like tone. Patrick's letter, when seen by the Home Secretary, is accompanied by a short note outlining the circumstances: 'Mr Patrick Ross prays for a consideration of the case, since it is nearly twelve years since his brother was sentenced.' An additional note says that Ross has served eleven years and five months, pointing out that this is a commuted capital case, 'but I think he might now have a licence' to which the advice is to 'bring up with prison report when he has completed twelve years on 31st Jan 1894'.

On 31 January, we duly find the following letter:

> *Sir, in compliance with the instructions contained in the Home Office referral paper No A12371B, I have the honour to report for the information of the Secretary of State that the convict 1416, John Ross, in Portland Prison, completed 12 years of his sentence on 30th Inst. His conduct during the whole of his sentence has been very good. Signed, M Longford* [to which is added the note] *Case considered alongside Richardson. Stabbing after drink and quarrelling. There was less provocation in the case of Ross than in that of Richardson. R has served 15 years, Ross 12. Ross to be placed on licence. Suggest Richardson might receive a like consideration.*

I don't know if Richardson ever received his 'like consideration', even though there had been more provocation in his case, but Ross was duly released on licence. On 23 April 1894, the date of the convict's release is proposed as 2 May. This is a notification of discharge, on licence, for life. He returns to Leeds, but, once again, keeps his head down and stays out of trouble. Little is heard of him between his release in 1894 and his death some twenty years later in 1914. Dated August 7 1903, when he has been out of prison for nine years, we find a letter from the Chief Constable of Leeds, the first of these official notes concerning the case to be typewritten, progress of a sort and certainly easier to read.

> I beg to inform you that during the last twelve months, the conduct of this man has continued satisfactory. He has alike reported himself and worked regularly.
>
> Ross has behaved himself consistently well and is now

even allowed to report by letter, which again suggests that he might be able to read and write. Perhaps he has learned while in prison. There would have been other prisoners with the skill. Even if he couldn't, the resourceful Patrick may have written it for him. 'Ross has been over nine years on licence and has been reporting by letter this last year. Chief Constable of Leeds reports good conduct,' is the official annotation to the letter.

He remains in regular employment and never once comes to the notice of the police during the whole of his licence period. He dies in 1914, of emphysema, a cruel disease, but he has probably been a lifelong smoker and has spent much of his life working out of doors in harsh conditions. He was working as a night watchman at the time of his death and, once again, the death certificate provokes a little pang of sympathy for a solitary man whose life was ruined by a moment of uncontrolled rage, and the coincidence that he had just smoked his pipe, and found his fingers grasping a tobacco knife at the exact moment when that rage descended on him.

It's worth glancing at his brother Patrick's own criminal career. There were a string of offences to his name, some committed before and some after the murder. Mercifully, and unlike his earlier crimes, none of these later offences involved John Ross, who, following his release from prison, was keen to stay out of trouble. After some years of good behaviour that coincide in large part with his brother's sentence in Portland Prison, on 14 April 1890, Patrick was caught housebreaking and – intriguingly – stealing books, for which he received a sentence of nine months. Perhaps he planned to learn to read and write. In 1894 he celebrated his brother's release from prison by stealing a watch. In 1895 he was charged with loitering with intent. In 1896 he assaulted a policeman, while in 1897 he was back to loitering with intent. By now, Patrick couldn't loiter anywhere without the police arresting him. Also in 1897 the loitering with intent became actual when he was charged with housebreaking. He had another period of relative honesty, but in 1901 he was charged with stealing nine gills (just over two pints) of brandy. Over and above this, there were various 'minor convictions' for assault, being drunk and disorderly and for being a 'rogue and vagabond' on the records. In 1904, when his notorious brother had been out of prison for some ten years, Patrick, then in his forties, had been working as a labourer but had been discharged. He was a marked man, but he didn't seem to care. Alcohol may well have been a factor in all this. There is a whole novel to be written about Patrick, although I'm perhaps not the person to write it.

There is no indication that either Mary or Bridget encountered the Ross family again, and all the evidence points to the two women moving away from the Bank area, onwards and upwards to what would eventually amount to a better, although still very difficult, life. Bridget made a good second marriage and called her first girl Elizabeth after her sister. Unlike her namesake, this new Elizabeth would have a long and fruitful life. Mary Terran moved over the River Aire too, along Whitehall Road, to where Lower Wortley met Holbeck, still an area of heavy industry, whose surviving street and place names – Springwell Street, Holbeck Moor, Water Lane, Meadow Lane – told of an earlier, more rural past, long buried beneath an Industrial

Revolution that carried all before it. Their lives were better. Their children were more likely to survive than otherwise. Poverty still haunted them, but not as relentlessly, nor as desperately as it once had. They had begun to have a few choices.

As for the murderer, the stories told in the family afterwards, even by people like my grandmother, a child when Elizabeth died and a young woman when John Ross died, indicated that the family had done their best to forget about him. The bald statement that he 'got away with it' was all that was handed down through the generations, along with a garbled (and untrue) tale that he had gone to Canada. When I began this quest, I had no idea what had become of him, but he didn't get away with it. Not really. And somewhere, even as I write this, he and his canny brother Patrick and his bright sister Kate, who cared enough about John to find him a solicitor, will be slotted into another family tree by some fascinated descendent, hopefully living in different and better circumstances.

Retrospectively, depending on closeness or otherwise, some family members seem to become major players within the drama of our personal family histories, while others are only bit-part actors, except when real notoriety intervenes. John Manley attained this kind of tragic notoriety even though we know so little about his life before he became a murder victim and therefore newsworthy. My grandmother spoke about him as though she knew him, but it's clear that wasn't possible. She was born a few years after he died and by that stage, the family were living in a different part of Leeds. What she did know, of course, was the story of his death, inextricably and permanently woven into the history of the family, a story that cast him in the rosy glow of what might have been.

The immediate family never forgot John Manley: cheerful John, fond of a joke, with his fine head of curly red hair and his smart, light-coloured clothes in honour of the Christmas season, so soon to be stained with his own blood. I'm sure these close relatives didn't forget Elizabeth either, although she was among the 'things that cannot be mentioned', one of the skeletons in the family cupboard. All families have them and most have more than one. The stigma of mental health problems, of the asylum, of presumed immorality too, clung about her memory, although not so closely that Bridget didn't recollect the well-loved sister and commemorate her in the name of her daughter.

When Friedrich Engels, visiting the Bank area of Leeds in the 1840s, wrote *The Conditions of the Working Class in England*, he concluded that these conditions were appalling. Not even Dickens seemed to be quite so graphic and accusatory as Engels in describing the horrors of the Industrial Revolution, the sheer venality of the times, pointing out that too many of the early factory owners knew there were plenty more desperate workers to be had, with more arriving all the time to take the place of those who succumbed to sickness and starvation or were injured by the machinery or the conditions in the factories. 'Hands' they were called and that's what they were: a chilly impersonal description for a chilly and impersonal state of affairs. He described the Bank, where the Manleys and the Rosses of Leeds struggled to survive, as having 'drainless streets, mud a foot thick, cellars . . . seldom dry'. It didn't prevent him from blaming the Irish for their own situation, describing them as 'excitable, fiery, generous to a fault and ruled primarily by sentiment'. He was not using that word 'sentiment' in any congratulatory sense, but rather in its meaning of the opposite of reason: sensibility as opposed to sense.

'Sentiment' is a word with constantly shifting meanings, but it was often ascribed to fiction written mainly, although not exclusively, by women, and in no good way, both during the Victorian period and after. Critics are still arguing about the inclusion of 'sentimental works' in the literary canon, which provokes the question as to why the word or indeed the description of a whole nation as being 'ruled by sentiment' should be pejorative in the first place, and also serves to demonstrate how far we have still to go in getting rid of our own prejudices, not just against women, but against other nationalities. Engels was using the word in its 'irrational and mawkishly susceptible' meaning. Not people like us, he might have added. These are people who can be discounted. 'Excitable, fiery and generous to a fault' would have been a very good description of my great-grandfather, James Flynn, if those who knew him had had access to that kind of vocabulary.

These are all qualities that, even now, English people might be heard ascribing to their foreign migrant neighbours. Back then, with regard to the incoming Irish, and apart from their generosity, which was eminently exploitable, there was a distinct disapproval of their 'fiery and sentimental' nature, and of the rural habits they tried to import into the industrial cities of the empire. Britain was happy to host Ireland as an exploitable colony. Glad of the 'hands'. Much the same complaint was made of many of the refugee Poles and other Eastern European migrants after the Second World War. Only recently, somebody asked me why Poles had refugee status after the war. Why did they stay? Why didn't they go back 'home'. I had to explain that most of them didn't have a home any longer. Borders had shifted. There was nowhere and nobody to go back to. Later, Asian and African émigrés were thought to be the problem and to bring the same troubles with them. Economic migrants. But all migrants, at all times, whether we're talking about those early Anglo-Saxons, moving west to populate parts of the British Isles, or the Vikings, marauding but also settling and intermarrying, or the waves of later migration, all are essentially economic migrants, driven by poverty or cruelty or war or some deadly combination of all three, seeking a better life for their children.

Now it's happening all over again with Central and Eastern European migrants: Schrödinger's immigrant, simultaneously taking other people's jobs and refusing to work. My Irish forebears would have recognised this slur all too well, although there were no benefits to be had, so they were blamed for stealing jobs and working for lower wages, while being dismissed as unemployable drunken layabouts at the same time.

17. A Good Living Person

With Elizabeth locked away in the Sheffield Asylum, Mary Terran married my great-grandfather, James Flynn. Mary and James were married in St Patrick's Church on York Road, on 13 April 1888. My grandmother, Honora, always called Nora, was born some months before the wedding, on 13 November of the preceding year, 1887, in Off Street. This was where widowed Mary had been living, and where the asylum in Wakefield thought she still was living when Elizabeth was transferred there in 1890. The couple must have been seeing each other – courting, as the old expression had it – for a little while. There is a mystery about my grandmother's birth certificate. Honora's father is certainly James Flynn, who at this time is described as a paviour's labourer. Later he would have the full title of paviour. The birth is registered some weeks later on 30 December 1887, but while Mary Terran has now changed her name to Flynn, her maiden name is given as 'late Green, formerly Black'. There is no doubt that Honora's mother is Mary Terran née Manley, that James is her father and that the couple will be married very soon after Honora's birth. James will provide a home for the Terran children as well as his own, firstly in Hound Street, Quarry Hill, again one of those areas designated as unhealthy by the authorities. But the 'Green, Black' names are odd and don't crop up anywhere else in the family records. The most likely explanation may lie somewhere in the difficult years between Charles Terran's early death in 1884 and Mary's marriage to James in 1888. Like Elizabeth in Glasgow, we can only guess at what poor Mary was forced to do, and with whom, in order to keep body and soul together, for her children as much as for herself. One thing is certain. James Flynn would have known all about it. In areas like this, unlike middle class homes with their net curtains, it is almost impossible to keep secrets.

At some point over the next decade, the Flynn family moves again, this time from Hound Street to Ascot Terrace in the Richmond Hill area, still north of the Aire, but the house seems a much better proposition altogether. This street of brick-built houses, with their tiny rear gardens, and with a convenient shop on the corner, survived into the 1960s and must have been an enormous improvement for Mary and James. Mary gives birth to Timothy in 1889 (this time his mother's maiden name is recorded as Manley on his birth certificate) and to Thomas in 1891, but this child dies in 1894. Her last surviving child seems to have been Michael, born in 1893. At some point, the family makes a bigger move, over the river to Peacock Yard in New Wortley, which is where we find them living in 1911.

*

It is James Flynn, small, wiry and neat, whose picture sits in my hallway, alongside the men he works with, including Tarry Arse the Fiddler. Official records about him are scant, but he was well loved in my immediate family. I'm looking at a copy of the 1911 census that he has filled in and signed himself. It is an evocative and intensely moving document that contains a wealth of information on this one, small piece of paper. To begin with, this is an image of the original form, warts and all, filled in by the individual householder. Previously, census forms had always been collected and copied into the enumerators' books, but the forms themselves had then been destroyed. Since many people in previous years could neither read nor write, the enumerator's job must have been a difficult one, especially when they were going from door to door in some of the more dangerous parts of the industrial cities. The census recorded employment, as well as children, living and dead.

As was not uncommon, James has included more information than was strictly necessary. The family is living at 2 Peacock Yard in New Wortley, about a mile to the west of the city centre and on the south side of the River Aire. The house has five rooms, of which one is the kitchen: a comparative luxury compared to the places where Mary had lived earlier in her life. New Wortley itself was an improvement for Mary, too, as was a healthy husband and children. This was still an area of immense privation, poverty and pollution. Throughout my childhood I was aware of tales of nearby houses such as those at Camp Field, east of Holbeck and just south of the river, to which once again many of the migrant Irish workers had been consigned, and where conditions were appalling. In the early to mid-nineteenth century, New Wortley and adjacent Holbeck had been just as filthy and insanitary as anywhere else in the industrial heart of the city, but cholera epidemics had prompted some early slum clearance and things were improving.

Holbeck – whose name means the stream in the hollow – had once been a rural village situated outside Leeds, at a convenient place for fording the stream or beck. In the eighteenth century, this was a place of hand-loom weavers and fine spring waters (still recollected in names such as Springwell Road and Water Lane) that, like the waters from the Spoutmouth in Glasgow, were so fresh and clear they were taken into Leeds for various domestic and medicinal uses. Old documents show a number of small breweries established here, also taking advantage of the good, clean water. Even writing in 1834, Edward Parsons can speak of 'the Eyebright Well, once supposed to afford a sovereign remedy for the eyes' at the Monk Pits. These were on meadowland just south of the Aire, not far from the present-day Monk Bridge, itself probably named after these adjacent 'pits'. These may have been shallow bell pits dug for coal or ironstone by the Cistercian monks of Kirkstall Abbey, an early example of small-scale industrialisation.

During the late eighteenth and throughout the nineteenth centuries, mills, foundries and other industrial concerns were established in ever-increasing numbers and all were greedy for water. These included the extraordinary Temple Works, so much a part of my own childhood that I simply took the building for granted. This was originally a flax mill built in the grand Egyptian style by the wealthy Marshall family, as fine an example of overweening industrial hubris as you are ever likely to meet. The office building was said to be based on the Anteopolis and the Temple of Horus at Edfu. The mill itself was modelled on the Typhonium at Dendera. Sheep were set to graze on the grass-covered roof, to maintain the humidity needed to keep the linen thread damp and flexible, and a hydraulic lift was devised to get them up there. There was even a chimney in the style of Cleopatra's Needle. What were they thinking? The factory opened in 1840 with a Temperance Tea for the workers, alcohol still being seen as the curse of the working classes. In spite of evidence to suggest John Marshall treated his workers rather better than many other factory owners, the mill functioned with what might be described as a truly Pharaonic disregard for the well-being of the numerous men, women and children employed there.

In 1832, little Eliza Marshall (obviously no relation) was interviewed by Michael Sadler, investigating the state of child labour for a House of Commons committee. She had worked at Marshall's Mill, another part of the Marshall empire, also in Holbeck, before moving to Burgess's worsted mill on Lady Lane. She told the committee that, while still only nine years old, she had worked from six in the morning till seven at night, but then her hours increased from five in the morning until ten at night. When she was younger, the overseer would beat her. She used to have to rub 'stuff' into her knees and joints since they were so stiff from the work. She had been 'straight' (that is, upright) before she started work, but now when she asks for her wages, the master tells her that she can't run about as she used to, the implication being that he wants to pay her less or get rid of her altogether. She has an iron on her leg because her knee is contracted. The surgeons at the infirmary tell her that the 'marrow is dried out of the bone, so there is no natural strength in it'.

Sadler asks her, 'You were quite straight till you had to labour so long in those mills?' to which she replies, 'Yes, I was as straight as anyone.'

In fact, the original John Marshall banned beatings for children and instituted some education for the better behaved, although with a seventy-two-hour working week, that isn't saying much. He even organised weekends away for the more deserving of his workers from Marshall's Mill, although the ubiquitous *Leeds Mercury* was soon on the case, cautioning about the advisability of a large body of people being away from home for two whole nights – and on the Sabbath Day too! Soon after the Temple Mill was built, there was a slump in the flax industry and it never regained its dominance in England, especially given the rise and importance of cotton.

Overall, the increasing siting of heavy industry in the area meant that the supply of spring water diminished and had to be pumped out of the ground from ever-greater depths. Holbeck and New Wortley also suffered from the same swift erection of housing for the workers as we have seen across the river in the Bank area, without much care for the conditions in which these workers would have to live. Still, James and Mary must have seen some advantage in the move. The street and pub name Peacock is not uncommon, but a hunt through old maps reveals that this particular Peacock Yard was part of yet another maze of streets near Whitehall Road, streets that had long since been demolished when I was young, in one of the later waves of slum clearance. Nevertheless, not all industrial housing was bad housing and this would probably have been progress for the family. The green space of Holbeck Moor with its annual 'feast', as we always called the travelling fairground, was only a short walk away, up Domestic Street with its variety of little shops. There was a fine library, opened in 1903, public swimming baths and other amenities.

On the 1911 census, James is 54 and he gives his wife's age as 52. He describes himself as a paviour and gives his place of birth as Ballinlough, County Roscommon. An earlier census gave his place of birth as Liverpool, and this error seems to have been perpetuated in various genealogies, but this may simply have been where he landed in England as a young man. This 1911 form, which he filled in himself, speaks of an Irish place of birth. Moreover, those in my family who remembered him well confirmed his Irish birth, described his strong Irish accent, his characteristically Irish singing, and the fact that he had come over to England as an adult, for a specific piece of road-building work. Somewhere along the way, Mary seems to have lost some eight years, since she was certainly older than he was, but neither of them is admitting it. He has carefully written the names of all of the Terran children on this form: James, Elizabeth, John and Mary, born long after Charles Terran's death. My grandmother Honora is also there, aged twenty-three, and working as a shirt machinist. Timothy is twenty-one, and a labourer in a chemical works, while the youngest son, seventeen-year-old Michael, who must have been born when Mary was in her very early forties, is working in an iron foundry. There is a little lad called Thomas in the house. He is four years old, and he is Mary and James's grandson. He was my grandmother Honora's first child, born out of wedlock and absorbed into this large family. Somebody – perhaps James, who realises he has got it wrong, or the exasperated enumerator himself – has crossed out the names of those children who are not actually in the house that night. Somebody named Catherine Flynn is on the census form, too, but her name is also crossed out and no age is given. She isn't described as a child of the family or a stepchild, and since she isn't actually in the house on the evening in question, we know no more about her than that she may have been a relative who was staying with them, one who James saw fit to include. James states that he and Mary have been married for twenty-four years. They may have been officially married for only twenty-three years, but they have certainly been together for longer. James declares that they have had five children from the marriage, of whom three are still living, and that two children are dead, presumably one of whom is the earlier Thomas who had died at the age of two. But who was the other? Was a child perhaps stillborn? We can't be sure and, after Michael's birth in 1893, Mary, who had given birth to eleven children in total – twelve if we count the possibility that Elizabeth was her child – may have been past childbearing age.

Two more babies had died in this house in Peacock Yard.

In 1910, Honora had given birth to twin girls, Gladys and Ethel. My grandfather Joe is not named as father on their certificates; he was some years younger than she, and overseas in the Navy for much of his youth, so it's possible, but not likely, that they were his. She never spoke of these baby girls to any of her other children. Neither my mother nor my aunt knew anything about them, until a distant relative, researching his own family tree, ferreted them out.

She gave birth to them in the building that had been, and still was in name at least, the Bramley Union Workhouse, although it was on the way to becoming a proper hospital, and would later become St Mary's Maternity Hospital, where I was born. The workhouse was never named on birth and death certificates. The address only was noted. She had given birth to Tommy at home, but perhaps she needed medical attention this time. Twins must have been a precarious undertaking, which perhaps explains why she was sent to the Bramley hospital, although the workhouse was still feared. She delivered them safely, and then she brought the little girls home to Peacock Yard, but, much like her mother Mary's twin girls in the previous generation, they didn't live for more than a few months. Gladys Flynn died of 'malnutrition and convulsions' at the age of two months, on 18 May 1910, while Ethel, who seems to have been named after one of Honora's close friends, lived a little longer, for eight months, and died on 11 October of that same year. The death certificate reads 'dentition and convulsions', but as with the deaths of infants in the previous generation, these infantile convulsions, so often associated with teething, may well have been the result of some underlying infection or sickness.

James wasn't allowed to write these names on his form, but he filled it in as best he could, and signed it in a careful, curly hand, much like my mother's in a later generation. He always calls himself James and it is only on his death certificate that he becomes Michael, while in the probate report for his will, we find the entry: '*Flynn, Michael, otherwise James, of 32 Whitehall Road, Leeds, died 18 July 1930, Administration Wakefield, 16 October, to Michael Flynn (his son) tailor's presser. Effects £68 16s 4d.*' This was the equivalent of three to four months wages for a factory worker, so James must have managed to save something, albeit not very much, during his reasonably long lifetime. His other son Timothy had predeceased him, dying of tuberculosis at the age of 36.

Several people who remembered my great-grandfather, including my Aunt Nora, who recollected him very clearly, pointed out that he had a strong brogue. Young Michael Flynn's daughter, Mary, also remembered that her grandfather had a broad Irish accent. She mentioned the name Ballyhaunis, just a few miles along the road from Ballinlough, so perhaps James Flynn had come from somewhere between the two places. She knew that he came to Leeds to build the original 'coal road'. This was probably the road that used to run from Seacroft to Harewood, and still exists at the Seacroft end. Coal was once transported along here from the Waterloo Main Colliery to Harewood House, although James's involvement with the road probably came after that. Ballinlough means the town on or at the lake. The nearby lake, large and well stocked with fish, in this rural area with its green fields and blossoming hedges, is named O'Flynn, so James's forebears belonged there. Michael, the youngest of the family, was described as 'ruined' – but only in the sense of being the petted baby of a big family. As a child, Michael's daughter remembered looking for her grandfather, James, when he was working on the roads, because if he saw her, he would give her and her siblings shillings and half-crowns instead of the usual coppers. She remembered too that he would work hard and save up his money, but then might blow it all on one huge binge. All in all, he was not a bad provider, and his wife, who had been Mary Manley and Mary Terran, saw some significant improvements to her life. In old age, she was described by one of her grand-daughters as a 'good living person, small and plump with grey hair', which is exactly how I remember her daughter, Honora: small and plump with grey hair. Loving and warm, but not to be messed with.

There are fragments of disconnected stories about James floating around in my memory. My aunt Nora remembered that he could sing the traditional mouth music sometimes known as 'lilting' that would be an accompaniment to dancing if no other instrument was available or that would just be sung for its own sake. He would dandle her on his knee and sing to her. Honora, my nana, remembered him as the most generous of fathers. He must have been big-hearted, for sure, kind-hearted too, to take on Mary's children and then his own, most of whom lived and thrived far better than poor Charles Terran's children. She too would tell tales of his good humour and his impulsive generosity, but it had its downside. If he saw a beggar in the street and he was wearing a good coat, he was as likely as not to hand it over to the more needy man.

'He couldn't keep anything,' she would say, shaking her head. 'It used to make my mother angry. He would give things away when they could ill afford it.' This was the kind of 'excitable and generous to a fault' behaviour of which Engels would certainly have disapproved, albeit for less practical reasons than those of domestic economy.

At some time in the 1920s, after Honora and Joe had married and moved to 32 Whitehall Road, and the widowed James was living with them, he was knocked down by a bus on Whitehall Road. He appeared to have no ill effects, but became unwell a little while later, and was taken into the Leeds Union Infirmary, otherwise known as the Workhouse Hospital, a place of ill-repute, in central Leeds. Not surprisingly, he was unhappy there, so he was moved to the Bramley Workhouse on Green Hill Lane, where Honora's twins had been born some years earlier. By then, Bramley had dedicated facilities for those who were elderly and unwell. The Leeds Union Infirmary was still a place of grim and discreditable reputation, but Bramley seems to have been a much more kindly place, already in transition between the workhouse and the maternity hospital it would later become. He must have recovered to some extent, because we know that he was sent home to his daughter in Whitehall Road.

In July 1930, he died at home, of arteriosclerosis and senility. My grandmother was 'in attendance'.

There is one last tale to tell about James Flynn and it concerns the old house in Whitehall Road where I spent the first seven years of my life. The main house was a narrow building, two rooms on each floor, with a couple of small shops next door, a back yard, a washhouse and an outside lavatory, all surrounded by heavy industry and railway lines. Even here, the family must have been crammed in, somehow or other, at the time when James Flynn was living with them. Mary Flynn had died some years previously, and James had his own small room at the very top of the house.

On the night after he died, James came upstairs to his attic room, one last time.

The rest of the house, at that time, was managing to

accommodate my Aunt Nora, then in her teens, her eleven-year-old brother George, my six-year-old Aunt Vera and my four-year-old mother, Kathleen, as well as my grandfather Joe and my grandmother Honora. I think the downstairs best room, always known only as 'the room', must have been pressed into service as a bedroom for the young ones, but George and Nora were upstairs, lying awake late into the night, when everyone else was asleep. More than once, over the following years, they related how James Flynn had often come in late and clumped up the stairs to his attic room in his working boots. It was a familiar and comforting sound and they would miss him.

They knew he had died the previous day, but both of them swore that they heard his heavy footsteps coming upstairs to the landing, pausing, and then moving onwards, up the next steep, creaking flight of stairs to the attic bedroom, where they abruptly ceased.

Into the silence that followed, George called to Nora, 'Did you hear that?' to which she replied, 'Yes! That was my grandad!'

It was a custom in Ireland, as it is in other countries too, to open a window in a house to let the soul of the dead person fly free to heaven. Perhaps that's where James was going. Onwards and upwards. Given his notorious generosity, his compassion, I don't think he'd have had much trouble with St Peter.

18. *Number Thirty-Two*

During the war, a British Restaurant had been built more or less on the site where Peacock Yard had once housed the Flynn family. These originally went by the unappetising name of 'community feeding centres' until Churchill decided otherwise, and chose the patriotic branding 'British Restaurants' to describe these not-for-profit concerns set up by the Ministry of Food, where nourishing meals were provided at a very low, subsidised cost during wartime. The food was of good quality, although cabbage, due to its availability and the commendable desire to provide vitamin C to the masses, was a staple. The one opposite our house had been built in 1942. After 1947 the restaurants were converted into 'civic' restaurants run by the local councils. The Labour Party had always seen them as a way of guaranteeing a decent diet for the very poor, and the one on Whitehall Road continued to serve the community throughout the 1950s. I was never in it, as far as I remember. My grandmother was too keen a cook for us to have to supplement her cooking and in fact eating out – other than the great treat of exotic hot dogs and ice cream in Marks and Spencer's café, or on occasional day trips or even more rare holidays, to the seaside at Scarborough or Bridlington – was largely the province of the middle classes. Marks and Spencer's café also served daring frothy coffee in the very newest thing in pale brown plastic cups, as well as delicious hot dogs with continental mustard and three flavours of ice cream in boat-shaped dishes. My very first proper restaurant meal must have been eaten circa 1959, and was spaghetti bolognaise in an Italian restaurant somewhere in the centre of Leeds. My Polish dad had come from a country where café culture was deeply embedded, but the opportunities for coffee and cakes in Leeds were limited. Lyons had cafés in Leeds; Bettys Café had opened in the city in 1930, and we certainly bought cakes there occasionally, but we invariably ate them at home.

Probably because of her early work as a shirtmaker, my 'nana' Honora, or Nora as Joe always called her, was a talented seamstress. She could cut patterns by sight, with only minimal measuring, and sew up clothes that fitted and looked good. She must have served an apprenticeship as a shirtmaker, perhaps in a small workshop or factory unit in Holbeck or New Wortley. This would have been piecework, difficult, finicky work, involving long hours in poor light. Thomas Hood's 'Song of the Shirt', written much earlier, would still have been not far short of the mark, although sewing machines would have been blessedly available by then, and my grandmother's old treadle machine sat in the back room throughout my childhood.

> Stitch! stitch! stitch!
> In poverty, hunger, and dirt,
> And still with a voice of dolorous pitch, —
> Would that its tone could reach the Rich! —
> She sang this 'Song of the Shirt!'

Honora had other, perhaps unexpected, talents. She

could swim well and she could play the piano. There were public baths in Holbeck by this time, first opened in 1898, and the Flynn children would have taken full advantage of them. How they acquired a piano I don't know, but it may have been one of James Flynn's periodic extravagances, probably bought second-hand, and would certainly explain the fact that my Aunt Nora, Honora's eldest daughter, was a fine pianist too.

My grandfather, Joe Sunter, had been living with his parents and his brother, George, in Pollard Street, another row of back-to-backs, further along Whitehall Road. His father, William, was a shoeing smith, although the family had come to Leeds by a circuitous route via Castleford, from Swaledale, where they had been lead miners, another unenviable occupation with a short life span for those involved. Joe was born in 1890, but his mother died young, his father remarried, and ten years later, Joe found himself fairly desperate to leave home, with a stepmother whom he disliked quite as much as she disliked him. His brother would join the army and Joe would go to sea, joining the Royal Navy in 1908 and serving for twelve years, right through the Great War. He went on to join the Merchant Navy after that before finally coming ashore to work in tailoring. Given that Nora Flynn was an Irish Catholic and Joe was a Yorkshire Methodist, they must have met because of the proximity of their houses. Or maybe at the public baths.

When they were first married, they had squeezed in with the Flynns at Peacock Yard, but by 1939, when a wartime register was taken of people and their occupations, Joe and Honora and their family were living at 32 Whitehall Road, although they don't seem to have had the shops at this time. Thomas, Honora's eldest, seems to have been brought up mainly by his grandparents, James and Mary Flynn, in Peacock Yard. My Aunt Nora was born right at the start of the Great War in 1914, while George was born just after its end in 1919. Vera came along in 1924 and my mother, Kathleen, was born in 1926. This was a house they eventually owned outright. Joe would have been paid war gratuities for his service. These were not generous, but perhaps he had saved up enough money for the purchase during his years at sea, since Honora wouldn't have had a spare penny to her name and most people rented. Perhaps his father left him something. In retrospect, and looking at old maps of this part of Wortley, I think the house must originally have been part of the inn next door, and the Goodman's Arms may have been a coaching inn, with stables and accommodation. When these extra buildings were no longer needed, perhaps they had been sold off. The house was attached to the pub by one wall, and certainly had the air of being an older building than anything surrounding it.

The ground floor of the house had two rooms. There was a living kitchen, with a table covered by an orange velour cloth when not in use for eating, a Yorkshire range in cast iron, with a 'fire oven' that was heated directly from the coal fire, a huge and very traditional bank of built-in cupboards and drawers on one side, and a sink that always smelled faintly of potatoes, set into the wall, on the other. There was a gas cooker that must have been greatly prized when first acquired. At the back, the good room had a circular polished wooden table, a dark veneered piano that may have come from Peacock Yard or may have been a later acquisition, an ebonised overmantle and an ornate wooden sideboard, my nana's pride and joy. This room was dark and rather chilly and was mostly used at Christmas or for the occasional family party, although the circular polished table with a claw-footed pillar beneath was often covered with a half-done jigsaw puzzle throughout my childhood. The family liked jigsaws and board games. These puzzles were old even then, so they must have belonged to the previous generation. There were two bedrooms above that: one at the front of the house where my grandparents slept, with a built-in bath in a panelled and tiled nook in the wall. My grandfather had installed this himself and it would have been an unheard-of luxury when first fitted. The water must have been heated by some complicated arrangement of plumbing involving the range in the room beneath. The back bedroom, with a window looking onto the yard, was where my glamorous Aunty Vera slept. She had a green satin eiderdown on her bed, jewellery and make-up on her dressing table. I would sit on the bed and watch her getting ready to go out, doing her thick, wavy hair in its Veronica Lake hairdo, choosing which costume jewellery to wear, putting on lipstick and powder, and pretty earrings in her bravely pierced ears. I loved her dearly. Beyond that, up more steep wooden steps, were the attics, uninhabited now that James Flynn was gone. It was dusty and spooky up there, full of cobwebs, and I seldom ventured up the steep steps without supervision.

Downstairs, between the room where everything happened and the room where almost nothing happened, except on high days and holidays when the fire was lit, there was a back door that led onto stone steps and a paved yard, surrounded by industrial buildings that emitted almost constant noise and chemical smells. In the yard was an old wooden hut where my grandad kept his bits and pieces, his tools, his odds and ends of wood and metal. Long before I was born, Joe, who had the soul of a Dalesman still, had tried to dig a duckpond in the back yard for three ducklings he had bought on a fishing trip. He would bring all kinds of good things back from his angling excursions to the countryside: there were big field mushrooms that were cooked whole in a frying pan with bread cakes to sop up the dark juices, fresh strawberries, sweet and misshapen apples, crumbly curd tarts, honey. We ate well in those days. He was fond of duck eggs, too. But he had been deceived in his purchase. The ducklings were much too young and drowned one by one.

Beyond the yard was an ancient stone-flagged wash-house where there was a copper for boiling water, a posser for pushing down the sheets and towels, a big wringer for squeezing out the surplus water, and 'the salvage': a hangover from the war years when newspapers had to be saved and were stored in a big bin, recycling being nothing new. When I was a small child, all of these things seemed surreptitious and hostile in the darkness, vibrant with the possibility of life. My mother once caught her hand in the wringer and, although no bones were broken, it would forever afterwards go a bluish-white colour, like a dead fish, and feel icy-cold on winter days.

At the back of the wash house was a doorless, white-washed lavatory, set behind a wall to give the occupant some privacy. The whitewash on the walls felt furry, gritty under my fingernails. It flaked off in satisfying lumps. The lavatory, with its warm wooden seat, smelled pleasantly of bleach and lime, a clean smell, but it was very dark at night. It had a high water tank, with a handle on a long chain, and a shelf with shiny, impractical Izal toilet paper. I never went there alone at night. Sometimes I would use the pot, the jerry' as my grandad called it, in the house. But if I did go to the outside 'lav', somebody always went with me. Often it was my aunty Vera, who would take the opportunity to smoke a cigarette, and there would be the comforting scent of it, and the little glow of it, coming and going in the dark.

In the living kitchen, where everything happened, there was a door straight from Whitehall Road, with a curtain over it to keep out the draughts, and an Anaglypta dado on the right-hand wall as you came in. Further along that wall was another door and this led into the chilly sweet and tobacconist shop that my nana ran, with the help of my mother, Kathleen. Beyond the sweet shop was a second shop with sawdust on the floor, where my grandad Joe worked on his fishing tackle, and where I would sit in my own small chair and watch him. I would pester him for the fizzy lemonade that always made me sick. He was endlessly patient with me but sometimes he would give in, unable to bear my pleading. I would drink the lemonade and then I would be very sick and blame him. 'He gave it to me,' I would say, treacherously. He sold maggots in jam jars to little fat anglers with waistcoats stretched over their pot bellies, retirement watches in their pockets with the chains draped across.

'Ey up, Joe,' they would say, faintly patronising. 'Ey up, Joe.'

There was a door from the street that led straight into the sweet shop. This was for the customers, and, beyond that, there was another street door that opened into a stone hallway. This gave access to the fishing tackle shop on the left, while in front, a flight of stone stairs led up to the small two-roomed flat above, where we three lived: myself, my Polish father and my Irish mother. For the first seven years of my life, I lived between that flat with no indoor lavatory and no bath, and my grandparents' house next door.

I was seriously asthmatic, but happy. I don't remember any sense of privation. I knew nothing else. We were by no means wealthy, but there was no risk of homelessness and there was enough money to feed and clothe everybody. The NHS was well under way, so the doctor was available when needed; the clinic at Holbeck gave out free cod liver oil and malt, and free orange juice. The treatments for my chronic asthma were inadequate but they helped, and there were antibiotics to treat my annual successive chest infections. Decent schooling was available, too. Nobody expected me to work a twelve-hour day in a mill. In the big living kitchen next door, my grandmother baked her bread in the fire oven to one side of the range. My mother worked in the sweet and tobacconist shop, standing on the cold stone-flagged floors to weigh out quarters of pear drops and cough candy. My father was happy, working hard, improving his English, cycling through the foggy streets to night school (that was free too); but he was always hoping for a better life.

19. *Still I Love Him*

In the 1970s, having lived in Scotland since I was twelve, I was one of the last students to do a postgraduate Master's course in Folk Life Studies at Leeds University. This was a weird and wonderful amalgam of social and oral history, under the leadership of the great Scottish folklorist Stewart Forson Sanderson. One of the first projects assigned to us was to produce a file of everything that we had learned traditionally, everything that had been passed down orally and not on paper: songs, rhymes, chants and stories that we had never seen written down, but that we knew well. We were in our twenties, so childhood was a vivid and recent memory. We were given plenty of time to do this, and simply told to note things down as they occurred to us over a period of a few months. It was an enlightening project, because most of us found that our notebooks ran to many pages. It was instructive to compare our lists, both for the differences and similarities between the great mass of rhymes and songs, chants and games, which had been passed down in different parts of the country. I doubt if it would be quite the same for students now, but the comparison would still be interesting.

My list ranged from snatches of the popular songs that my mother had sung to me when I was ill to the many skipping and ball game chants I had learned at school, from '*She is handsome, she is pretty, she is the girl of the golden city*' to '*Dip diptation, corporation, how many pigs went to the station?*' Some, we had heard on *Listen with Mother*, on the wireless. ('Are you sitting comfortably?' Daphne Oxenford would say. 'Then I'll begin.') Most, however, I had learned at home and at school. At school, we would circle, hands held, chanting '*Wallflowers, wallflowers, growing up so high, we're all pretty maids and we all have to die, except for Catherine Czerkawska, she's the youngest girl, ah for shame, ah for shame, turn your back to the wall again,*' whereupon the chosen girl would face outwards, holding hands again. This would continue until all the dancers were facing outwards, still circling hand in hand. Much later on I found our rhymes, or versions of them, in a book called *The Singing Game*, by those dedicated collectors of children's rhymes and games, Iona and Peter Opie.

Looking back on that project, I realise just how much was passed down from my grandmother, Nora, with whom I spent so much time as a child. Like my mother, she would sing to me, but while my mother sang popular songs, such as 'Russian Rose' and 'Goodnight My Love', melodies that remain with me to this day and remind me of her, the songs my nana sang seemed to be older and more mysterious. She would sing:

> Good night, number one, good night number two,
> goodnight number three and number four the same to you.
> Goodnight number five, goodnight number six,
> and when you retire, in case of fire,
> don't forget to snuff your little wicks.

I had no idea what these dangerous wicks were, which had to be 'snuffed' in case of fire, even though we did have candles in the house in case of power cuts. But for Nora's mother, Mary Manley, they must have been very real.

There was another rhyme that went:

> You know last night and you know the night before,
> three tom cats came knocking at my door,
> one with a fiddle, one with a drum
> and one with a pancake stuck to its bum.

Quite apart from its delicious rudeness for a very small girl, it sounds like part of a street game, probably a skipping game. It wasn't a rhyme we used at school, but it might have been one that Nora had learned from her mother. It may even have been something that Elizabeth knew and sang and skipped to, because those young Manley sisters must once have skipped in the street. Skipping was a girls' game. A length of rope was always available, no matter what. You could skip alone with a short rope or, more skilfully, with a girl at either end of a long rope, calling in one child after another, until several girls were skipping at once. Chants kept the time and instructed the participants. '*Dirty dirty lady, touch the dirty ground, dirty dirty lady, turn yourself around*,' we sang. Sometimes the rope had to make a full circle, sometimes it was swayed from side to side, so that the participants jumped back and forth over it, two feet together, tricky to keep time, especially when more than one or two girls were involved. 'Bumps', perhaps the hardest of all, involved the rope making a double turn before the skipper hit the ground.

Elizabeth and her friends must have chalked hopscotch

on the paving stones, or bounced two balls, if they could get them, against a wall, in complicated patterns, as I once did. They may have bowled a hoop down the street. My nana certainly remembered doing this when she was a child, and my primary school had a set of hoops in the games cupboard, although they were judged old-fashioned even then, and seldom brought out. Whips and tops were still popular, though, and everyone used them, boys and girls alike. The 'top' was a small wooden cone, with a flat surface and a metal stud at the base, on which it would spin. With it came a 'whip'; a stick with a leather bootlace would do just as well. Whips and tops had their season, starting around Pancake Tuesday, when the weather might start improving. You wound the leather lace around the top of the whip, and then, holding the top in your left hand and the whip in your right, you swung both down, pulling back the whip to release the top at just the right moment, close to but not on the ground. The swift unravelling of the leather would give the top enough momentum to set it free, and the idea was to keep it spinning by whipping it as it went. There was a knack to it, and I remember being able to do it, but I don't remember learning it. Girls in particular would use coloured chalks to make patterns on the flat tops, so that when they spun, the effect was pretty.

There was another chant, a fragment only, of a rhyme about the 'knocker upper'. *'Knocker upper down street, three doors left'*, recalled the human alarm clocks, men and woman who used to go along the streets in the towns and cities of the industrial north, tapping on doors and windows with long poles to wake workers for an early shift. This custom persisted well into the twentieth century in some places, but must have been a feature of Leeds life back when Nora was a girl, and even earlier when the young Manleys were living with their parents in Brussels Street.

It would be hard to exaggerate just how Irish we felt, how the culture, traditions, history and beliefs of Ireland informed so much of our lives when I was young. We knew about the famine. We knew about the treatment meted out to the Irish. Now, I find that I know the words of a dozen rebel or famine songs without ever being conscious of learning them. Even my grandfather, a Dalesman who had served in the Royal Navy, would speak with disgust about the 'Black and Tans', the hated and undisciplined Special Reserve Constabulary, about what they had done in Ireland and how much they were despised by 'proper' soldiers, like his elder brother George, who had been in the West Yorkshire Regiment, and who had died right at the start of the Great War.

There is a traditional song called 'Still I love Him' that seemed to resonate throughout my childhood, since my grandmother and my mother would both sing it. I have seen this described as an English song, and unlikely to be older than the First World War, but identifying the age of a song from its first published appearance is a precarious business. There are many different versions of the song, in Scotland and Ireland as well as in Yorkshire. The melody 'feels' Irish, the formula/formulaic – 'if you want any more you can sing it your- self' – is found in various traditional songs in England and elsewhere, bread rolls are called cakes in Yorkshire, but the plaid shawl might be Irish or Scottish. Whatever its origin, the song has a definite nineteenth-century urban quality. The young man comes down the girl's alley, he goes to an ale house, he goes off with the jeweller. Perhaps it is simply a song of disappointed young women everywhere, giving unconditional love and receiving little but abuse in return, although it is never sung as a sad song. There's a jaunty, defiant quality to it, quite at odds with the words. It could have been Elizabeth Manley's theme song. I doubt if she was ever formally married, but it does seem likely that she was unscrupulously abandoned and that, in the face of misery, she remained defiant to the bitter end.

When I was single, I wore a plaid shawl
Now that I'm married, I've nothing at all
Oh, but still I love him, I'll forgive him
I'll go with him wherever he goes

He came up our alley and he whistled me out
But the tail of his shirt from his trousers hung out
Oh, but still I love him, I'll forgive him
I'll go with him wherever he goes
He bought me a handkerchief, red, white and blue
But before I could wear it, he tore it in two
Oh, but still I love him, I'll forgive him
I'll go with him wherever he goes

He brought me to an ale house and he bought me some stout
But before I could drink it, he ordered me out
Oh, but still I love him, I'll forgive him
I'll go with him wherever he goes
He borrowed some money to buy me a ring
Then he and the jeweller went off on a fling

Oh, but still I love him, I'll forgive him
I'll go with him wherever he goes

There's cakes in the oven, there's cheese on the shelf
If you want any more, you can sing it yourself
Oh, but still I love him, I'll forgive him
I'll go with him wherever he goes

Something else that was handed down to me from my grandmother, without ever being written down, was her baking and her cooking. I never knew her to follow a written recipe, but she would make Yorkshire puddings, rich fruit cakes that my grandad ate sliced with Wensleydale cheese on top, curd tarts, bread pudding, custard tarts with nutmeg, meat and potato pies to make the meat go further but delicious anyway, stews and soups with root vegetables and pearl barley, spare ribs of bacon boiled with cabbage. Double decker was a favourite: the cheapest cuts of beef, chopped carrots and onions, put straight into a heavy, high-sided saucepan, two layers of them, with suet crust in between, and beef stock or an Oxo cube in hot water poured between the layers, simmered for hours at very low heat on top of the stove, filling the kitchen with the glorious scent of cooking meat and vegetables. Some of this must have been food the Manleys would have recognised, food that they must have eaten when they could afford it, always making the expensive meat go just a little further, or managing to do without it altogether.

Everything was eaten with bread because it filled you up, and my grandmother baked a couple of times a week. Pastry would be made on the cool marble slab of an old washstand that sat in the kitchen for that purpose. Bread, though, was always made on a big wooden board and baked in the oven to the side of the range rather than in the gas oven. The flavour was better. The Manleys and the Terran family may have had some kind of cooking facilities in their various homes, or access to an oven at least. By the time Mary was married to James Flynn, and living in a five-roomed house, it's likely that she had a basic Yorkshire range very similar to the one at 32 Whitehall Road, and it would have been on this that Honora had first learned to cook and bake. She would make a large quantity of dough and I would help. I would be allowed to put a little sugar into the block of yeast, and watch the miraculous process as the sugar appeared to melt the yeast and then, with the application of warm water, began to froth. This mixture, with more warm water, would be poured into the middle of the flour, and left to froth still more. Then the energetic process of adding more water while kneading and stretching began. My small, plump nana, in her clean gingham pinafore, her hair tucked back into a slide, would work the dough vigorously, punching and pounding it to smoothness. She would leave a bowl or jug of water on the side and dip her hand into it, introducing extra liquid gradually.

When it was smooth enough, she would leave the dough in her brown baking bowl, covered over with a tea towel, close to the range for a few hours, and then the oven would be brought to the right temperature by the simple expedient of putting more coal on the fire until it blazed bright and hot. She would throw a little flour into the oven to test the temperature. She needed no thermometer, just as I never remember her using a recipe for anything. Too pale and the oven was not hot enough, too dark and the bread would burn, so the fire would have to die down before the baking could begin. Meanwhile, she would shape the dough into loaves and big, flat, tasty breadcakes, each with her thumb print in the middle. Fruit was kneaded into some of the dough to make teacakes. Then they would all be set to prove again before being baked. Oven-bottom cakes were flat breadcakes baked in the bottom of the fire oven so that their bases were more crisp and tasty than the others. Shortcakes were made by rubbing fat into flour, along with dried fruit and a little milk: flat, dense cakes, which were also baked quickly in the bottom of the oven, with soft insides, for buttering, and crisp, slightly scorched outsides, all to be eaten warm and delicious. Something called Irish teacake was made in much the same way, a big circular scone, with less butter, but with sour milk or buttermilk making a soft dough, again baked in the fire oven.

The recipes for many of these things would have been handed down to Honora by her mother, not on paper, but taught, mother to daughter. Mary Manley had known times of poverty, none more so, but these were people who were used to making much out of very little and Honora had learned these skills from her mother. They may have struggled with hunger and a lack of resources, but when plain ingredients and a source of heat were available, these people knew how to make the best of them. Their limitations were all to do with poverty and not a lack of knowledge. Breadmaking was a skill that had been handed down from mother to daughter for a thousand years and more, and there were traditions associated with it, the thumb-print in the middle, the firm belief that the dough, or the baked bread, should not be allowed to fall, and that if anything were dropped in the baking process, it must be blessed with the sign of the cross.

There is a strange tale told in the family that Honora went to Canada, while Joe was away at sea, before the couple were ever married and well before the start of the Great War. She is supposed to have worked there for a while, before coming home again: a huge undertaking at that time. Certainly there are female Flynns on the shipping registers, but it's hard to be sure. Maybe she did go. Maybe it wasn't what she thought it was going to be and she was homesick. Or perhaps she still had a hankering after Joe Sunter. The story goes that she was back home in Peacock Yard, down on her knees, scrubbing the front steps, when Joe came down the street.

'I've been to Canada. Where have you been?' she said.

My grandmother cooked and baked delicious food, with simple ingredients bought in Leeds market, or produce that my grandfather brought back from his trips to the countryside with the angling club. Now the kind of dishes I ate in my childhood feature on the menus of on-trend restaurants, at high prices. I still occasionally read about the dreadful English cooking of the 50s, but I don't recognise any of it. Then it strikes me that so much of the 50s cuisine that was later scorned by middle-class food writers must have been that of their or their parents' childhood, dishes from homes where the post-war servant problem had doomed middle- and upper-class women with no traditional skills to wrestle with unfamiliar ingredients in alien kitchens and produce food with pretensions. This was about as far removed from the oven bottom cakes, the double decker, the Yorkshire puddings and the meat and potato pies of my childhood as it was possible to get. Even so, I sometimes wonder if Nora had some experience of working in a commercial kitchen. Is that what she did, briefly, in Canada? Some of her baking, darioles, for instance, carefully decorated with jam and coconut, and other fancy, light-as-air cakes had the flavour of something far grander than she might ever have learned from Mary Manley.

20. *Aliens*

The years succeeding the Second World War brought another, more exotic influx of foreign migrants to Britain. The refugee Poles who stayed here after that war had something of the cheerful and vivid temperament of the Irish about them, but with less patience and perhaps more confidence. Like the Irish, too, their sad history had all been with their immediate neighbours: Stalinist Russia and Nazi Germany. They had far more liking for their English and Scottish hosts and, for a while, the feeling was mutual. They had done their bit in the war, not least in the Battle of Britain, and the general feelings of the native population towards them, initially at any rate, were more positive than my Irish forebears had ever experienced.

All the same, my father was an alien and that made me and my mother half-alien, too. Julian Czerkawski was born near a village called Dziedzilow to the east of Lwow, in the turbulent Polish borderlands of Galicia. All of these places are now in the Ukraine. Lwow is Lviv. Dziedzilow is Didyliv. My grandfather, Wladyslaw, had been a landowner, one of the Polish minor gentry known as the *szlachta*: fiercely proud, impulsive, unconventional. The more usual form of Dad's name in Poland would be Juliusz, but Wladyslaw was an anglophile and liked the English-sounding version. There was also a more pressing family reason. The estate at Dziedzilow had once belonged to another Julian Czerkawski, a doctor and politician who had been one of the Polish representatives to the Austro-Hungarian parliament. He was my grandfather's great-uncle. I have a copy of his obituary, fulsome in its praise of him. He was a collector of old Polish artefacts, including the ornate, finely woven silk or wool *kontusz* sashes, part of the traditional *szlachta* costume. He also, reputedly, owned a set of the formidable winged armour that, when worn on horseback, had proved so terrifying in battle, so instrumental in a number of victories for the soldiers of the old Polish commonwealth.

Unmarried, he had welcomed his great-nephews and nieces including my grandfather, Wladyslaw, on frequent visits. That branch of the family lived forty miles south of Dziedzilow, where there was another Czerkawski estate. Their mother was Anna Brudzewska, from a rather grand family, major rather than minor nobility, and their father was another Wladyslaw. My grandfather was Dr Julian's favourite, though. Young as he was, he would dare anything, especially on horseback, and was full of the kind of devilry and mischief that would probably be termed anti social behaviour nowadays. It was no surprise to the rest of the family when, upon Julian's death, they discovered he had left the entire estate at Dziedzilow to this great-nephew, my grandfather, who was still much too young to look after it. Anna, by now a widow, but by no means elderly, employed an estate manager, travelled back and forth between the two estates to keep an eye on things and – eventually and somewhat scandalously – married the manager, much to the disapproval of the rest of the family. She gave birth to a daughter, so perhaps the marriage was inevitable. It wasn't only the poor like Mary Manley and Honora Flynn who found themselves in these kinds of difficulties.

Wladyslaw would become one of the last of the great Polish lancers. Not that they ever charged tanks on horseback as the foolish and slightly mocking stories go, but when he was in his teens, he had certainly run away from school to join his elder brothers in fighting the Russians. This was probably the conflict known as the 'Defence of Lemberg' – the Austro-Hungarian name for Lwow – in 1918 and, according to family legend, my grandfather was fourteen years old when he took himself off to fight. He was born circa 1904, ten years before reformed murderer John Ross died of emphysema in Leeds. Accounts of the extraordinary defence of the city tell us that, after the initial clashes, conventional Polish forces were joined by many hundreds of volunteers, including large numbers of students and school pupils, affectionately known as the 'Lwow Eaglets'.

My knowledge of my father's own wartime experiences is sketchy at best. For me, they too seem like snapshots in time, much like the handful of surviving Polish and English family pictures. He didn't like to talk about any of it. I think it was too traumatic and so – in the same way that my grandmother Nora never said much about her own early life – he buried it and got on with things. He was in Lwow in 1939 when the city was caught between the rock of the Nazis and the extremely hard place of Hitler's then-allies, the Russians. His mother tried to get him out of the country. There were relatives living on what was then the border with Romania, and so she sent him off, aged no more than thirteen, with a suitcase – one of those sad, brown, wartime suitcases you see on television dramas – to try to find his way to the border, 300 kilometres distant. He got a long way south, but eventually, learning that the border had been closed, he trudged back to Lwow.

Looking back, there is a part of me that wants to know what happened to him and a part of me that is very glad I never *did* know exactly what happened to him on those interminable walks south and north. I remember him saying it had been a harrowing journey, and that there had been bodies in various states of decay along the sides of the road, where skirmishes had taken place. When he got back to Lwow, he was so covered in filth and lice that his mother made him undress before coming into the house, and his clothes had to be burned, his hair cut very short, to get rid of them.

Dad was an alien. It says so on his papers. I have them still, stored in a box in the room where I write. I've been sifting through them more than once recently, in the hope of reinstating the Polish nationality I acquired at birth, by blood rather than location, and then lost again. It was surrendered for me, although there were, at the time, valid reasons. When I was born, Dad's status made me half-alien too. Actually, it made me three-quarters alien, given that my mother was half-Irish. As soon as she married him, my mother acquired her husband's nationality as well as her own. So there we were, aliens by virtue of birth or assimilation in this brave new post-war world. The borders had arbitrarily shifted and my father's home wasn't even in Poland any more.

Somewhere among those precious papers is a battered

volume of English idioms. My father had arrived in England with a reasonable knowledge of English. He could 'get by', largely thanks to that young anglophile father who had been imprisoned by Stalin, and released, only to die of typhus on the long march east with General Anders's army towards what was then Persia. He is buried at Bukhara on the Silk Road. Dad, meanwhile, had come to a resettlement camp in Yorkshire via Italy and Monte Cassino, where he was lucky to survive. Major Hardy Parker, writing in his memoirs of the day, *Diary of a Soldier*, described how:

> we learnt that the Polish flag was flying over the Monastery. It was very fitting that this should be so, for the Poles have suffered dearly. Georgi, the Polish Liaison officer, told me that the hills behind the Monastery were absolutely indescribable. Hundreds of dead lay all over the hillsides, Americans, French, New Zealanders and now Poles.

Now that he was here, in the place his father had yearned for, Dad set out to improve his command of the language. The volume of idioms is annotated with scribbles here and there in pencil. On one page, he has written out the words of 'You Are My Sunshine', a song he used to sing to me, one which, when I suddenly came across his book all over again a few years ago, long after his death, made me cry. Among other things, he used to write notes and letters for some of the Poles in the camp if they wanted to contact the English girls they might have met at the dances in Helmsley village hall. His English may not have been perfect at that time, but it was good enough for a love letter.

Some time in the late '40s, Dad was demobbed from

the camp at Duncombe Park with his pinstripe suit, his raincoat, a couple of shirts, a spare set of underwear and very little else. British servicemen and women had to be reabsorbed into the day-to-day life of the country, but most of them had homes to go to, however difficult the adjustment. The refugee aliens, much like the Irish of the previous century, had nothing except the scant handful of personal possessions they had been able to bring with them. In the case of the Polish refugees, it was generally a few family photographs, their essential documents, and the civvies they had been given. Dad had also managed to bring a tiny silver hand mirror that had belonged to his mother, out of her travelling vanity case. Many of the demob suits were made by Montague Burton, which meant that they were probably made in Leeds, by members of the family into which Julian would soon marry. The demob raincoat must have been serviceable, because I remember it from my own childhood. There are several snapshots of him wearing it, looking mean and moody (which he never was) and very foreign, very alien indeed. He looked what he was: a Slav from the East with high cheekbones and black wavy hair.

There were reserved occupations at that time and Julian had to choose between mills and mines, so he chose the mills. Again like my Irish forebears, he went to work as a textile presser in a woollen mill somewhere in Leeds. The Poles were helped to get digs, usually a room in a lodging house with a landlady who supplied an evening meal. It was a dreary, circumscribed kind of life, until he met my mother. Kathleen Irene was the youngest daughter of Joe Sunter and Nora Flynn and, like Julian, she was born in 1926. She had been just young enough to be evacuated to the countryside during the early years of the war, but she hadn't liked it much and had simply got on a bus – with the same kind of brown suitcase that my father had hauled about in much worse circumstances at about the same age – and had run away back home to 32 Whitehall Road.

Kathleen had several siblings. Nora and George were older, but the two youngest sisters, Kathleen and Vera, were very close. George was in the Royal Navy like his father before him, and Nora had been in the WRNS, so hadn't lived at home for the duration of the war. There were plenty of refugee Poles in Leeds and, given that they could be charming and attractively exotic, they were not always popular with the local lads. Everyone went dancing in the city centre, and Julian and Kathleen met in the Mecca Ballroom. There was a Master of Ceremonies and you weren't allowed to sit out without a good excuse. You came there to dance, and dance you did. On the night when they first met, Kathleen had a cold sore developing on her lip and, never one to bother over much about appearances, had her hair tied back with a shoelace and was wearing no make-up. In spite of that, she was a remarkably pretty young woman and this is true in practically every snapshot I have of her from that time.

My parents were in love for the whole of their married life. I think it had been a *coup de foudre*, love at first sight. Now, when I look at photographs of them, black-and-white snapshots from that time, they seem invariably happy: joyful beyond the usual smiles for the camera. Sometimes there's a picture of Julian looking alien in his demob raincoat and once like a gangster, inexplicably in the middle of a field, in his demob suit. Sometimes there's Mum, smiling at the man behind the camera. She's wearing a full tartan skirt, with soft pleats, quite short for the forties, showing off her long legs. In these pictures, Mum's hair is always a dark tangle, while Dad still has his wartime thinness, spare, dark and foreign.

They married on 21 January in 1949 and spent their honeymoon in Scarborough: a long weekend, so that Julian could go back to work and Kathleen would be around for the shop on Monday. There had been a few problems in arranging the wedding. The refugee aliens had great difficulty in accessing official papers after the war. My mother, like all the Flynn Sunter children, had been baptised and brought up as a Catholic, albeit not what you would call a 'red-hot' Catholic. My grandfather Joe, nominally Methodist but in reality not much at all in terms of religious belief, wisely kept his own counsel. Nora's marriage to a Methodist had been unusual, but also characteristic of her steely determination to do whatever she wanted with her life. Nevertheless, the children had been brought up as Catholics. My mother kept the faith her whole life long. She didn't go to church very much, but she believed as confidently and assuredly as she believed in the sun rising in the morning and setting at night.

There was no problem in Kathleen marrying a Pole in church, and no problem in assuming that he was a Roman Catholic, since he clearly knew what was what when questioned about the tenets of the faith. What did cause a huge potential problem was the suspicion that the occasional Eastern European refugee might have left a wife and family behind in Poland and conveniently 'forgotten' all about them. Some proof that this was not the case might be demanded, and it was almost impossible to obtain, now that the Iron Curtain was very firmly in place. I used to imagine it as a literal curtain, gleaming metal folds dividing a whole continent. The state authorities seemed to accept the information given by the army about individuals, but the church was inclined to be more suspicious. One of my father's fellow lodgers in his digs fell for, courted and almost married the landlady's daughter, until somebody pointed out that he did indeed have a wife and child back home in Poland. It wasn't commonplace and, besides, Julian had been too young to have acquired a wife when occupation turned his world upside down, too busy surviving to think about marriage.

It was, predictably enough, Kathleen who first lost patience with the priest; Kathleen who pointed out sweetly but forcefully that if they couldn't be married in church, she was quite prepared to be married in the nearest registry office, whereupon the priest capitulated immediately. Spider silk again. Julian wore his demob suit and Kathleen wore a smart 'costume', although whether it was lovingly tailored by one of her talented sisters or bought in the city centre with carefully hoarded clothing coupons, I don't know. They took taxis to and from the church, an unheard-of luxury, and on the way back, Charles Trenet was singing 'La Mer', and that was their song forever after. My father, the kindest of men, seeking peace after the turbulence of the past years, must nevertheless have brought with him a sense of widening horizons.

The flat they returned to was a very far cry from the large house in the countryside in which my father had spent much of his childhood, but I don't think he ever complained. I think he was too happy to have found a kind of sanctuary with my mother. They had a couple of years alone together before I was born in December 1950. Julian worked long hours at the mill, pressing woollen cloth, my mother still helped out in the shop, weighing out quarter pounds of pear drops, cream-line toffees and cough candy for the millworkers and forge workers and the suit makers at Maenson, who came through the ginnel beside the Goodman's Arms every morning and went back again at night. They would still go dancing at the Mecca or to the pictures at the Gainsborough on Domestic Street. In summer they would take the bus out to Ilkley and walk on the moors above the town, visiting the little white building called White Wells or clambering about the Cow and Calf rocks. In autumn there would be blackberries to pick and take home to make into jam or pies. At some point during those early years, Julian began to study, not just to improve his English but to fill in the gaps in his education, especially in maths and the sciences, for which he was displaying a real aptitude.

I remember a happy, if unhealthy, childhood for the first seven years of my life. But the truth is that although I was well loved and well fed and comfortable, for my parents and extended family, there were troubles enough. The water in the glass by the bed froze overnight. The frost coated the insides of all the windows in dense, beautiful patterns by morning. The house was beset by persistent industrial fumes from Petty's, the printing company next door, as well as smoke from the railways nearby, fumes from all of the factories between New Wortley, Holbeck and the polluted river. The canal was seriously polluted too, filthy with rainbow slicks of oil and scummy foam. When I look at the handful of surviving pictures of that slightly crumbling house now – so cheerful inside – I can see that it is not really how I remember it. Some nights I wheezed so much that my parents couldn't distinguish between the wheezing and clanking of my lungs and the noises from the railway goods yard only a little way along the road. The smog came in and left thick yellow trails around the lights. The dust and grime got in too and coated everything. My father was dubbed an alien and now my mother and I were half-alien, too, with all that that implied. There was a sense in which Kathleen had leaped from the Irish migrant frying pan into a Polish refugee fire. She would tell how somebody, chatting to her in the local grocery shop, had remarked that they should 'send all those Poles back, now that the war is over, don't you think so?' to which my mother replied, 'Not really, seeing as how I've just married one.'

Whenever a crime was committed in the city, whenever a foreigner was involved – and foreigners were always suspected, just as the Irish had always been suspected in a previous generation – the police would come calling, hammering on the door at the bottom of the stairs to check that Dad was at home and not involved in nefarious pursuits in central Leeds. Or they did until Kathleen, with a new baby and a short fuse, one that she had clearly inherited from all those women like Honora and Mary and Elizabeth, who had managed to be both cheeky and defiant on the verge of death, sent them packing, telling them in no uncertain terms that if they ever came back again she wouldn't be responsible for her behaviour.

They never did come back. One more indication of

change, perhaps. Or just another indication of the merry-go-round of acceptance and suspicion that characterises our attitude to incomers.

21. *Hunt the Thimble*

Late in the 1950s, Dad had learned fluent English, taken some qualifications, managed to get a BSc and was studying for a PhD on some kind of fellowship, as well as teaching chemistry to young printing students to help fund it. My parents would later joke that they could afford only a single pair of pyjamas between them. We three had moved away from the pollution of Whitehall Road and my health was improving, albeit slowly. We were living in a big, chilly council flat, part of an old vicarage in Bellevue Road on the other side of Leeds, near Woodhouse Moor. Impractical as a vicarage, it had been sold to the council for conversion into flats. The water still froze in the glass on winter mornings. In addition to the essential paraffin heaters and hot water bottles, my father, very keen on problem solving, had made a patent bed-heating device we called the Rat Lamp: a rat cage from the grim experimental basement of the School of Medicine, with a light bulb rigged up inside it. He would put it in my bed an hour before bedtime and switch the lamp on, so that the sheets would be nice and warm as I crept in.

Although we had moved house, I stayed on at the same school, Holy Family Primary in Armley, and my mother walked me across town so that I could catch the bus the remaining half-mile to school every morning. Then she would go back and help out at home or in the sweet shop, as long as it remained open. But Nora and Joe were becoming frail and needed care. For a while, she also worked for Phyllis Naylor, in her newsagent's shop in Holbeck, just along the road from Lake's Corner, where my grandmother's friend Ethel Lake kept a grocery shop with her husband Fred. The shop sold the best butter, which came in big yellow mounds, and the shop always smelled of good things: bacon and cheese, fresh vegetables and the faint, appetising scent of the stews Ethel always seemed to be cooking for their dinner. Just along the road, Phyllis Naylor had a television and two fierce Alsatian dogs to protect it and her shop. Hardly anybody had a television in those days, not in Holbeck anyway, so we went there to see Princess Margaret's wedding on a tiny black-and-white screen with a crowd of people huddling around to watch.

In the mornings, especially on winter mornings, I would often be flagging by the time we got close to 32 Whitehall Road, wheezing or coughing. On those days, rather a lot of days, I never quite made it to school, spending the time reading and drawing and baking in my nana's kitchen instead. When I was seven or eight years old, I managed to catch measles, mumps and whooping cough, all in the same year. Later, when we were living in Bellevue Road, I contracted hepatitis B (the school lavatories left a lot to be desired) and spent weeks on a diet of boiled fish and other bland foods. The doctor, as blithely autocratic as doctors were back then, recommended a holiday for me to recuperate. He didn't understand that convalescent holidays were way beyond our means, but we managed a week at Cayton Bay on the Yorkshire coast, staying in a small, damp and rickety caravan that smelled of Calor Gas. It was early in the springtime and very cold. Snapshots show me muffled up in a duffle coat and scarf. We picked vast bunches of primroses and I felt better, although still dazed from the sickness. I think if I had been born even fifty years earlier, I would have met with the same fate as those other children who had not survived infancy, but I was lucky.

I was a strange child, with a handsome foreign father, a forthright Irish mother and a head full of fantasies. I never knew quite where I belonged. My accent was the broad Yorkshire accent of my Leeds family and playmates, but my name was tricky. When first I went to school, it took me a long time to learn how to spell it. I knew some Polish words. I knew my name in Polish: Katarzyna. I had a Polish 'costume' that my mother had sewn for me: a red felt skirt, an embroidered waistcoat, long socks with tassels on them, carefully made by my dad.

I drank Ovaltine at night, and listened to the Ovaltineys singing on the wireless, although their cut-glass accents and their keenness on games and sports were about as far removed from my life back then as it was possible to be.

Every Christmas, Ronald Tunbridge, Professor of Medicine at Leeds University, threw a party for the children of all those who worked in the department, from the lowliest PhD students and the young post-doctoral fellows to various heads of lesser departments. The house was striking, with an enormous garden. We went by bus, of course. It was somewhere in Headingley, well above the smoke. I remember a posh but kindly woman who must have been his wife, and the professor himself, towering over me, a benevolent man, cheerful and welcoming.

I knew nobody. There was a Christmas tree and a big fireplace with a fire as cheerful as the professor. They were burning logs. We burned only coal, lighting the fire with newspaper twists and little pieces of dry wood we called chips. Sometimes you had to hold a sheet of newspaper in front of the fire to make it draw, to get it started, until the flames roared up the chimney and singed the paper. This fireplace looked much too big for any newspaper to fit. The rooms were vast, full of chattering adults and children who were obviously familiar with one another. Perhaps they attended the same schools but they were not my friends, nor did they speak like me. My only advantage, the only things about me that fitted into this milieu, were my clothes, perhaps even my general appearance. My hair was long and thick and dark and my mother would have plaited it and coiled it up on top of my head. My dress was a typical, fashionable late-50s party dress in pale organdie, with little blue and green roses, a full skirt and a dainty matching paper rose pinned at the neck. My mother was a fine seamstress, too, like Nora before her, like her sisters, and my clothes were always striking, although I didn't realise it at the time. They didn't look home-made, or only hand-made in the way that couture clothes are hand-made. People must have wondered where on earth I got them, since my father was on a minuscule salary. She made splendid clothes for me and for herself, but never could bring herself to wear a hat, at a time when middle-class women generally did. That marked her out as different too.

The food seemed wonderfully sophisticated at those parties: dainty, warm sausage rolls and soft little bread rolls with delicious fillings, pretty cakes that disappeared in one delectable mouthful. This was nothing like the occasional parties at home, where the food was appetising and plentiful but plain. It was nothing like the Christmas parties at school, with not-so-appetising bread and jam, and orange squash so dilute as to be only just distinguishable from plain water. I loved those professorial parties and I hated them. As soon as I opened my mouth, I was pigeon-holed. My accent was all wrong. I may have been articulate, but I spoke the Leeds of my home and my schoolmates. And I was shy. Hopelessly, helplessly, achingly shy.

We played party games.

These were well-organised, middle-class party games. We played hunt the thimble and I singularly failed to find the thimble. Half a century and more later, I can still feel the hot-cheeked dizzying embarrassment of it all. The rules of the game were that when you saw the thimble, you left the game and sat down. Being a nice, well-brought-up little girl, it never even occurred to me to lie, so I wandered around, increasingly panic-stricken, hunting for the damned elusive thimble. I remember a room full of grinning adults and tittering children. I knew what a thimble was, of course. My mother and my nana used them all the time. But this didn't seem to be the kind of environment in which a thimble would ever be found. With hindsight, I can see that the professor's wife probably did fine embroidery, much as my mother did beautiful embroidery, whenever she could find the time for it.

I wandered around in my organdie dress with the blue roses, and my patent-leather ankle-strap shoes, which I had been so proud of at the beginning of the afternoon, looking here, there and everywhere for the thimble. I have no memory of what my parents were doing, but I can only assume that they were paralysed with horror. At last, Professor Tunbridge, who was a kindly man, and – in retrospect – must also have been desperate for the game to end, said, 'Think, Catherine. Where would you expect to find a thimble?'

I went straight to the mantelpiece, with its toffee-coloured tiles and its Christmas decorations. It was where almost everything was randomly put down, everything that would be needed again soon, in my grandparents' big living kitchen, in our two-room flat and even in our new flat on Bellevue Road. There was always sewing going on in our house, and the thimbles were always somewhere within easy reach, usually on the mantelpiece, with the matches, the random ornaments, a bit of spare change, Dad's pipe, a pencil or two. There were sewing boxes but somehow the thimbles never made it back into them.

My, how they laughed.

I remember the roar of laughter from the assembled company, young and old. I remember the heat, flaming on my cheeks, and not knowing whether it was the heat of the fire or something else. To this day, the memory of it is enough to bring me out in a retrospective flush of embarrassment. The thimble was, of course, neatly placed on some elegant female finger. She waved it at me. And they all laughed again.

They were as far removed from me as I was I from them. Our experiences were so utterly different and that went for my father too, in spite of or perhaps because of his aristocratic background, that we were as alien to one another as Elizabeth Manley would have been to the doctors and attendants who repeatedly questioned her during her stays in the various asylums. They might as well have been asking her to hunt the thimble. The differences were as great as that between a big institution and a small cabbage. At that moment, I was the smallest of small cabbages.

Some time later, I passed my Eleven Plus exam, which meant I was destined for grammar school, where I wore a fancy uniform (still made by my mother to patterns supplied by the school) and mixed with girls called Deborah and Penelope, instead of the Bridgets and Bernadettes of my primary school. So I have some inkling of differences, of embarrassment and helplessness in the face of the chasms that lie between the experiences of different sets of people. Even with the reality of all that stored in my memory, I can't really know the lives that these people led, can't know the life that Elizabeth Manley led, the desperation, the vulnerability, the constant battle against filth in appalling conditions, the desire for something better, the longing to escape, the betrayal in whatever form it took, and the sense that there was no help available from anywhere. I can try to imagine, as I try to imagine every time I write a piece of fiction, but I can't really know. None of us can.

22. *People Like Us*

Earlier in this story, I wrote about the historical novelist wanting to know what something 'felt like'. The trouble is that we can never really know what it looked like, can never really smell and taste the past, so knowing what it felt like to those most closely involved is well-nigh impossible. Even with the most vivid imagination in the world, we can't go back. Not only is there no time machine, no Tardis waiting to whisk us into the past, but we can't unlearn what we know, our own insights, beliefs and prejudices. We can offer a more or less good approximation, we can illuminate, that's all. Where social history is concerned, especially the social history of women, so many of whom tend to be excluded from the bigger picture, it's almost impossible to know anything for sure.

Television, even good, well-made television with high production values, sanitises. Film goes further and glamourises. As far as the relentless cruelty of those times goes, the unenviable position of poor workers in the industrial north, even the very best fiction tends to offer an escape, a resolution. Some people, like Mary and James Flynn, or like my grandmother and grandfather, Nora and Joe, escaped, after a fashion. But the social changes of a new century were instrumental in that escape. The tragedy of a war that deprived my father of his own family allowed him to seek a new one, thousands of miles away. For many thousands of Irish and other migrants living and working in nineteenth-century British cities, there was no way out. For many, even now, there is no way out. And yet the temptation for anyone telling their stories is always to shape, to resolve, as well as to illuminate. Even this story has a satisfying shape of sorts, although it is not fiction, but a true story, or as true as I can make it. I succumbed to the temptation myself, foresaw some kind of happy ending, right at the start, gazing at that joyful picture of my mother and my aunt, striding out into the future with their friends on a seaside jaunt: fine, brave, brilliant young women with the world at their feet.

Even as I was writing that, I found myself thinking about their elder sister, my Aunt Nora, who was a fine pianist. I'm not sure where she learned, but if it's true that Honora could play as well, perhaps she taught her eldest daughter, Nora. There was an old, upright, black veneered piano in 'the room': the posh back room of that house at 32 Whitehall Road. Nora could play it, and she could play so well that when she was a young woman, she was offered a scholarship to Leeds College of Music, one that she never took up, because 'people like us' didn't do that. Besides, even with the scholarship, there wouldn't have been enough money. She had to work. She was more than ten years older than my mother, born to Honora and Joe in 1914, around the start of the First World War. When Nora was young, she took a job playing for the silent movies in one of the nearby cinemas, and when she was older, she would sometimes play at family gatherings. I can picture her doing it, vigorously, almost angrily, stumbling over the notes a little, but still with the flair and talent that must have characterised her earlier performances.

It was a sign of the changing times that, up in the attic, in the room once inhabited by James Flynn, was an extraordinary toy called a Galloping Scooter. Two prancing ponies in front were propelled by pedals attached to the carriage in which a small child could sit. My grandfather, who was serving in the navy, had bought it for his little daughter Nora in Hamleys when he was passing through London on his way home on leave or more likely at the end of the war. A rather dour Yorkshireman – although never when he was with me – he was occasionally prone to these extravagant and loving gestures. It was a sign of the *unchanging* times that the first time my grandmother took Nora out on the galloping scooter, in Holbeck, they were so mobbed with children that the toy was consigned to the attic and never taken out again. It was a toy more suited to Headingley than to Holbeck. It stayed there in pristine condition until my aunt donated it to the Castle Museum in York, many years later.

But Honora and Joe were, by this time, much better off than working-class families would have been a century earlier, much better off than the Manleys and the Everons, escaping famine only to meet with extremes of poverty and prejudice. Charles Dickens, perhaps our finest English-language exponent of the plight of the working poor, had been forced to work in a blacking factory at the age of twelve, while his father was in a debtor's prison. The rest of the family, his mother and siblings, moved nearer the prison, so that they could support their father, leaving Charles to live alone. This experience of poverty and solitary hardship informs so many of his books, from *A Christmas Carol* to *Oliver Twist* and – his own favourite – *David Copperfield*. These experiences were unforgettable and he was to describe them in a number of his novels. Charles returned to school when his father received an inheritance and was able to repay his debts. But in 1827, at the age of fifteen, he was again forced to leave school and work as an office boy. This fine writer, with a difficult childhood and a keen eye for the injustices he saw around him, may have got closer to the truth of the state of the poor than almost any English-language novelist of the time, and shocked a nation in consequence, not least in *A Christmas Carol* with its intentional sting in the tail.

> 'This boy is Ignorance. This girl is Want. Beware them both, and all of their degree, but most of all beware this boy, for on his brow I see that written which is Doom, unless the writing be erased. Deny it,' cried the Spirit, stretching out its hand towards the city. 'Slander those who tell it ye. Admit it for your factious purposes, and make it worse. And abide the end.'
>
> 'Have they no refuge or resource,' cried Scrooge.
>
> 'Are there no prisons,' said the Spirit, turning on him for the last time with his own words. 'Are there no workhouses.'

All the same, swathes of middle-class writers, Victorian and later, tried and failed to illuminate the terrible conditions in which vast numbers of people were living and working, because those most badly affected had no voice of their own.

How could they be otherwise? They could neither read

nor write. The voices they once had, the Irish, the Highland Scots, the Dales people who, like my grandfather's antecedents, had fled terrible conditions in the lead mines of Swaledale, economic migrants all of them, had effectively been silenced. The languages and dialects they spoke were denigrated or proscribed. The Gaelic languages in particular were so disparaged that they could, in all seriousness, be hated and mocked by Friedrich Engels, a native German speaker, when they were heard on the streets of Manchester. His English friends would have agreed with him. The songs these people sang and the stories they told were mocked. The traditions they held dear were dismissed as superstitious nonsense. These people were scorned simply for being what they were. Those who found their voices were too often castigated for speaking out. For such people, in later years, it was almost impossible to describe the times they had known and most of them didn't even try, although they did still sing the songs and tell the tales, nostalgic for the country they had lost, while acknowledging the impossibility, for them at least, of ever going back. For too many years, Ireland's greatest export was people, although this looks like a trend that is set to be reversed.

The true plight of working-class women in particular in industrial Britain is hardly ever evoked in any meaningful way. Henry Mayhew's verbatim accounts are the closest I have ever come to hearing the voice of the industrial poor, men and women, picturing and hearing them as I read, although when he is writing about the Irish, sympathetic as he is, even he transcribes their words into a kind of fake brogue. Elizabeth Gaskell's factory workers, as fine a writer as she is, seem like minor characters beside the true heroes and heroines. Bessy Higgins is as beautifully drawn and sympathetic a portrayal of a young working-class woman as you will find, but even so, she is there mainly to teach tolerance to Margaret Hale. Such characters are seldom permitted agency, seldom allowed to be defiant or angry on their own behalf, as we perceive that Elizabeth Manley – mad or not – seems to have been both defiant and deeply, viscerally angry about her fate. There have been stories about upper-class women in Victorian Britain wrongly consigned to insane asylums, brave stories tackling domestic abuse, such as Wilkie Collins's *The Woman in White* and Anne Brontë's *The Tenant of Wildfell Hall*. But where are the stories about the Elizabeths of this world: the young women whose lives seemed to be worth less than nothing in the grand scheme of things?

It is too easy to see her only as a victim. She had some happy times. She would have felt joy and sorrow, love as well as pain. She had her hopes for a better future. We know she did, because there would have been little reason except the hope of something better and more fulfilling to take her all the way to Glasgow. We know something of the songs she sang, the stories she told and the games she played. She would have skipped in the street as I once did. Everyone 'played out' in all weathers, because the houses were too small to permit anything else. She too may have chanted about the girl of the golden city and giggled about the tom cat with the pancake stuck to its bum. Her mother would have taught her how to bake bread, how to sew, how to wash clothes. Did Mary Manley senior speak and sing in the Irish language? It's quite possible that she did. She came from an area where the language was spoken. The decline had begun before the famine, but it was still widely, albeit often privately, spoken about. Sometimes people wouldn't admit to knowing it, since they had been made to feel ashamed of it. For those contemplating migration, English was essential. Did Elizabeth speak, as I did, with the dialect of the city where she was born, or had she picked up at least some of her words and ways of speaking from her Irish parents? Did she learn how to use yellow 'donkey stone', handed out by the rag and bone man in exchange for a few rags, to craft careful and beautiful designs on the steps of the house in Brussels Street, as my grandmother Nora did, desperately making silk purses out of sows' ears?

Even factual accounts from those times are either disapproving or remote. Or – like Engels's manifesto – powerful but prejudiced. The truth is that the reality of what it must have been like for these people constantly slides away from us, just as it slid away from me, as I was writing this. Ultimately, I came to the conclusion that the reason for the almost constant knot of anguish I felt somewhere inside me, as I tried to write this story, perhaps most of all as I tried to write and come to terms with Elizabeth's story, was the fear that even though I was writing something very close to home, there was no way of getting to the heart of it.

*

Every once in a while, I dream about 32 Whitehall Road, the house in Leeds where I spent the first seven years of my life. Sometimes I'm outside, in a different part of the city, looking for the house, knowing that it is still there, if only I can find it. Buses are running but I have forgotten how to get there, forgotten which buses to take. The city has changed beyond recognition, but the house is still there, only I have lost my way.

Sometimes the house is as I remember it: warm, a little dusty, with a fire that smokes when the wind is blowing in the wrong direction. I can see the steps at the front door that my nana carefully decorated with donkey stone and the curtain to keep out the draughts and the Anaglypta dado. It is full of heavy furniture and the scent of baking, just as it was then. Sometimes it is empty and distressing, but occasionally in the dream, it is not derelict. It is an ancient house, richly ornamented, the stones older than I ever realised, tunnelling deep under the bedrock of the city, and those are the strangest dreams of all.

We must have gone back on a visit to Leeds when the house was derelict, before it was demolished, before the new millennium, when the nice old pub next door was demolished too, and the land was absorbed by Petty's, the big printing company that had grown and surrounded it as efficiently as any parasitic plant. Perhaps it was when I was travelling to Leeds University for my postgraduate course. I don't remember the time, but I do remember that peculiar, unmistakable smell of an abandoned building: lathe and plaster, mould, mice, the few remaining fragments of the rich and complicated lives that we lived there, hanging like shreds of wallpaper.

Two things stick in my mind from that visit. One is the mildewed remains of a once-treasured photograph of my grandfather, Joe Sunter, a handsome seaman, in oriental dress. The photograph – along with a vivid dragon tattoo that once fascinated my younger self – was one of the few reminders of his time at sea and all his travels. He might have had it done in Singapore. My grandparents were dead by the time of that last visit, and the house had been empty for years, but there was the picture of Joe Sunter, ghostly, all but destroyed by damp and hungry mice. Besides that, there was an old toy dog. Brown Dog Dingo I had called him. A visiting cousin, also called Joe, had come on an infrequent visit. He had brought Brown Dog Dingo and a silk bomber jacket with an embroidered dragon on the back and tiny dragons on the front. This was from Hong Kong, where he was stationed with the army. I can remember wearing it, remember being five or six years old with envious boys pointing at me.

They had seen nothing like it in 1950s Leeds. Nobody had.

I grew out of the jacket and Brown Dog Dingo, too. Going back, he seemed ridiculously small, although when I was a little girl, he had been enormous. When we moved, when I was seven, my dolls and teddies had all gone with me. But not the dog. The woolly dog was mildewed and threadbare and for some reason, we had abandoned him on the floor, in the attic bedroom where James Flynn had once slept. James who knew how to lilt and was generous to a fault; who had rescued Mary Terran and her children from abject poverty and abuse and brought them over the river. Who could do nothing at all to rescue poor Elizabeth, thought mad and treated accordingly, when she had possibly been passionately, angrily sad. Elizabeth, whose story brought and still does bring a lump to my throat and a sensation of rage on her behalf so strong that I don't know what to do with it. And my nana, Honora, who sometimes spoke about her poor, red-headed uncle John, who was murdered in the street on Christmas Day, but who never once spoke about his sister, whose life was also ruined, just as she never spoke about her own twin girls, but kept those remarkable losses tucked away under the softness of her gingham pinafore, against which I was content to lay my head.

In both versions of the dream, whether the house is derelict or not, I find myself going down into the cellars, although I seldom saw them in real life. The uneven stone cellar steps were dangerous, and I wasn't allowed to go down there, except once in a while, when my father or my grandad was fetching coal, and I ventured cautiously in their wake, before being sent back up to the living kitchen. It was dirty down there, full of coal dust and cobwebs, and the cellars seemed to stretch on and on, as perhaps they did. These were very old houses, in an old part of the city. I don't know if anyone had ever lived in these cellars as they had once lived in the cellars over the river, in Brussels Street and Off Street and Brick Street, as some of my forebears themselves had almost certainly done.

Maybe the house, with its adjacent buildings, had been part of the inn next door, fortuitously situated on one of the main routes into the city, as the Gallowgate had once been a main road into Glasgow. There had been springs too, like at Spoutmouth, until the clutter of the Industrial Revolution, the mills, the factories and forges, the roads and bridges and railways, slowly but surely choked out every hint of green.

In every version of the recurring dream, the cellar is not what it was, a dark, dangerous, cobweb-ridden place. The cellar is a treasure trove, full of long-buried items, collections of precious things, gleaming, built up over time, layers and layers of artefacts. The cellar goes on and on, beneath the city. And in every dream, I find myself exclaiming over my finds and wondering, 'How could I not know about these things when I lived here for seven years?' But it is only a dream, and it comes very seldom, perhaps because I find it at once tantalising and distressing. I want to stay, I long for the dream to go on and on

The truth is that the house is gone, demolished to make way for a factory that is partly gone itself. Sometimes the house is as it was on that last visit, derelict, with only the cellar sheltering hidden treasures. Rarely, I open the door and exclaim, 'But it isn't so bad after all. You could make something of this! It's all right. You could do something with this! You could even live here.'

A little while ago, the dream came back to me again, and this time, there was no need to go down into the cellars. The house itself was warm again, full of life and light, full of people who had once been loved and had loved in return, people who had suffered terribly, who may have behaved badly, but who had also laughed and sung and survived, who were still loved and remembered. That may have been the most enticing and distressing dream of all. Waking, it occurred to me that all of these things had been heading for the surface, like moles casting up fresh earth. *I am flesh of the flesh of these lowly, I am bone of their bone.* The time had come to take these things out into the light, and examine them at last.

THE END

Appendix

John Ross Trial Transcript

Regina v John Ross, tried before the honourable Mr Justice Cave and convicted of murder.

Leeds Assizes, 10 February 1882.
Mr Barker and Mr Walton for the prosecution.
Mr Lockwood for the defence.

Trial transcript

James Rooks, cloth dresser, Mason's Buildings, York Street, Leeds

I was with Manley, the deceased, on Xmas day from 9am, went with him to Railway Hotel, York Street, shortly after 6pm. Manley was not sober. None of us were. I knew what I was doing. Ross came in while we were there about 9.30 or 9.40pm. He asked for a pint and the landlord would not fill him it. I was sitting right-hand side in the dram shop with Manley. Ross came into the dram shop alone. You go through the tap to get to the bar. [There would have been a tap-room, where the beer was served, and the dram shop must have been something like a snug.] *Manley and I were quarrelling about fighting and Ross interfered. Manley said if he'd been there he would have hit McDonald. Ross said he couldn't. Manley said he could and they were quarrelling a bit. Ross said he could hit him* [Manley], *Ross and Manley pulled sixpence out and matched to fight between me and Ross in the morning. Ross said he could pay the pair of us. Manley said he wasn't a fighting man and didn't want to fight. We were quarrelling a bit and the landlord came in and turned us out. Outside we were all three quarrelling and Ross said if he'd any one with him he'd fight the pair of us. He then gave a bit of a turn and put his hand in his pocket. He pulled a knife out and stuck it into Manley's neck before he fell but not after. Doherty ran after Ross. Manley's hand were in his coat pocket when he was struck.* [Cross-examined]: *Had only been to one public house that day. Was there in the morning from 12.30 to 2.30. From 2.30 to 6 I was drinking with Manley. The fight between McDonald and Brannagan had come off that day. We were quarrelling a quarter of an hour or twenty minutes with Ross before we were turned out and we were quarrelling six or seven minutes outside. Only remember Kilvington outside. Think I should have seen Mrs O'Connor if she had been there. I did not see her there. All three were standing close together when the blow was struck. There was no quarrel between Ross and Manley. They were always friends. Did not see Manley put his hand up – was not watching him all the time. The knife was left sticking in Manley's neck. It was a pocket knife, such as is used for cutting tobacco. Ross was between me and Manley.* [Re-examined]: *Could see both Ross and Manley.*

Edward Kilvington, moulder, 9 Lumb Street, Leeds

Was at Railway Hotel, York Street on Xmas Night until house was cleared. Saw Manley. Rooks and Ross there. There was no fighting between them in the house. I left with them. I was the first to go out and remained outside. I heard Ross and Rooks quarrelling about fighting outside. Manley stood behind Rooks on left-hand side. He was talking to a young fellow behind. I saw Manley fall. This was about two minutes after he was talking to the young man. Heard Ross say if he had a knife he'd put it through his [Manley's] *heart. When Manley fell, I saw Ross turning around to run away and he ran away. He dropped his cap and I picked it up. He did not stop for it.* [Cross-examined]*: One sixpence was staked with me by Ross to fight Manley. No one staked on the other side. Will swear Manley did not produce sixpence. Did not see Mrs Connor outside. He said if he had a knife he'd put it through Manley. He said he'd put it through his heart. He didn't say if he had a knife he'd rip the pair of them. I was in the Railway Hotel about 1pm and stayed there till 2.30. I went again between 6.30 and 7 and stayed till turning out time.* [Re-examined]: *They were quarrelling outside about three minutes before Manley fell. I was stood a few yards off them.*

John Hardaker, landlord of Railway Hotel

Manley came in soon after we opened at 6pm on Xmas Night. Rooks and Kilvington and two or three others were with him. Ross, the prisoner, came in with two men at 9.20 or 30. I stopped them in the passage.

I would not let them go in because the other two were very drunk. Ross asked to be allowed to look into the tap-room for someone. I allowed him. He went into the tap-room and in a few minutes came again into the vault where Manley was sat down. After Ross got in, they began talking about fighting. I noticed some money being put down. I put the light out and asked them to leave when I saw the money being put down. This was a few minutes to 10. They were talking about fighting – making a match.

Elizabeth Manley

I live at Number 5 Brussels Street. John Manley was my brother. He was twenty-two years old. Xmas Day last, I was with him at the Railway Hotel and remained there until closing time. I went out first and went to the bottom of the street about nine or ten yards from the hotel – I could not hear what took place outside. I heard a woman scream and saw Ross running down past me. I said, 'Oh, you've killed my brother!' He never spoke. He had nothing on his head. I then went to where my brother was. He was lying on the ground, bleeding. I saw no knife. My brother had known Ross for years. Have heard of no quarrel between them. [Cross-examined]: *They had been good friends as far as I know. Heard Ross say he would back himself for sixpence.*
My brother said he would never fight for sixpence.

Mary Ann Burke, single woman, Phillips Yard, Leeds

I was at Railway Hotel, Christmas Night last. Manley and Ross were there. Saw Ross talking to Manley about fighting. Ross said all he had was sixpence and he'd put that down. Manley said before he'd fight for sixpence, he'd fight for fun. They went out before me and I followed them out and saw Ross talking to Rooks. Ross drew knife out and stuck it in Manley's neck and with that Manley fell to the ground. When Manley was struck, his hands were in his pockets. Saw the knife in Manley's neck when he was on the ground. Ross ran away. He let his cap fall. [Cross-examined]: *Was stood at the side of Manley. Was 2 or 3 minutes in the public and came out after Ross and Manley. Manley had a light coat on and light trousers and waistcoat and billycock hat. I understood the fight was to be between Manley and Ross. I heard Rooks say he'd fight Ross if Manley didn't. Manley did not raise his hands as if he were going to strike.* [Re-examined]: *There was no fighting in the public or outside and no hand raised to fight.*

Michael Kelly

(No questions asked)

Ann Connor, wife of William Connor, Sykes Place, Leeds

Saw Manley and Ross outside Railway Hotel at 10pm. They were quarrelling. I drew nearer but could not hear what they said. I saw John Ross open a knife and stab Manley under left ear and then ran away. Manley had one hand in his pocket and the other out. The one out was down by his side. [Cross-examined]: *The only light was the gas lamp over the door.*

John Fee, marble polisher, Leeds

Christmas night, was passing Railway Hotel, York Street, saw Ross strike Manley. Manley fell.

Patrick O'Doherty, cloth dresser, 8 York Street, Leeds

I was standing by Railway Hotel, 9.55 Saw Manley and Ross and seven or eight more. Manley was about one yard from Ross. Saw Ross strike Manley. I got hold of Ross by collar of coat. I asked what he did it for. He swung out of my arms and then I struck at him. I don't know whether I hit him. He ran away and I ran after him for about 30 yards.

Charles Henry Harral, surgeon, Leeds

At 10.25pm on Xmas Night saw Manley. He was dead. Found wound on left side of neck quarter inch below and inch behind ear. It was horizontal and half inch in length. Post mortem next night and found extended to depths of three and a quarter inches. He died from the wound in the neck. One artery and two veins wounded. Light blow would not cause such a wound.

James Nortcliffe, chief of the detective police, Leeds

Jan 24th. Found Ross in custody at Wolverhampton.

Verdict – GUILTY

Foreman desires to state that some of the jury wish to recommend the prisoner to mercy.

Sentence – DEATH

Bibliography

Andrews J. et al. 1997. *The History of Bethlem*. Routledge.

Annan, Thomas. 1977. *Photographs of the Old Closes and Streets of Glasgow 1868 –1877*. Dover Publications.

Anonymous. 1826. *Glasgow Delineated*. Wardlaw and Cunninghame.

Archibald, Malcolm. 2013. *The Real Mean City: True Crime and Punishment in the Second City of Empire*. Black and White Publishing.

Barnard, Sylvia M. 2001. *Viewing the Breathless Corpse. Coroners and Inquests in Victorian Leeds*. Words@Woodmere.

Barnard, Sylvia M. 2009. *To Prove I'm Not Forgot. Living and Dying in the Victorian City*. The History Press.

Brears, Peter. 1992. *Images of Leeds, 1850–1960*. Breedon Books.

Brontë, Charlotte. 1847. *Jane Eyre*.

Brontë, Emily. 1847. *Wuthering Heights*.

Brotchie, T C F. 1925. *Tramway Guide to the Borderlands of Glasgow*. Corporation of Glasgow.

Burt, Steven and Grady, Kevin. 2002. *The Illustrated History of Leeds*. Breedon Books.

Collins, Wilkie. 1859. *The Woman in White*.

Davis, Andrew. 2011. *The Gangs of Manchester*. Milo Books Ltd.

Davis, Mark and Kidd, Marina. 2013. *Voices from the Asylum: West Riding Pauper Lunatic Asylum.* Amberley Publishing.

Davis, Mark. 2014. *Asylum. Inside the Pauper Lunatic Asylums.* Amberley Publishing.

Dickens, Charles. 1843. *A Christmas Carol.*

Donnelly Jr, James S. 2001. *The Great Irish Potato Famine.* Sutton Publishing.

Engels, Friedrich. 1845. *The Condition of the Working Class in England.* Otto Wigand.

Foreman, Carol. 2002. *Lost Glasgow. Glasgow's Lost Architectural Heritage.* Birlinn.

Glasgow Past and Present, Illustrated in the Dean of Guild Court Reports. 1848, 1849. David Robertson and Company.

Hartley, Marie and Ingilby, Joan. 1990. *Life and Tradition in West Yorkshire.* Smith Settle.

Hartley, Marie and Ingilby, Joan. 1990. *Yorkshire Album. Photographs of Everyday Life 1900–1950.* Dent.

Higgs, Michelle. 2009. *Life in the Victorian and Edwardian Workhouse.* The History Press.

House, Jack. 2013. *The Heart of Glasgow.* Neil Wilson Publishing.

Kay-Shuttleworth, Sir James Phillips. 1832. *The Moral and Physical Condition of the Working Classes Employed in the Cotton Manufacture in Manchester.*

Kenna, Rudolph. 1990. *Old Glasgow Streets.* Strathclyde Regional Archives.

MacDonald, Hugh. 1910. *Rambles Round Glasgow in the 1850s.* John Smith and Son (Glasgow) Ltd.

MacDougall, Carl and various others. 1990. *Glasgow's Glasgow. The Words and the Stones.*

McUre, John. 1737. *History of Glasgow.*

Mahood, Linda. 2005. *Policing Gender, Class and Family in Britain, 1800–1845*. Routledge.

Mayhew. 2008. *London Labour and the London Poor.* A Selection by Rosemary O'Day and Englander, David. Wordsworth Classics of World Literature

O'Donovan Rossa, Jeremiah. 2004. *1838–1898, Memoirs of an Irish Revolutionary*. The Lyons Press.

Opie, Iona and Peter. 1985. *The Singing Game.* Oxford University Press

Patterson, Mary. 1993. *The Ham Shank*. University of Bradford.

Payne, Brian and Dorothy. 1974. *Leeds as It Was in Photographs*. Volume One. Hendon Publishing Co Ltd.

Pearse, Padraic. 1924. *The Collected Works of Padraic H Pearse.* Phoenix Publishing.

Riddell, Fern. 2014. *The Victorian Guide to Sex: Desire and Deviance in the 19th Century.* Pen and Sword Books Ltd.

Shepard, Leslie. 1973. *The History of Street Literature.* David and Charles.

Small, David. 1896. *Bygone Glasgow.*

Stevens, Mark. 2014. *Life in the Victorian Asylum: The World of Nineteenth Century Mental Health Care.* Pen and Sword History.

Walkowitz, Judith R. 2013. *City of Dreadful Delight. Narratives of Sexual Danger in Late Victorian London.* University of Chicago Press.

Online References

Ancestry: https://www.ancestry.co.uk/

Beatty, Aidan. The Irish Story: http://www.theirishstory.com/2015/08/03/frederick-engels-and-ireland

Bramley Union Workhouse: http://www.workhouses.org.uk/Bramley/

British Newspaper Archive, The: https://www.britishnewspaperarchive.co.uk/

Climey, Paul: https://www.commonspace.scot/articles/10050/asylums-glasgow-buildings-where-madness-was-managed

Cox, Catherine and Marland, Hilary. 'A Burden on the County': Madness, Institutions of Confinement and the Irish Patient in Victorian Lancashire. *Social History of Medicine*, Volume 28, Issue 2, 1 May 2015, Pages 263–287: https://doi.org/10.1093/shm/hku082

Ellis, Samantha. The Brontës' Very Real and Raw Irish Roots: https://www.irishtimes.com/culture/books/the-bront%C3%ABs-very-real-and-raw-irish-roots-1.2932856

Finn, Michael Anthony: The West Riding Lunatic Asylum and the Making of the Modern Brain Sciences in the Nineteenth Century, http://etheses.whiterose.ac.uk/3412/1/Michael_Anthony_Finn%2C_eThesis.pdf

General Register Office: https://www.gro.gov.uk/gro/content/

Hayes, Joseph: https://www.atlasobscura.com/articles/railway-madness-victorian-trains

History to Herstory, Yorkshire Women's Lives Online: http://www.historytoherstory.org.uk/

Leodis. A Photographic Archive of Leeds: http://www.leodis.net/

Marshall, Eliza. Child Labour Documents: https://www.bestlibrary.org/files/child-labour-documents.pdf

Milliners and dressmakers in Victorian London: http://www.victorianlondon.org/professions/dressmakers.htm

Moriarty, Esther. 2010. The Great Famine – an Irish Tragedy and Its Impact on the English Town of Huddersfield from 1845 –1861: http://eprints.hud.ac.uk/id/eprint/8802/1/MoriartyEsther_final_thesis.pdf

National Archives, The: http://www.nationalarchives.gov.uk/

Old Scottish Genealogy and Family History: https://www.oldscottish.com/

Saracen's Head, The, Glasgow: http://www.saracenhead.com/welcome/4533493626

Scotland's People: https://www.scotlandspeople.gov.uk/

Wakefield Asylum: http://www.wakefieldasylum.co.uk/

Word on the Street, The. National Library of Scotland: https://digital.nls.uk/broadsides/

World War II Today: http://ww2today.com/18-may-1944-polish-troops-capture-monte-cassino

Acknowledgements

This has been a uniquely challenging project for me, uncovering tragic events that were part of my relatively recent family history, some of them involving people I had loved, many more involving people I had heard about, not just from old documents and new websites, but in intriguing family stories.

As anyone who has ever undertaken serious family history research can testify, the difficulties are compounded by the fact that for every certainty, unanswered questions, potential and actual errors, spring up like hydra heads. I became aware of this early in the process, while researching my immediate Leeds Irish family and finding online errors about relationships between people I had known well. Of necessity, and while most of this story is as factually correct as I can make it, there are elements of speculation, questionable connections and mysteries that will never be solved. The reasons for this are many and varied. Sometimes the records simply don't exist. They may have been destroyed or they may never have existed. Often different documents contain conflicting details. The very poor – too often perceived en masse rather than as individuals – were not documented nearly as precisely as the great and the good, unless they had committed some dreadful crime or had been declared insane – both, sadly, circumstances that assisted me. Many of these people were illiterate, and were relaying information verbally to overpressed officials.

Sometimes the records lie. People don't always tell the truth and they may have their own reasons for falsification. The temptation in assessing this information is to employ William of Ockham's razor and shave away unnecessary assumptions, but we also need to remind ourselves that life can be complicated, that at times of intractable need, people will do what they must for the survival of themselves and their children, and that fact can sometimes be much stranger than fiction.

This whole project would have been well-nigh impossible without the help of a number of people. Foremost among them, my friend, Sooh Sweeney, was generous with her time and her genealogical expertise. I've lost count of the number of times she managed to ferret out the kind of complicated and immensely useful information that would have taken me months, possibly years, to discover without her invaluable help. I can never thank her enough.

I also want to thank my cousins, Vera's children, especially David Watson, who has – over many years – expressed an interest in the history of our family, conducted an interview with a family member I never knew, and has been willing to chat about all of this, as well as supply encouragement and enthusiasm. Thanks are also due to his sisters, Jane and Carol, for reconnecting with me and for reminding me about the resolute and persisting strengths of the women – our forebears – whose stories I have tried to tell.

As ever, with projects like this, many others have helped me along the way. Among these, I must name Penny Lewis and Fergus Smith of Old Scottish Genealogy and Family History, who generously shared the parts of the story that (all unexpectedly) involved Glasgow. Michael Gallagher, Archivist of Glasgow Life at the Mitchell Library also supplied the documentary evidence that clarified so much about Elizabeth's last weeks in that city. Harriet Harmer and Alison Depledge, West Yorkshire Archive Assistants, gave me valuable assistance in the pursuit of Elizabeth Manley's asylum history, and the history too of the Bramley Union Workhouse that figured in the lives of other family members. Alan Pugh of the Friends of Beckett Street Cemetery was able to confirm burial details of Elizabeth Manley and James Terran.

Among the many friends who have encouraged me, Dr Alison Bell, as ever, has followed the project from the beginning, as has fellow Saraband author Olga Wojtas. Dr Valentina Bold in particular directed me to information about Broadside Ballads among other things. Many thanks are due, of course, to Sara Hunt and Craig Hillsley at Saraband, to the best editor of all, Ali Moore, to proofreader Madeleine Pollard, and to my patient and supportive husband, Alan.

Finally, I must name those I have loved and lost: my indomitable and affectionate nana, Honora, and grandad, Joe, Uncle Georgie Big Eyes, Aunty Nora, but especially my wonderful, glamorous Aunty Vera ('Hoo aboot it on the rug, Vara?'), my beloved mum, Kathleen, and my incomparable, alien dad, Julian. I couldn't have done it without any of you.

CATHERINE CZERKAWSKA